RADICAL EDUCATION

Robin Barrow is the author of many books in the philosophy of education and classical civilisation. These include *Plato, Utilitarianism and Education* or *The Liberal Democratic Dilemma*, probably his most important work, in which he argues strongly against the thesis put forward in the first volume of Sir Karl Popper's *Open Society and its Enemies*, and suggests that a closed society, such as that envisaged by Plato, might be more truly just than an open society and that a utilitarian philosophy is more adequate than a liberal-democratic one.

In a more practical vein his *Common Sense and the Curriculum* has received wide acclaim. His latest books include *Radical Education, An Introduction and Commentary on Plato's Apology* and *Moral Philosophy for Education*. Educated at Westminster School and Christ Church, Oxford, Dr Barrow has subsequently lectured in the philosophy of education at the University of Leicester, England. He is currently Visiting Professor of the Philosophy of Education at the University of Western Ontario, Canada. He likes George Gissing, Elvis Presley and Hector Berlioz.

By the same author:

RADICAL
EDUCATION

*a critique of
freeschooling and deschooling*

ROBIN BARROW

A Halsted Press Book

John Wiley & Sons · New York

First published in 1978 by Martin Robertson & Company Ltd,
17 Quick Street London N1 8HL

Published in the U.S.A. by Halsted Press,
a Division of John Wiley & Sons, Inc., New York.

Library of Congress Cataloging in Publication Data
Barrow, Robin.
　　Radical education.

　　'A Halsted Press book.'
　　Bibliography: p.
　　Includes index.
　　1. Educational innovations.　2. Free schools.
I. Title.
LB1027.B2574　　　　370.1　　　　78–1972
ISBN 0–470–26329–6

Filmset in Great Britain by
Northumberland Press Ltd,
Gateshead, Tyne and Wear
and printed by
Richard Clay (The Chaucer Press) Ltd,
Bungay, Suffolk

Contents

Abbreviations to sources

The following abbreviations are used throughout the text in order to keep the sources most often referred to as brief as possible. Where a group of consecutive quotations in one paragraph have the same source, the reference is given only once. Full publication details are included in the Bibliography.

CA	*Celebration of Awareness* (Illich, 1973a)
CM	*Compulsory Miseducation* (Goodman, 1971a)
D	*Deschooling* (Lister, 1975)
DS	*Deschooling Society* (Illich, 1973b)
E	*Emile* (Rousseau, 1972)
FL	'Freedom and Learning: the Need for Choice' (Goodman, 1971b)
GA	*Growing Up Absurd* (Goodman, 1960)
MS	'Mini-Schools: a Prescription for the Reading Problem' (Goodman, 1975)
PUE	*Plato, utilitarianism and education* (Barrow, 1975)
S	*Summerhill* (Neill, 1961)
SC	*The Social Contract* (Rousseau, 1935)
SD	*School is Dead* (Reimer, 1971)
TSA	*Teaching as a Subversive Activity* (Postman and Weingartner, 1971)

Acknowledgements

I should like to thank the University of Western Ontario (in particular John McPeck), whose invitation to me to come over as Visiting Professor of the Philosophy of Education revitalised me. Thanks too to Patrick Gallagher, with whom I first discussed the idea of this book some years ago, and who, though now far away, is not forgotten. Thanks to Dr Sara Delamont, who had a hand in pushing me forward with the project, and to Miss Victoria Barrow, who typed the manuscript under somewhat trying conditions.

I owe thanks of a different kind to: my wife, who puts up with me when my mind is on my work and without whom all is impossible; to Edward Elgar, who made it as easy for me to write this book as a publisher can; and to Dr David Elmo Morrison, a true friend, a scholar and a gentleman.

Canada

To my parents, with admiration and gratitude

Difficile est Saturam non scribere
[Juvenal 1.30]

CHAPTER 1

Introduction

In this book I shall examine the arguments and educational ideas of Jean-Jacques Rousseau, A. S. Neill, Paul Goodman, Everett Reimer, Ivan Illich, Neil Postman and Charles Weingartner. It may well be asked what links these superficially very different individuals – a Frenchman, a Scotsman, some Americans; an eighteenth-century philosopher, a nineteenth-century practising teacher, a one-time Catholic priest. In particular, in what sense of the word is it fair to regard them all as radicals?

Our word 'radical' derives from the Latin word 'radix', meaning a root. What I mean by a radical is one who wants change that involves going to the root of the matter, as opposed to one who wants no change at all, or one who wants superficial change. That is all, and that is precisely what I mean by a radical. For many people the word conveys rather more than that. It is often associated with left-wing political views, and consequently for some people the word has strong emotive overtones, whether favourable or unfavourable. But then the matter is further complicated by the currency of such phrases as 'the radical Right', which usage puts all the emphasis on the idea of extreme views of whatever kind. My use of the term involves none of these associations. It is worth repeating that I mean simply one who favours root-and-branch change; a radical proposal is one that strikes to the heart or foundations of the matter. The term, in this usage, is intended to be evaluatively neutral. Striking to the heart of the matter and insisting on a fundamental change is, in itself, neither good nor bad. Much must depend on what we propose should be changed in this way, and when and why we do so.

If I am asked why I insist on using the word 'radical', while admitting that it very often carries implications that I want to ignore, the answer is partly that the same is true of any alternative word that I can think of, and partly that the term has already been proudly applied to some of the people I am concerned with by their publishers, themselves and each other. But the only sense in which it is true to say that writers like Goodman and Illich are radical is in the sense that I have outlined. Alternative labels, such as 'progressive', 'revolutionary' or 'anarchic', are equally ambiguous and probably, in most of their senses at least, less appropriate. Besides, if these people want to be called radicals and are called radicals, why shouldn't they be? They *are* radicals in the specific sense of people who propose fundamental change, which is the sense that the word will consistently have in the remaining pages of this book. These are not educationalists who propose tinkering with the educational system as it is: they propose blowing the system as it is to pieces.

There are a number of more specific affinities between these writers, too. To a greater or lesser extent, they are all romantics in the sense of idealistic and sentimental: they tend to see the past as a Golden Age (Goodman even reverts to precisely the same classical examples as Rousseau had done two hundred years before) and the future as potentially perfect. The notion that individuals might be responsible for evil and misery because they are selfish and nasty is one that they find it difficult to embrace: they prefer to put it all down to circumstances. Towns and industrialisation they hate. They are suspicious of book learning, seeing something more in keeping with human dignity in working with one's hands (outside of industry). Illich's recent interest in the abuses of the medical profession matches Rousseau's interest no less obviously than a match can be made between their views on education (see Illich, 1975). His central thesis, that the medical profession as an institutional body creates rather than cures sickness, is Rousseau's objection to the medical world of his day.

There are also strong stylistic similarities between all these writers. Without exception they overstate, generalise and personalise. They substitute metaphor for argument; they commit elementary logical errors such as interpreting an event as the cause of another simply because it precedes it in time. They use emotive and obscure terms at vital places in their argument; they confuse means and ends, and empirical and evaluative issues. Even those most anxious to stress what is important in the work of the contemporary radicals are forced to admit, as is Lister, that 'much of [their] evidence is circumstantial or anecdotal: both Goodman and Holt tend to buttress their assertions with the statements of friends who agree with them. When "hard" data ... are presented they have often been selected to support the thesis being argued' (*D* p. 11).

Specifically these radicals share the following views. They value individual happiness highly, sometimes regarding it as the supreme value. They also claim to value critical autonomy, or thinking for oneself, and (superficially at least) a high degree of social freedom. They tend to value, and to equate in a rather vague way, whatever is natural, spontaneous and sincere in man's behaviour. They are adamant that learning is not dependent on overt teaching, and that more effective learning will take place without overt compulsion. In one way or another they envisage the community or environment as a whole as being educative and thereby inducing, perhaps with the help of adult guidance and inspiration but certainly without naked instruction, the natural and good, moral and intellectual, development of the individual.

On the negative side, all are united in objecting to what they see as the typical pattern of education in their own time, which pattern they are inclined to depict as a somewhat oversimplified stereotype. They are no less hostile to what they see as dominant aspects of society in general. They are particularly vehement against the schools' tendency to teach what they regard as useless and irrelevant knowledge. They resist any conception of knowledge that sees it as some kind of static commodity or as a collection of packaged and unchanging truths. They strenuously oppose what they see as an artificial separation between school and life, and each in his own way is proposing an alternative that would in his view minimise, if not obliterate, such a distinction. Although Rousseau was not familiar with such terms as 'hidden curriculum', 'grading' and 'diploma', the ideas are none the less grist to his mill; he, no less than A. S. Neill or Neil Postman, is aware of and concerned about the phenomenon of unintended consequences arising from incidental influences on children, not to mention competition and grading. All these authors see standard patterns of education as socialising children into an unequal, insincere and unacceptable form of society. Despite their nominal allegiance to autonomy as an ideal, most of them are at best ambivalent and obscure in their attitude towards rationality, and all of them place more emphasis on a combination of developing feelings and practical skills than on what might be termed academic skills.

Generally they are passionate enemies of hypocrisy, humbug and hate. It is not surprising therefore that their work is imbued with the characteristically Platonic idea that no one willingly does wrong. The real or true inner man, in every case, would be frank, loving and sincere, if only he were not misshaped by upbringing and misled by society. By the same line of thought it can be implied that we would agree with all that is being said if our vision and understanding had not been distorted by the world in which we live. That line of thought is one example of many similar, which together render these theories what I shall call 'likely stories'. By a 'likely story' I mean one that at crucial junctures, and hence as a whole, rests upon assertions that are unfalsifiable and unverifiable. I do not mean assertions the truth or falsity of which we happen not to be sure of; I mean assertions the truth or falsity of which we are in no position to set about establishing. To assert that those who do not agree with one thereby indicate the truth of one's assertion that they have been rendered incapable of seeing the truth by the world in which they live is to place oneself beyond the possibility of rational discourse. Adherence to the dictum becomes a matter of blind faith. At rock-bottom all the educational theories we shall examine appear to be 'likely stories' in this sense.

Rousseau, in his *Emile*, presents a classic statement of the radical thesis: a comprehensive blueprint for uprooting contemporary schooling and building a new kind of society by means of a new kind of education. Although the other authors considered here differ from him in various ways, and do not represent a line of continuous development, they can all be seen to take up and develop ideas that are to be found in his work. The emphasis changes quite considerably from writer to writer, but there is very little of importance in any of the later writers that cannot be found at least embryonically in Rousseau. To him the social setup in the France of his time was insupportable; but the educational system of the day was clearly supporting it. A totally new type of society was needed, a complete revolution in political and social organisation; but all this could be achieved only through a totally new kind of education. What was needed was not improvement within the current practice and procedure, but the annihilation of current practice and procedure. A new conception of education was needed, one founded on a completely new set of principles.

Rousseau roundly challenged the hitherto almost unquestioned assumption that ideally children should be placed in the care of professionals in special settings which thus became institutionalised; he challenged no less the presumption that they should be fed a body of information and socially hallowed maxims, that they should be veneered with knowledge, and that they needed moulding, shaping and directing if they were to become responsible adults. Emile, by contrast, is to have a natural education: the real world will be his classroom and he will learn from experience.

It is the idea of education according to nature that provides the main connecting link between Rousseau and A. S. Neill; otherwise the similarities are for the most part negative ones. Despite a popular idea to the effect that Neill's school, Summerhill, is the embodiment of Rousseau's theory, there are very important differences between them: Summerhill children really *are* to a large extent left to grow up as they will, given the arbitrary constraints of the group as a whole, whereas Emile is certainly not. But Rousseau and Neill do seem to share a belief in some kind of innate human nature which is at odds with the fashions and fancies of respectable society, the latter being preternaturally obnoxious when they are made the basis of the school curriculum. One other point of similarity should be noted here: both men see themselves as pioneering a new kind of education appropriate to a truly democratic society, as opposed to what is called a democratic society. Rousseau imagines that Emile will think and vote in accordance with the terms of what he calls the General Will, which is the basis and safeguard of the truly free and just society. Neill claims that children educated along the lines that he advocates will both gain vital experience of the democratic process and grow up to be hostile to externally imposed authority and well disposed to the interests of fellow citizens.

Paul Goodman clearly felt a lot of sympathy with what he took to be A. S. Neill's views.[1] Both men would agree that by and large the typical school fails even on its own terms. Schools purport to be institutions geared towards promoting proficiency in certain clearly defined areas, but they do not deliver the goods: the majority of children gain little in the way of such things as mathematical ability or a mastery of basic chemistry. Second, they both believe that the traditional school cages and distorts human nature. Third, they believe that learning and compulsion are incompatible. Fourth, both men are hostile to examinations, certification and grading; they regard such labels as 'clever' and 'stupid' as misleading, if not actually false, because they are the product of preconceived conceptual schemes on the part of adults or the nature of the organisation of the school itself – anything, in fact, except the appropriate name for the actual characteristic of a particular individual; and they both recognise and object to the 'hidden curriculum', by which I mean the things that the school teaches without explicitly drawing attention to the fact that it is doing so, perhaps being unaware that it is doing so, although Neill does not actually use the term 'hidden curriculum'.

Their proposed solutions, however, are different. Whereas Neill thinks that it is possible, and in some respects even advantageous, to operate within something approaching a school situation, Goodman shifts the emphasis to the point of beginning to see the institutionalised setting as itself the cause of all evils. Neill proposes, metaphorically speaking, to build a wall around his children, thus protecting them from the outside world, and to populate their private world with sympathetic adults, thereby giving the children the opportunity to develop as he, like Rousseau, terms, 'naturally' (notwithstanding the fact that he and Rousseau are making different proposals). Goodman proposes almost the opposite: to break down the wall and let the children grow up as members of society.

Both Goodman and Rousseau stress the importance of education taking place in and for the real world, but they have decidedly different views of what constitutes reality. Goodman, very surprisingly, allows the prevailing social conditions to define reality; Rousseau, more consistently with the sort of ideal that both men share but perhaps also more impractically, defines it in terms of the negativisation of social norms. Goodman also departs from Rousseau in rejecting the latter's emphasis on the idea that the child is not a miniature adult but a person who functions in a manner quite distinct from that of the adult. He argues that we should revert to treating young people as precisely that – young people.[2] The refusal to accept a concept of childhood as something distinctive qualitatively is common also to Reimer and Illich, who, together with Goodman, are usually regarded as the holy trinity of the deschooling movement.

The term 'deschooling' is vague and it is used in different senses by different people, sometimes to refer to views that do not involve getting rid of schooling. It was coined accidentally by Illich, to his subsequent regret. And as Lister well puts it, 'it is less of a concept than a general drift of thinking' (*D* p. 93). It involves explicit emphasis on two ideas that are to be found in Rousseau: first, a recognition that education and schooling are not necessarily the same thing or that form and substance, ritual and content should not be confused; second, that the institution of schooling by virtue of being an institutionalised process itself automatically and inevitably causes damage. 'The mere existence of schools discourages and disables the poor from taking control of their own learning,' says Illich (*D* p. 89), partly for economic and organisational reasons, but more significantly because they make us believe that they are the proper and only channel for genuine learning. 'What goes on in schools is not necessarily education' (*D* p. 79), but it is schools that insidiously make us believe the opposite, and thereby legitimate their own dubious activity. Nor is it simply that, as a matter of fact, the schools do not educate. By their nature they cannot, for 'institutions create certainties which deaden the heart' (*CA* p. 13). And so 'all over the world the school has an anti-educational effect on society' (*DS* p. 15). Illich talks of 'deschooling' society and of 'disestablishing' the schools, for what deschooling implies is being rid of the ritual imprisonment that schools achieve because they are institutions. Institutions are the enemy. We must indeed get rid of schools, but if that were all we were to do we should still school people. To *deschool* society we must get rid of all institutional and other schooling mechanisms. It betrays a misunderstanding of what deschooling is all about, therefore, to say that the way forward is 'possible only through deschooled schools' (Hentig – *D* p. 37). There is no such thing as a deschooled school: there are, at best, only more or less free schools, and a free school is a school for all that.

The fact that Goodman looks with a favourable eye on free schools only goes to show how uneasy is the alliance between the three members of the deschooling triumvirate, for neither of the other two will have any truck with them. To Illich they are more dangerous and unacceptable than the traditional schools, for free schools 'produce the mirage of freedom. Attendance as the result of seduction inculcates the need for specialised treatment more persuasively than reluctant attendance enforced by truant officers' (*D* p. 3). Illich's wording here is characteristically baroque and opaque, but like Reimer his basic objection is that Neill's 'Summerhill and schools after it . . . still teach dependence on the school' (*D* p. 3). A committed deschooler, for whom a central tenet is that the influence of an institution as such must be avoided, must feel towards the free school rather as a marxist must feel towards any apparently genuine and important class reconciliation – namely, resentful, since such compromises and temporary solutions merely get in the way of momentum towards the real and final confrontation and victory.

Deschooling theory asserts both that we fail to see what schools *qua* institutions must necessarily do, and that we ask too much of them and thereby invite failure. How can the same individual be judge, jury and executioner? And before the mind has time to question the validity of the analogy we are asked how the same individual can be nanny, prophet, indoctrinator and guide as we expect the teacher to be. Defining the school in terms of compulsory attendance and grading (*SD* p. 34),[3] they conclude that a school must effectively achieve only 'the shaping of man's vision of reality' (*D* p. 67), in unacceptable form, by means of the hidden curriculum. Hence there must be no such institutions.

Postman and Weingartner share this critical attitude to schooling and society. But they propose to operate within schools, and even within classrooms. Their hope is that, by eliminating school preoccupation with subjects and by means of a curriculum based on open-ended questions, we can develop in each individual the ability to see and condemn the evil and absurdity inherent in the accepted manners and beliefs of contemporary society. Therein lies the link with the other radicals: Postman and Weingartner, too, see in a new kind of education the hope of a new kind of society, one in which sham and superficial conventions are cast aside by individuals who, free of manipulation, indoctrination and docile acceptance, will forge truth anew for themselves.

Finally by way of introduction attention should be drawn to the fact that a considerable part of the work of Reimer and Illich originates in relation to the Third World and is particularly concerned with economic arguments, both matters that are beyond the scope and interest of this book. One of their main complaints is that the Third World has been invaded by a mythology that is irrelevant and disastrous to it. The suggestion is that a particular Western culture and a Western type and system of qualification has been imposed quite inappropriately, at great material and spiritual cost, on alien cultures facing different circumstances.

It seems highly likely, *a priori*, that the imposition of a schooling pattern evolved in Western industrialised democracies over a long period of time would be inappropriate if transplanted rapidly and wholesale to other contexts. But the deschoolers themselves claim that what they have to say is directly relevant to Western industrialised democracies themselves. It is not therefore the inappropriateness of one type of schooling to some types of society that is really at issue. Theirs is not simply the rather banal (albeit very important for those involved) theory that there is no such thing as the universal pattern of true or correct education; it is 'the general futility of world-wide educational institutions' that is at issue, and according to Illich, 'accumulating evidence now indicates that schooling does not and cannot produce the expected results' (*CA* p. 89). It is true that much of the evidence referred to turns out to be nothing other than what has been culled from the experience of Latin America, and to that extent it may look as if it will be difficult to separate the general deschooling thesis from the Third World context. But we do not have to rely on such evidence, and in fact we clearly ought to ignore it: partly because it really will not do to draw deductions from one specific situation and assume they will be applicable to any situation, and partly because in any case the real problems in deschooling theory are not empirical ones at all.

Lister refers to the lack of solid evidence and the absence of systematic empirical research in the work of the deschoolers and suggests that such deficiencies need to be remedied (*D* pp. 15, 92). In the final analysis that must surely be so – should there be need for a final analysis. But the real problem is one that precedes any problem about evidence, one indeed that must be solved before the question of evidence could possibly arise, and that is the problem of what the various claims made by the deschoolers actually mean, whether they are internally coherent and whether they are mutually consistent. For example, the concept of usefulness figures prominently in their work; nor does it cause much trouble in the context of the Third World: in societies where daily survival, increased productivity and blatant exploitation constitute the immediate and obvious problems, there is no difficulty in seeing that the study of Latin is not immediately useful in a way that learning to operate a particular piece of machinery is. But when we transfer the criterion of usefulness to more complex societies such as our own, the immediate problem is not one of carrying out some empirical tests to see what would be most useful in the changed conditions. The prior problems are first that of working out whether the criterion of usefulness is still so important (and, if so, there may be a case for shifting the emphasis as between immediate and long-term usefulness) and second that of working out what constitutes usefulness in these very different conditions. Neither of these problems has much to do with empirical research. Take the opening words of Bullfinch's preface to *The Age of Fable*:

> If no other knowledge deserves to be called useful but that which helps to enlarge our possessions or to raise our station in society, then Mythology has no claim to the appellation. But if that which tends to make us happier and better can be called useful then we claim that epithet for our subject.

Well, does it or doesn't it? That is the kind of question that most pressingly requires an answer.

It is for this reason that the economic arguments of the deschoolers can also in this context reasonably be set aside. Terms like 'wealthy' and 'poor' are relative, and what a person can afford is generally a matter of making judgements of priority. Whether a nation can afford a particular system of schooling is not simply a question of looking inside the nation's money-box. It is a question of deciding what the nation regards as a worthwhile deployment of resources. The question of whether we can afford the current system of schooling cannot be divorced from the question of what it is worth to us. We must first know what this and alternative systems actually involve and achieve; then we need to establish priorities. Only then can we say whether or not we can 'afford' this, that, or the other system.

Similarly I shall not pursue the question of the differences between the contemporary American and British situations and whether they are such as to make a material difference to the significance of various proposals. That there are differences is indisputable: Vaizey has gone so far as to say that 'the diagnosis of the American problem is almost wholly inapplicable to the British situation' (*D* p. 122). But even if that were true, there would still be important ideas and proposals embedded in that diagnosis which it is worth our while to examine. In any case we need first to establish what the diagnosis and proposed remedy are in order to make up our own minds as to whether or not they do have application to Britain as well as North America as the deschoolers claim.

It is, then, with the clarity, coherence and logic of the arguments and ideas of the radicals that this book is concerned. Its brief includes asking such questions as whether a particular author contradicts himself, makes his meaning clear or argues fallaciously. There are those who feel – and 'feel' is the right word – that, provided that somebody produces an idea that they, the audience, lack the perspicacity or wit to conceive for themselves – provided, that is, that they, the audience, are stimulated, excited, amazed or otherwise alerted – then the person who shows this remarkable talent for stimulating, sparking off, promoting creative responses, etc. is for that reason alone to be enshrined as a guru and sold in W. H. Smith's stationery shops or drug and variety stores. Such people are not infrequently to be heard muttering 'Oh, you *know* what he means. Don't quibble.' This book is not for such people. (There ought not really to be *any* books for such people. Giving them books is rather like giving them erratic bombs – you never know quite what will go off when or where.) It is for people who expect arguments to be sound, reasons relevant and good, and assertions well founded or suitably qualified and hypothesised.

The overriding interest in the logic and coherence of what is said has to some extent dictated the plan of the book. In the case of each author I have tried to give an accurate statement of his argument and to pinpoint the weaknesses and difficulties in it. Issues that crop up in relation to more than one author (and there are many) are dealt with in the context of the author who seems most concerned about them. (In some instances the placing as between one author and another is rather arbitrary; in others themes insist on recurring, but the Table of Contents should prove a sufficient guide.) I have refrained as much as possible from making judgements and drawing conclusions at the end of each chapter, preferring to give the radicals rope with which to make us all a ladder or to hang themselves.

CHAPTER 2

JEAN-JACQUES ROUSSEAU
1712-88

THE SOCIAL CONTRACT

'I had come to see', writes Rousseau in his *Confessions*, 'that everything was radically connected with politics, and that, however one
proceeded, no people would be other than the government made
it' (Rousseau, 1975). Accordingly he wrote the educational treatise
Emile and the political treatise *The Social Contract* as two parts
of the same work. The manner of education advocated in *Emile* is
supposed to be the prime means of ensuring the success of the kind
of society idealised in *The Social Contract*, which, in turn, will allow
the natural Emile to thrive, which he certainly could not have done
in the society of his day that Rousseau so much despised.

On the first page of *The Social Contract* Rousseau writes: 'Man
was born free, and he is everywhere in chains' (*SC* p. 5). Such is
the nature of human society that one's every movement is dictated
by convention, whim or artificiality. When Rousseau refers to chains
he is not talking about literal slavery, class or economic exploitation.
What he conceives of as the free man is one who casts off the shackles
of custom and prejudice. At birth, he seems to suggest, we are not
yet tainted by particular cultural norms and we are not like peas
in a pod. There is no necessity for us to develop all alike, bound
by accepted attitudes. We should be individuals. We should be our
natural selves.

But inclinations may be perverse and interests may clash. What
we need to ensure is that the interests of all get equal consideration,
that none are enslaved to others, and that perverse inclinations do
not gain sway. That cannot be achieved unless society is organised

on a basis of agreement. There must be a social contract, not between the rulers and the ruled but between all the citizens. But if this contract is to achieve its purpose it must be such that each individual in obeying its demands 'renders obedience to his own will'.

Whether such a contract can in practice be devised or not will depend upon the proposed terms of the contract. We may all agree to adopt a rule about driving on one side of the road or even one to the effect that payment should be made for goods received. But what about more contentious issues? How do we ensure that the terms of the social contract are generally recognised as desirable? The contract must embody the dictates of the Universal Voice or the General Will. The General Will, we are told, is always right, and in forcing the individual to obey its demands we are merely forcing him to be free. But what precisely does Rousseau mean by the General Will?

It is not to be equated with majority opinion; it is to be distinguished from the Will of All, which is the phrase that Rousseau applies to the sum of the wills of all the various individuals. The dictate of the General Will is that which each individual would see to be the best policy if he were truly to consider both his own and everybody else's interest. What remains obscure is how, in actual instances, we are supposed to set about deciding what is in everybody's interests and hence what is actually demanded by the General Will. We know that we do not arrive at the General Will by counting votes; that would only give us the Will of All, unless we could rely on every individual to vote in accordance with the demands of the General Will. But how could each individual do that when none of us know what it does demand? Furthermore, even assuming that I, as an individual, do happen to know what the General Will demands, why should it be presumed that I will therefore vote in accordance with it?

At this point one might be forgiven for cynically summarising Rousseau's General Will theory as the view that it would be nice if everybody were able and willing to consider everybody else's interests as well as their own, assuming that we knew how to determine what was in the best interests of everybody. But it is at this point that we have to remember that *The Social Contract* is not supposed to be taken in isolation. Rousseau never imagined that, once he had explained the theory, we would all at once accept it and accurately discern what the contents of the social contract should be. As things are, we are all corrupt. We are full of received opinion, artificial values, humbug, hypocrisy and selfishness. In the state in which mankind actually finds itself it is not to be expected that it should either embrace the idea of the social contract or be able to interpret and abide by the General Will. But, according to Rousseau, if we had not been brought up in the absurd manner in which we have been, but had been educated properly, then we would be naturally inclined towards the dictates of the General Will.

Rousseau sees education as the means whereby we fail or succeed in producing adults capable of making something worth while of society – individuals who can and will discern the common interest. And the key both to a sound education and to a stable and just society lies in letting natural man emerge. All will be well, as soon as we cease to regard 'the received opinion of those with influence and power' as synonymous with true wisdom, and recognise that what is going wrong is that we are being moulded by society in all its artificiality rather than creating society in our natural image. 'Everything is good as it comes from the hands of the author of Nature; man meddles with it and it deteriorates' (*E* p. 5). That is the real problem.

Rousseau is careful to stress that the interplay between education and social arrangements is reciprocal. Not only is the correct education essential to the idea of realising the perfect society founded on the social contract, but the reverse also holds: the proper type of education needs a just society in which to be set; it is not appropriate to the very imperfect world known to Rousseau. 'Under existing conditions a man left to himself from birth', which is the essential first step of the education Rousseau advocates, 'would be more of a monster than the rest' (*E* p. 5). The claim then is *not* that the education provided for Emile is without further change appropriate for the here and now, but that it will contribute towards changing the social here and now into something nearer the ideal, which in turn will constitute a setting more appropriate for further education of the ideal type.

This notion of a spiralling interplay between the ideal education and the ideal society goes some way towards rendering Rousseau's theory what I have termed a 'likely story'. For it seems to be both unfalsifiable and unverifiable. No evidence that particular children educated along the lines that he recommends turn out disastrously as adults can be taken as conclusive proof against the claim; for it can always be argued that, were society less corrupt, the consequences of a natural education would not have been disastrous. By the same token we cannot be expected to validate the full claims made for this education by producing examples of individuals with whom it has proved successful. Rousseau himself, therefore, by binding his political and educational theory so closely together, forces us to estimate the coherence and value of his position in logical terms alone, seeking not empirical evidence that it works, but reasons for regarding it as plausible.

Rousseau's basic aim is to bring people up in such a way that they may pursue a free, happy and secure social existence. This leads him to present a stark dichotomy between natural and civilised man. In Rousseau's use the latter term has none of the favourable emotive overtones that 'civilised' as contrasted with 'uncivilised' in the sense of 'primitive' may have for some of us. Rousseau's civilised man is rather like the prisoners in Plato's Allegory of the Cave, who see nothing but the shadows of reality, so hopelessly are they limited and bound by their own ignorance and lack of ability to discern the true nature of things. To the civilised man 'what he is is nothing; what he appears is everything' (Grimsley, 1973, p. 20); what matter that he is in very truth a liar, a cheat, a knave, provided only that he cuts a good figure and commands general adulation and respect? He is a victim of fashion and current prejudices; his knowledge, divorced from any real human context, separated from any actual daily purposes or interests, has become 'vain science and futile curiosity'. Mere slavish prejudice is confused with wisdom, while 'what passes for philosophy is little more than reflection inspired by pride and vanity' (Grimsley, 1973, p. 11). Centuries before advertising had become the all-pervasive creature that it is today, Rousseau was alive to the distinction between true needs, or needs common to the human condition, and created needs, and he was aware that many apparent needs were in fact artificial so that man 'is alienated from his original being'.[1]

The indictment on civilised man, whatever degree of truth it may possess, is gloriously unrestrained. But the depths of bathos are plumbed when we are presented with the contrasting romantic and idyllic picture of natural man which includes all the clichés of the genre from Wordsworth at his worst through to country and western songs at their best: the country is better than the town; the farm is better than industry; the family is better than the wider social group. One half expects to be told that city slickers ain't no good, while country girls is pure, pretty and true ('they wear dresses cut country tight'). Unashamedly, we *are* told that in natural surroundings 'all men would be tall, strong and well made' (*E* p. 11). Natural man has what might in current jargon be termed authentic existence; in him, what belongs incontestably to human kind is rightly and fully developed. Among men, in a state of nature, there is 'a real and indestructible equality, because physical differences [are] not important and certainly not great enough to make one dependent on the other' (Grimsley, 1973, p. 53). An interesting point, to the effect that inequality can arise only where interests are subordinated and not when they are merely different, is being made here; but one could be forgiven for missing it, such is the schmaltz and popcorn flavour of most of Rousseau's vision of hillbilly heaven.

Life is the trade that he would teach children, and the life he would have them lead is one that would be free and independent, yet involve them in being co-operative and social individuals, while happiness would be its reward. He sees both freedom and happiness in terms of facing up to and harmonising with reality, or enmeshment between the individual and his situation.* 'A conscious being,' he writes, 'whose powers were equal to his desires would be perfectly happy. . . . True happiness consists in decreasing the difference between our desires and our powers, in establishing a perfect equilibrium between the power and the will' (*E* p. 44). Similarly, a man is free 'who desires what he is able to perform and does what he desires' (*E* p. 48). According to Rousseau this equilibrium, this harmony between what is feasible and what is wanted, is the state of affairs in the beginning, by which he would seem to be suggesting both that in the history of mankind such equilibrium used to exist and that it is there at the birth of each individual. But the process of history has long since upset the balance and distorted the harmony for mankind in general, and with each individual the equilibrium is similarly rapidly lost by the creation, through the society of civilised men, of artificial desires, felt as opposed to real needs, and false expectation. True education would preserve and maintain the initial harmony and thereby enable people to live prosperously and happily.

---

*The term 'enmeshment' was coined by myself in my detailed analysis of the concept of happiness in *Plato, Utilitarianism and Education*, which is worth further study in relation to Rousseau. Plato, Rousseau and myself all share the same view of the nature of happiness and individual freedom.

EDUCATIONAL PROVISION: INFANCY AND CHILDHOOD

Every Emile should have his own tutor who will remain with him from the moment of his birth until his marriage. Emile is representative of the normal child, and the first thing that his tutor should do is remove him from human society, including even the company of his peers.[2] The potentiality for development along desirable lines is presumed to be within Emile at birth, and consequently it is assumed that such development would naturally come about in natural surroundings. But in the world as it is we cannot rely on the surroundings being natural, and that is where the tutor comes in, for his primary task is to keep the unnatural elements of civilisation away from the young child.

Book One of *Emile* is a sensible enough, if at times slightly trivial, essay on infancy. Rousseau argues forcefully against the practice of swaddling babies on the grounds that it is unnatural, since it involves attempting to alter the form that physical development would otherwise take, and that the claims made about it are not borne out by experience (for instance, that to discontinue the practice 'might injure the proper development of their limbs' (*E* p. 12)). He insists that the mother should suckle her own young rather than hire a wet nurse, on the grounds that this is more natural. In general he advocates steering a middle course between neglect and spoiling the child. His message for the early years is clear: let the child run free. Let him learn from nature in the sense both of learning what nature has to teach and of learning by means of natural experience.

Indicative of Rousseau's outlook is the injunction to 'let the child's vocabulary be limited' (*E* p. 40) on the grounds that the shrewd peasant folk, the exemplar of something approaching perfection and natural man, have 'few ideas, but those few ideas are thoroughly grasped'. This is the germ of a recurring theme to the effect that what George Gissing once termed 'the half-knowledge that turns life sour' is considerably more damaging and deplorable than simple ignorance. The insistence that 'the only habit the child should be allowed to contract is that of having no habits' (*E* p. 30) is typically overstated, but the emphasis accords well enough with the overall theme.

The second stage of Emile's education, that of boyhood, which is envisaged as lasting from the age of two to twelve years, now begins. He will learn all that he learns as a result of becoming aware of the natural consequences of whatever he does. Conduct is not to be prescribed; rules are not to be drummed into him. Prudence, thought by many to be a virtue, is roundly condemned by Rousseau, who does not want Emile organising his life in response to fearful calculations of what might happen (*E* p. 46). Emile is to be free of all worry. He will simply learn, through experience, to avoid what harms him.

When Emile is hurt Rousseau will not go near him until he stops crying, and in that way he will soon learn not to waste unnecessary tears. Rousseau here takes up a theme (also introduced when discussing medicine) that is still of importance among contemporary radicals: what we experience is the product of our expectations and ways of looking at the world rather than the inevitable outcome of the world being the way it is. Thus we are told that 'it is not the blow but the fear of it which distresses us when we are hurt' (*E* p. 41), and are given to understand that Emile will actually be the less badly hurt by his fall in so far as nobody around him takes it very seriously.

Emile must learn what can or does harm him and the surest way to learn that lesson is to be hurt. Other children, Rousseau admits, may receive fewer injuries, but they pay a heavy price in that their physical safety is the outcome of their being perpetually 'thwarted and constrained'; they are safe but sad. But might not Emile be in serious danger sometimes? No, replies Rousseau. He won't do himself any real harm unless he 'has been foolishly left on a high place, or above the fire, or within reach of dangerous weapons' (*E* p. 42).

Here we meet for the first time in this book what I have elsewhere termed the Manfred Syndrome, resort to which is unfortunately all too common a device among some of the authors with whom we are concerned (*PUE* p. 11). The Manfred Syndrome refers to the technique of insisting that an unlimited amount of X is required or demanded and then adding, usually very quietly or in some aside, a more or less meaninglessly vague qualification such as 'provided that it is not too much'. The mnemonic is taken from W. S. Gilbert's line in *Patience*: 'A little of Manfred, but not very much of him'. How much *is* a little, but not very much? How useful is it to read page after page advising us to leave Emile alone so that he can learn from natural consequences, and then to be told at the last minute that, of course, any undesirable natural consequences must be guarded against? Emile must fend for himself, the cry rings out. But then it turns out that this is supposed to apply only in a carefully constructed nursery. At this point we can merely note that Emile is evidently *not* left to learn anything and everything from experience and by means of suffering natural consequences. Some things at least are guarded against by Rousseau, though precisely what things and how it is determined which they should be is not at present very clear.

We should try to ensure that Emile never acts from obedience, but only from necessity, by which Rousseau means that Emile must think that he sees the need or reason for acting in a particular way. He must see his conduct not as something demanded arbitrarily by another being, but as required by circumstances. The thinking behind this advice harks back to the observation in *The Social Contract* that an harmonious state depends among other things on the individuals within it feeling that they are subject to impersonal laws rather than the personal whims of other people. For 'it is in man's nature to bear patiently with the nature of things but not with the ill will of another' (*E* p. 55).

Emile will receive no moral preaching, indeed no verbal lessons at all, during boyhood. 'The education of the earliest years should', Rousseau claims, 'be merely negative. It consists not in teaching virtue or truths, but in preserving the heart from vice and the spirit of error' (*E* p. 57). Implicit in that remark is the cardinal tenet that, unless it is externally corrupted, the heart is already from the beginning in some sense whole and pure. Whether Rousseau really believed that is difficult to say, but passages such as this certainly suggest that he did. Again we may note the very characteristic reference to the idea that honest ignorance is inevitable and infinitely preferable to dogmatic but ill-founded certainty. It really does not matter that Emile is not acquiring a great stock of information. What would matter and be quite disastrous from Rousseau's point of view would be if Emile were to acquire a stock of conventional wisdom and treasure it as if it were holy writ.[3]

During this second stage the tutor's essential task is to re-impose or otherwise ensure that Emile has a natural environment in which to grow up. There will be no academic teaching of any sort and no moralising. While Emile is free to move about and learn what he·will in his protected environment, the tutor may engage in the exercise of learning with him, but he may not overtly instruct him. Or perhaps it might be safer to say that the tutor must not be detected by Emile in the act of teaching; for Rousseau makes it clear that he does see the tutor as both controlling and taking advantage of situations in order to advance learning. He does not sit back and do nothing until asked to do something by Emile. None the less, between the ages of two and twelve Emile will learn only what he can through his environment and by means of natural consequences. And it is apparent that Rousseau neither expects nor particularly wants a great deal, in traditional terms, to be achieved: 'If only you could bring your scholar to the age of twelve strong and healthy, but unable to tell his right hand from his left, the eyes of his understanding would be open to reason as soon as you began to teach him' (*E* p. 57). That is the point: this second stage is designed to protect Emile from the artificial and false knowledge of the civilised world, to prevent corruption, and to nurture him in such a way that he will be properly receptive to the lessons of the future.

The basic elements of a moral education are also supposed to be cultivated during this second stage of education. 'The first notion of justice', according to Rousseau, 'springs from what is due to us' (*E* p. 61), and he illustrates the claim with the story of Robert the Gardener. The tutor helps Emile to plant and cultivate some beans, continually forwarding the idea that they are his property and the product of his labour. But it turns out that the spot chosen for planting in fact belongs to Robert and they have ruined his Maltese melons. Emile will sense that Robert should have his due, just as he senses some things as due to himself. But the development of the moral spirit is not to be left at the level of mere sense of property. We must also set a moral example as tutors, particularly during these early years. 'At an age when the heart does not yet feel anything, you must make children copy the deeds you wish to grow into habits' (*E* p. 68). And when Emile does do wrong, his 'punishment' 'should always come as the natural consequences' of the fault in question, for, Rousseau argues, it is quite inappropriate to think of punishing children in the normal manner and sense of the word. 'Thus you will arrange that all the ill effects of lying should fall' (*E* p. 65) on the head of the person who tells the lie and those ill effects will constitute a natural 'punishment'.

Rousseau does not think that Emile will actually tell many lies.

But in the exceptional case when he does, he will see the wrongness of it (which at this point seems for Rousseau to be practically synonymous with the profitlessness of it) by the consequences of the act: consequences, such as being mistrusted and unpopular, which the tutor will ensure do fall on his head – just as, to revert to a more prosaic example, Emile will learn not to break windows as a result of finding himself extremely cold at night when he does so.[4]

Moral lessons are certainly not to be derived from books. In fact, 'Emile at twelve years old will hardly know what a book is' (*E* p. 80),[5] and it goes without saying that he will not be full of what Rousseau regarded as the normal useless educational fare of the time such as 'heraldry, geography, chronology and language'. He will not know such fine details as the position of Pekin on the map of the world, as the typical child of the time might be expected to; on the other hand he will be able to use a map and to find his way across France, as the typical schoolboy could not. His knowledge will be useful, practical, relevant knowledge rather than vain book knowledge.

Another familiar practice of the time, the use of morally enlightening fables as a means of moral instruction, is also roundly condemned on the grounds that such fables are incomprehensible to children as moral allegories and that they usually carry a hidden, often pernicious message, to be distinguished from the overt point of the tale, which is less seductive. For example La Fontaine's fable of the Fox and the Crow, whatever we might think to be its point, is quite likely to teach the 'six year old child that there are people who flatter and lie for the sake of gain' (*E* p. 79).[6]

Rousseau insistently claims that, because 'children are not to be required to do anything as a matter of obedience, it follows that they will only learn what they perceive to be of real and present value, either for use or enjoyment'. 'Present interest, that is the motive power' (*E* p. 81), he asserts, anticipating the main tenet of contemporary progressive thought. Furthermore he believes that, were a situation devised in which present interest could more or less determine what went on, present interests would not be all that remote from the traditional interests that the school typically likes to cultivate. For example, although Emile will at no stage be made to take up reading, Rousseau is confident that he 'will learn to read and write before he is ten, just because I care very little whether he can do so before he is fifteen' (*E* p. 81). By the end of this second stage Emile, like the Spartans who were 'not taught to stick to their books' but 'were set to steal their dinners' (*E* p. 84), is familiar with his environment, can cope with it on a day-to-day basis, and is otherwise without opinion or prejudice.

Book Two culminates rather unexpectedly with a series of practical tips. Emile is to wear little or nothing on his head. He is to learn swimming, which is a useful ability, rather than horse-riding, which is merely a fashionable accomplishment; he is to run around barefoot so as to harden himself to natural conditions; he is not to be innoculated against smallpox since, at least in a natural environment, nature herself will guard him against smallpox. His taste in food will be simple. Emile may look rather a 'rough little boy' as a result of this upbringing, Rousseau concedes (*E* p. 127). But is that to say anything more than that he is not the typical product of the fashionable homes of the time, with a head full of irrelevant rules and information and a body cramped into a sailor suit?

EDUCATIONAL PROVISION: ADOLESCENCE

Rousseau's aim is to provide for Emile 'a small store of [knowledge] which really contributes to our welfare', for that alone 'deserves the study of a wise man' (*E* p. 129). During the second stage of his education, Emile learnt something of how things are and the law of necessity. He learnt, for example, that there is cold that benumbs unless it is guarded against. Now he must learn to sort out what is useful from what is not as a prelude to the fourth and final stage of his education, in which he will 'come to see what is fitting and right'.

The environment still provides the subject matter, but whereas previously the environment was interpreted to mean the immediate environment, now, because Emile has developed to the point at which he sees beyond his immediate environment, the concept of environment changes to incorporate the wider physical world. But still we are concerned with what is grounded in perception and sense experience. 'The intellectual world is still unknown to us, our thoughts are bounded by the visible horizon' (*E* p. 130). And Emile is still to learn through experience. 'His geography will begin with the town he lives in' (*E* p. 134). He will progress in science by means of or through problems that he perceives as problems confronting him. The teacher does not instruct. 'It is not your business to teach him the various sciences', asserts Rousseau (meaning 'teach' in the sense of 'instruct'), 'but to give him a taste for them and methods of learning them when his taste is more mature' (*E* p. 135). Here we see the notion of 'learning how to learn' making an early appearance in educational literature. 'You have not got to teach him truths so much as to show him how to set about discovering them for himself' (*E* p. 168). The point is illustrated by the (rather long and boring) story of how Emile is fascinated by a conjuror at a fair who makes a wax duck follow a piece of bread about. The secret lies in a concealed magnet, and as a result of his initial fascination Emile is led to learn about both magnetism and the mechanics of compasses.

The emphasis is still on the child's immediate perceptions; Rousseau is now concerned to go beyond mere sense experience to look for explanation, but he still wishes to keep theory at arm's length. 'I have said already that purely theoretical science is hardly suitable for children ... it is only objects which can be perceived by the senses which can have any interest for children' (*E* p. 140). 'Things, things', he insists. 'We lay too much stress upon words' (*E* p. 143), which presumably means that we should look about us more and theorise less.

None the less, Emile is now introduced to his first book, which is Defoe's *Robinson Crusoe*, chosen not for any presumed literary merit but as a manual of self-sufficiency and a hymn to learning through experience rolled into one. Emile must also now be set to learn a trade, provided that it is a trade that is honest and useful, as Rousseau makes clear: 'I would rather have him a shoemaker than a poet; I would rather he paved streets than painted flowers on China' (*E* p. 160). This unveiled putting of art in its place is yet another example of Rousseau anticipating a theme of much contemporary educational thought: what use, we are repeatedly asked, is the study of such things as literature or classical civilisation? It is interesting to see here the close affinity between some aspects of radical educational thought and the untutored demands of the man in the street.

Emile's moral education continues, but now 'the idea of social relations is gradually developed in the child's mind' (*E* p. 156) to supersede the self-oriented seeds of a notion of justice developed in the preceding phase of education. 'Emile sees that for him to get tools for his own use, other people must have theirs, and that he can get in exchange what he needs and they possess.' In other words, the basis of morality is discerned as lying in prudent self-interest. (But Rousseau does not in any way combine that view with a cynical attitude to morality.)

Emile's intellectual development is presumed to continue through this third stage of education, and Rousseau attempts to explain the process whereby Emile makes the transition from being a receptor of sense experiences to being able to form ideas. 'From the comparisons of many successive or simultaneous sensations and the judgement arrived at with regard to them,' he says, 'there springs a sort of mixed or complex sensation which I call an idea' (*E* p. 165). This apparently means that the mind registers certain things such as a cat, a tree, a brick, a throwing, a toe, a screaming, and labels them accordingly. Then we begin to judge the various perceptions and to think about them, including thinking about the way in which we perceive and label them. Ideas are, in Rousseau's terminology, those things that are beyond direct sense experience. Thus a particular cat leaping up with a yowl when a brick falls on its toe is a perception. But if one proceeds to entertain the notion that animals can feel pain, one has an idea.

In sum, Rousseau makes the following claim for stage three of his educational programme: Emile, though still lacking skill in abstraction and still without a sense of the social virtues, will be unaffected, realistic, and temperamentally disposed to learn things for himself; well prepared, in fact, for the fourth and final stage. And it is worth remembering, since most pundits and commentators do not, that that is what the first three stages are designed to be: they cannot be assessed in their own right, if we are trying to be faithful to Rousseau's intentions, for they have no value in their own right. They are put forward as the necessary prelude to the fourth stage.

That final stage of education, according to Rousseau's plan, covers the years between fifteen and twenty. At this point Emile is to begin meeting with other people and living among them for the first time.[7] Consistently, with what he has so far said about moral development Rousseau refrains from making any claim to the effect that Emile will turn out to have any instinctive concern for the wellbeing of others when called upon to live in close contact with them. His view is that 'our natural passions are few in number' but they are those passions that 'tend to our self-preservation' (*E* p. 173). Indeed, he seems to go even further when he says 'the origin of our passions ... the only one which is born with man ... is self-love'. However, if self-love is the child's first sentiment, 'his second, which is derived from it, is love of those about him'. Thus, without going back on his premiss that a concern for self-preservation is natural and that a philanthropic spirit is not, Rousseau suggests that the former can become the latter by a natural process. 'I would have you so choose the company of a youth that he should think well of those among whom he lives ... teach him to know the world that he should think ill of all that takes place in it. Let him know that man is by nature good ... how men are depraved and perverted by society' (*E* p. 198).

It is not entirely clear *how* Rousseau imagines that Emile will achieve *amour-propre* (his term for the form that natural self-love, *amour-en-soi*, will take in a social setting where it will prove morally acceptable), *why* he should do so if he has any choice in the matter, or *in what way* it differs from self-love. We know that formally it is self-love made good. But what in substantive terms makes self-love good? All that is certain is that by this stage Rousseau believes that Emile is ready for the culmination of intellectual and moral development which will be aided by his experience of society and the quickening of his imagination by reading (*E* p. 179). (The phrase 'ready for', as the context shows, is not to be interpreted to mean that Emile says that he wants something; he is ready for the final step in the sense that he has been well prepared for it, even though in this particular instance the preparation involved has been largely negative.)

The study of history, along with literature, is suggested by Rousseau as a key means of achieving his objectives. He is not concerned with historiography or schools of historical thought. What he hopes to do through historical study is to show Emile what the so-called civilised world is really like, which in Rousseau's view amounts to a mishmash of humbug, conceit, lust, prejudices, airs and fancies. Rousseau thus presents us with the nice paradox of studying history, the record of what actually happened and what people were actually like, as a means of coming face to face with falsity and unreality. He is aware of the obvious objection that people have long since studied history, and yet it does not appear to have succeeded in opening their eyes to the superficiality and falsehood of mankind. He argues that that is because we live in an imperfect world and our study of history hitherto has taken place in corrupt conditions. 'Weighed down by books from our earliest years, accustomed to read without thinking', when we read our history books we do not perceive the awful picture of mankind they actually present 'because we already bear in ourselves the passions and prejudices with which history and the lives of men are filled. All they do strikes us as only natural, for we ourselves are unnatural and we judge others by ourselves' (*E* p. 263). Because of the fallen state we are in, history placidly confirms our assumptions where it should be shocking our prejudices.

But Emile has to learn the very practical lessons of 'how to get on with other people' (*E* p. 214), and he will not learn that from books alone. Rousseau, true to his manner, accordingly swings right round and, ignoring what he has just said about literature and history, asserts that '*all* the lessons of the young' should 'take the form of doing rather than talking; let them learn nothing from books which they can learn from experience'. So, without further thought of the lessons of history, it is proposed that Emile should be made to go out and help the poor and in other similar ways face up to and learn about what life is really like and how to come to terms with it. Emile, it is said, will move among the unfortunate, and 'the sight of suffering makes him suffer too'. Why so? Because, Rousseau confidently asserts, 'this is a natural feeling' (*E* p. 213).

Throughout the book Rousseau drops hints and sometimes makes explicit statements about the specific values that he expects Emile to acquire – for example, Emile must be no respecter of blood or wealth. But it is probably fair to say that the goal of the moral education provided is supposed to be the emergence of a capacity for autonomous reasoning in moral matters, which, it seems to be assumed, will conveniently coincide with the dictates of natural morality. This presumption that autonomy, reason and nature can for all practical purposes be brought together, and all potential conflict smoothed away, is given expression in the concept of conscience that Rousseau now introduces. He assures the reader that conscience is 'an innate principle of justice and virtue [residing] at the bottom of our hearts' (*E* p. 252). If it is *allowed* to emerge, as it generally is not in civilised society but as it has been in the case of Emile, then it inevitably *will*. Nor is the emergence of this unfailing intuitive sense of justice dependent upon academic learning or philosophy of any kind. As Rousseau memorably puts it,

'Aristeides was just, before Socrates defined justice' (*E* p. 271).

Emile has reached the age of twenty, free of useless information, fashionable tastes and conventions. On the other hand he is very well informed as to particulars that concern himself. He has an innate sense of justice which governs his behaviour and judgement. He is intellectually curious and has the ability to set about learning for himself whatever he feels he needs to learn. He is a willing member of the community because he sees the need for certain social rules that benefit himself and others, and those are the only kinds of rule that the society he belongs to has.

This brings us to the fifth and final book of *Emile*, which cannot fail to astonish the reader. For after close on four hundred pages, which have unambiguously asserted that we should ignore and turn upside down current assumptions relating to the education of the boy, Rousseau now introduces as representative of the female Sophy, who is brought up to be a caricature of the conventional devoted wife and dumb blonde rolled into one, on the grounds that such a role is natural! If it is, it doesn't take a philosopher to see that it must be 'natural' in a different sense of 'natural' to that in which Emile's upbringing was natural. 'Woman', says Rousseau, 'is specially made for man's delight . . . it is the law of nature' (*E* p. 322). 'To be pleasing in [man's] sight, to win his respect and love, to train him in childhood, to tend him in manhood, to counsel and console, to make his life pleasant and happy, these are the duties of women for all time, and this is what she should be taught while she is young' (*E* p. 328).

Meanwhile, as Sophy, speculative thought being beyond her womanly grasp and her studies therefore being thoroughly practical (*E* p. 349), is being brought up to marry him, Emile is made to complete his education by travelling, in order that he may gain first-hand experience of political matters. Finally he returns and, still guided by his tutor, who is showing all the signs of becoming a very Pandarus, enters into marriage with Sophy who was truly, as the song says, made for him.

MEDICINE, PUNISHMENT AND CHILD-CENTRED EDUCATION

Medicine
Declaring that medicine 'does less to ward off death than to make us dread its approach' (*E* p. 22), Rousseau effectively ignores sickness in children, eschews such preventive medicine as smallpox vaccinations, sweeps doctors away, and provides Emile with a rough and rigorous Spartan upbringing on the grounds that 'experience shows that children delicately nurtured are more likely to die' (*E* p. 15).

We must make some allowance for the state of medical science in Rousseau's time; and no doubt some doctors, then as now, were corrupt, vain and greedy. No doubt also we must recognise that medicine is not necessarily an unmitigated blessing. It may be a power for evil, as it was in Nazi concentration camps. The fact remains that Rousseau produces no convincing argument to back his slicing indictment not merely of the profession, but of the science of medicine itself. The argument about delicate nurture appears, by means of the ambiguity of the phrase 'more likely to die', to confuse two quite distinct propositions: that children delicately nurtured are more likely to die than other children, and that they are more likely to die than they would otherwise have been. The former claim may be true, although if that is what Rousseau means he offers no evidence to back his intuition. But even if it were true, it would not show that one should not delicately nurture certain children, for it might still be the case that certain children would be even more likely to die if not delicately nurtured than if they were delicately nurtured. To establish that one should never nurture children delicately one would have to establish the truth of the second alternative. But experience could not possibly show that children who are delicately nurtured are more likely to die than they would have been had they not been delicately nurtured, since in the nature of things if we bring them up in one way we cannot see how those same children would have reacted to a different kind of upbringing. At best an inference can be hazarded on the basis of the fact that many delicately nurtured children do die. But in the absence of any evidence at all, an equally plausible inference would be that more delicately nurtured children die because the sort of children who are delicately nurtured are by and large the more physically delicate in the first place. Such children might very well have fared badly or worse if left to the not-so-tender mercies of Rousseau.

Having soundly and correctly rebuked the medical profession for interpreting any outcome as all the better for their involvement, Rousseau here puts himself in exactly the same untouchable position in respect of smallpox vaccination. The doctors, he sneers, will claim the credit if the patient gets well, and will say that the matter was beyond repair if he dies. But Rousseau himself justifies his refusal to allow Emile to be innoculated against smallpox by claiming that if he were to die (without innoculation) it would merely show that nature would have had him die anyway. The absurdity is not quite as transparent as that only because Rousseau also retreats behind his other all-embracing defensive shield: naturally, he concedes, *as things are* a child might die without innoculation; but we are envisaging a better world, a natural world in which that would not be the case. We get a good light cast upon the general thesis that Emile will grow up to be good in a good world, when we realise that it is paralleled by the claim that he will grow up physically healthy in a world without sickness.

No good reason is given for the objection to innoculation. It seems to be the product of an instinctive feeling that innoculation being unnatural must be wrong, just as being ill is made all right, if not actually sanctified, by being natural – more generally that medical science must be an unnatural practice since it is concerned to fight germs and infections which are undeniably part of nature. But if being ill is natural, it is so only in the sense that it happens, and in that sense of 'natural' all sorts of things are natural that we do not therefore conclude ought to take place. (Evil is natural in this sense.) Indeed, Rousseau evidently senses that he is becoming confused. He has to admit that medicine can be of value and therefore he comes up with the carefully worded admission that 'the science which instructs and the medicine which heals are no doubt excellent, but the science which misleads and the medicine which kills us are evil' (*E* p. 22). That is true and singularly uninformative.

No such caution holds him from a typically overstated conclusion. The child 'knows how to be ill ... it is the art of nature ... hygiene is the only useful part of medicine and hygiene is rather a virtue than a science' (*E* p. 23). The argument is absurd: if being ill is natural and therefore should not be interfered with then everything that happens, including the practice of medicine, is natural and should not be interfered with. The comment on hygiene suggests that Rousseau imagines that hygiene grows on trees. He seems entirely oblivious of the fact that what is hygienic is a matter for scientific inquiry: it is not a given, but the product of medical science. It was not nature that taught doctors that handling corpses could lead to disease and death in others, but medical science.

However in his determination to blacken the name of medicine Rousseau does offer some interesting insights. 'I do not know what doctors cure us of, but I know this: they infect us with very deadly diseases, cowardice, timidity, credulity, the fear of death' (*E* p. 21). In a nutshell this is the essence of Ivan Illich's current attack on the medical world as a service industry that causes more illness than it cures as it unconsciously grows ever more voracious in its appetite. But from the truth of the proposition, 'without medical science certain illnesses would not exist', it does *not* follow that medical science does more harm than its non-existence would do. Consequently we may concede that the medical profession creates a certain amount of sickness (by causing anxiety, by defining as sickness what others might not have done, by making mistakes, by creating new drug-resistant bacteria, by making the doctor the licensed judge of whether you are sick or not) without concluding that we would be better off without it. And indeed it is difficult to see how such a contention could be established for the increasingly familiar reason that to establish it would necessitate the impossible: a comparison of the present situation with medicine and that same situation without medicine.

Part of the significance of this medical interlude for us is that it embodies a particular instance of an important theme running through radical thought, namely the hidden curriculum theory: the idea that what it is thought is being done may obscure what is actually being done. It is by reference to that idea that Rousseau is enabled to suggest that the medical profession creates sickness: it unintentionally makes people timid, anxious and afraid and suggests to them that they can only be ill if a qualified doctor asserts that they are, and that they must be if he does.

It is by combining that idea with a belief in innate or natural goodness that Rousseau comes to the conclusion that education should be negative and should involve a deliberate attempt to ward off any influence from the child. One might attempt to surround the child with good influences, and that perhaps is what the typical teacher thinks that he is doing. But the trouble is that 'with your endless preaching, moralising and pedantry, for one idea you give your scholars believing it to be good, you give them twenty more which are good for nothing' (*E* p. 21). It is this same appreciation of the phenomenon of the hidden curriculum that explains Rousseau's rather violent objection to the use of moral fables with the young: were it simply that children were not capable of understanding the moral significance he might have remained caustic and cool. But Rousseau recognises that, not only is the designed purpose not being achieved, but also positive harm may be being done. Similarly he remarks, in the context of what we would call sex education, 'it is plain from the way you set about it, that they are meant to learn what you profess to conceal'. The fundamental point is that 'we draw with our mother's milk a taste for the pleasures of the age and the maxims by which it is controlled' (*E* p. 351), and hence, since Rousseau heartily dislikes his age, his determination to provide an altogether new environment for children to grow up in. However, just as the hidden curriculum theory gives rise to the desire for a negative environment, so, strictly speaking, it makes it impossible to have one. Short of a literal vacuum, the environment will inevitably preach some kind of lesson. It would therefore be more accurate to refer to Rousseau's proposed setting for Emile as different rather than negative. At any rate, the hope is that in this new setting Emile will avoid taking in the hidden curriculum of the age with his mother's milk.

Punishment

Rousseau correctly observes that young children logically cannot be wrongdoers deserving of punishment. The argument here is primarily a conceptual one. Rousseau is well aware that children may as a matter of empirical fact do what we would regard as wrong acts. His point is that the child 'may do much damage without doing wrong, since wrongdoing depends upon the harmful intentions which will never be his' (*E* p. 57). In other words, we must distinguish between breaking a window while high-spiritedly playing with a ball and wilfully and maliciously breaking it to annoy: the latter perhaps involves wrongdoing, the former certainly does not. But Rousseau is saying more than that intention is part of the concept of wrongdoing. He also wants to say that young children, and in his scheme of things quite old ones too, cannot perform certain kinds of wrong act because they lack the cognitive maturity. Telling lies, he argues, does not come naturally to children. If they were not persistently expected to meet the claims of obedience, they would not need to make excuses and to misrepresent the facts of the matter, which constitutes one type of lying. And they can never properly be regarded as lying in the other sense of making false promises, because they lack the adult capacity for looking ahead. When the child says 'I'll do it later, I promise', he means it, even when it is a safe bet from the point of view of an outsider that he will not do it. The final stage in this particular line of argument is reached with the observation that the meaning of punishment is such that it can only be said to be taking place when unpleasantness is deliberately and with due authority inflicted on somebody for breaking a rule. The child who tells an untruth cannot be punished because, recognising no rule, he has broken no rule. And at the back of all this lies Rousseau's continued awareness of the hidden curriculum: who knows but what an inappropriate system of so-called punishment is teaching the child that the main thing in life is not to get caught?

All of this is excellent, because it is essentially sound argument. But then dramatically Rousseau undoes all the good by leaping to a conclusion that is in the same degree unsound. In deducing that 'children's lies are therefore *entirely* the work of their teachers, and to teach them to speak the truth is nothing less than to teach them the art of lying' (*E* p. 66), Rousseau's love of paradox leads him to what Flew has termed 'buggery in Bootle' (Flew, 1976, p. 16). Flew's mnemonic is coined to expose the paucity of thought involved in reducing all reality and truth to a matter of ideas, concepts and labels – the view, for example, that delinquency in all its various forms is solely the product of arbitrary adult attitudes, labelling, categorising and perceptions rather than a feature of the real world, so that any rise and fall in the incidence of homosexual activity in Bootle must be purely the product of varying ways of looking at the world on the part of media, police, etc. That Rousseau is guilty of this fallacy is evident, for to him the manifest fact that some children do sometimes lie is to be explained not in terms of their character, situation or environment but as a direct consequence of (i) our classifying as a lie what is not really a lie and (ii) our putting the idea into their heads in the first place (*E* pp. 65ff). Whereas the fact is, for all the truth of the points made by Rousseau, there remains a kernel of hard empirical matter in all of this: once we get beyond babies who cannot talk and *a fortiori* cannot lie, there is the possibility that some children will lie, bully or steal intentionally. We help nobody by pretending that such behaviour is always entirely the work of teachers – worse, we confuse an empirical claim with a conceptual one. Prior to the overstated conclusion the argument had been conceptual (such is the meaning of 'lie' that certain conditions must obtain for there to be an instance of telling a lie). But from there on it is an empirical matter whether or not those conditions do obtain, and the issue is hardly settled by Rousseau's comforting assumption that in the ideal situation that he envisages Emile would not wilfully break windows, consciously mislead and so forth. In so far as it is true to say that 'to teach them to speak the truth is nothing less than to teach them the art of lying' (*E* p. 66), it is so because knowledge of X logically involves knowledge of not-X. That is to say, to develop a concept of truth logically involves a concept of falsity. For all the reasons given this may lead some to lie – it may put ideas into their heads – but it is mere foolishness to reduce the whole matter to one of putting ideas into people's heads. The whole point about moral behaviour is that we do certain things *despite* having the tempting idea of doing the opposite in our heads.

Child-centred education

Rousseau's overall analysis of the problem of society and education involves the view that what is basically wrong with both is that what is being taught, whether by design or not, is an uncritical acceptance of the *status quo*. That is the message of the hidden curriculum. The overt curriculum, meanwhile, requires students to imbibe a lot of incomprehensible formulae. But 'once you teach people to say what they do not understand', or to mouth utterances they have merely learned by rote, 'it is easy enough to get them to say anything you like' (*E* p. 218). In all of this Rousseau anticipates most of what is sensible in the writings of subsequent radicals. He also anticipates them in a point of detail when (citing the Roman Varro, which shows how long ideas can take to make any obvious impact) he insists on the importance of distinguishing education from related concepts such as discipline and instruction (*E* p. 10). Implicitly, he recognises that the standard schooling of his day may well be providing sound instruction according to its own lights. But he is not interested in instruction. He wants education for Emile, and he does not think that the school is the proper place to get that. This is partly the consequence of his requiring a wider environment in which Emile can learn from experience, and partly the consequence of his fearing and objecting to institutional dominance. But it is not only a consequence of these negative considerations: it is also the consequence of what some consider his crowning achievement, namely his conception of child-centred education.

The term 'child-centred education' has become something of a slogan with more emotive than descriptive meaning and is therefore in itself of little use in serious discussion. But in order to appreciate what it stands for in this context, we can legitimately break it down into a number of more specific claims, all of them explicitly made by Rousseau. All child-centred enthusiasts would no doubt unite behind Rousseau's imperative 'Hold childhood in reverence'; but so, despite the cloying phraseology, would almost everybody else. What we need to know is what form of reverence is implied by Rousseau's idea of child-centred education.

1. The first element in his conception is the view that the teacher's approach should be governed by the nature of the child rather than by some preconceived plan or blueprint for action (*E* p. 71). On the first page of his preface he notes with cheerful sarcasm that 'the wisest writers devote themselves to what a man ought to know, without asking what a child is capable of learning'. Rousseau does not take the view that educationalists ought not to have any preconceived plan of what should be known by the child. But nor does he think that teachers should proceed with a preconceived master plan of objectives, goals and stages, such that it is to be presumed that something is seriously wrong, probably with the child, if he fails to reach a stage or meet an objective according to plan. Thus Rousseau would counsel the teacher not to entertain the preconceived idea that the child should be reading by the age of ten. He himself, as we have seen, doesn't care if Emile has not learnt by the age of fifteen. But, despite what he may seem to say, Rousseau certainly intends and expects Emile to read in the end. What Rousseau wants from teachers is a calm acceptance of the limits imposed upon them and their plans by the actual capacities of their pupils at any given time. He is not advocating the view that there should be no preconceived aims and objectives.

2. The second element is the suggestion that education should be related to children's readiness. By this he means that any particular lesson or bit of teaching must wait upon the child in question being ready in the sense of being suitably prepared, and not necessarily in the sense of expressing eagerness or feeling that he is ready. Rousseau seems inclined to think that the two will go hand in hand and that therefore, in practice, the teacher may rely on the child's showing an interest in learning something as an indication that he is ready to do so. None the less, despite the inclination, it is clear that by 'ready' he means suitably prepared, that he includes in the idea of education related to readiness the need to prepare ground in the first place, and that readiness provides a necessary but not a sufficient criterion. That is to say, the child should be ready for X before he is taught X, but it does not follow that he necessarily should be taught X just because he is ready for it.

3. Interests have already been mentioned, and a third aspect of child-centred education in Rousseau's sense is that education must take account of the child's needs and interests. As far as needs are concerned it is quite certain that Rousseau means that the tutor should be guided by what the child does need and that that is to be distinguished from what the child may think or feel he needs. 'Give him not what he wants, but what he needs', we are told (*E* p. 49). But, to distinguish needs from felt needs or wants in this way is already to have conceded that somebody other than the child, and therefore in this context the teacher, may have to determine what his needs are. The interpretation of this claim must therefore be that teaching should take account of what children actually need, their need being a further question on which nothing is here said, except that it cannot be equated with what they want or say they need. As far as interests are concerned the matter is again fairly straightforward. 'Present interest that is the motive power, the only motive power that takes us far and safely' (*E* p. 81), Rousseau claims. It is in point of fact hard to see any warrant for this dogmatic assertion – there are countless other efficacious motive powers besides present interest – but it is at least clear that Rousseau's point is a simple motivational one: education should look to what interests children because that will increase their motivation. Thus Rousseau suggests that 'his geography will begin with the town he lives in' (*E* p. 134) because his town, besides being a more useful thing to know about than the position of Pekin on the map, will be of interest to him.

However, although it is clear what Rousseau means by saying that interest is important, it is not clear how important he thinks it is. As with readiness, he certainly does not regard it as a sufficient criterion for determining what should happen – the fact that the child is interested in doing something is not sufficient to show that he should be allowed to. He remarks at one point that there is 'all the difference in the world between a liking and an aptitude' (_E_ p. 161); if Emile is to be a painter he must have an aptitude and not merely a liking. But where does an interest fit in? Is it akin to an aptitude or, as seems more plausible, a liking?

At any rate, the main points are clear: it is important that the teacher should have some regard to the child's present interest, for that is a very strong source of motivation – according to Rousseau, the only truly effective motive power. No reference is made or implied to the idea that the child's interest in an activity makes that activity automatically something of value in itself. The fact that Emile is interested in doing something is not in itself an overriding reason for allowing him to do it, but in practice one feels Rousseau would be tempted to do so. But behind all that, Rousseau is adamant that being interested, in the sense of being enthusiastic about or liking something, is not to be confused with being able to do something that requires aptitude or ability. All in all, his stress on needs and interests, though important, particularly considered in its historical context, is none too informative and not as sweeping as is sometimes suggested.

4. A fourth element is the stress on the importance of learning through experience. 'How strange', Rousseau remarks, 'the art of doing is never touched upon' (_E_ p. 211). He sees the typical schooling as being preoccupied with mental abstraction and divorced from practical knowledge. The stress on experience thus covers two points: the idea that knowledge of practical matters and skills may be of importance, and the idea that any knowledge may be better acquired through experience (see below, Chapter 3).

5. The individuality of the child provides a fifth dimension to this conception of child-centred education. It may be subdivided into two parts itself. First, Rousseau makes the observation that the child is not a miniature adult and should not be regarded or treated as such. He is different in kind, and hence we must face the fact that the young child does not merely judge immaturely; he is 'incapable of judging' at all, judgement being an adult characteristic. His

memory is not less well developed; he has 'no true memory'. He is a creature of instinct not reason, a creature of sensation not reflection. Children do not grasp fables inadequately as a novice bricklayer might lay bricks inadequately; they do not grasp them at all – 'only men can learn from fables'. The child is not *more* innocent than the adult; he is quite literally *an* innocent, and therefore a different kind of being.

The second point that Rousseau makes on this issue is that, just as the child is something unique when contrasted with the adult as a type, so each individual child will be a particular being and may differ importantly from other superficially similar children. As he admits, therefore, 'my example may be right for one child and wrong for the rest' (*E* p. 155). A child-centred educator in Rousseau's sense, then, must also proceed on the assumption that he is dealing with children who need to be understood as such, and with individuals any one of whom may defy or set at nought the generalities of the social scientist and the psychologist.

6. Finally, it would be impossible to lay claim to having given a complete picture of the various elements embedded in Rousseau's picture of child-centred education if one omitted to mention the particular nature of the relationship between Emile and his tutor. The specific proposal of a one-to-one relationship between master and pupil, crucial as it seemed to Rousseau himself, is as fanciful and impractical as the other fundamental idea in *Emile*, namely that this upbringing should take place for the most part in complete isolation from the rest of mankind. None the less, many people have been profoundly influenced by the picture of the relationship between Emile and his tutor. An important question however is whether those who have been so influenced have got the picture quite right, since Emile and his tutor in no way form the society of equals, a duo with mutual admiration and respect, that has sometimes been popularly supposed.

The tutor is to pose as a father to Emile. Better, we are told, 'a sensible though ignorant father' than 'the cleverest master in the world', which remark emphasises that the nature of the child's relationship with all who bring him up is more important than their intellectual capacity. The general rule for the tutor is that he 'must not give precepts, he must let the scholar find them out for himself' (*E* p. 19). His task is therefore primarily one of superintendence and example.

But, despite the reference to a father–son relationship, the further one reads this enigmatic book the more it dawns on one that it is far more important, as far as Rousseau is concerned, that Emile should *think* the relationship to be a close one between equals than that it should be. It is finally apparent that the close relationship is fraudulent in as much as the tutor has, throughout, been doing a job. He is a professional; Emile, as the individual person Emile, is of little consequence to him.

That is overstated, perhaps. (It is difficult to be sure.) But, for the sake of accuracy, it is important to appreciate that there is little warrant for seeing Rousseau as the precursor of those who see a loving relationship or even respect for persons as crucial to the business of education. Rousseau's tutor is a detached and manipulative figure. Emile's confidence in his tutor 'should rest on the authority of reason and a superior knowledge, advantages which the young man is capable of appreciating while he perceives how useful they are to himself' (*E* p. 209). In other words, Emile senses the advantage to himself of his continued association with the tutor. In revealing passages Rousseau admits that the tutor is effectively but subtly using force to control Emile and that the use of guile may promote trust which will then become habitual (*E* p. 281). Indeed, this tutor is not above a bit of emotional blackmail – playing on the feelings of affection that he has deliberately cultivated in Emile – when it suits his purpose. What really marks out the tutor from the typical teacher, the pedant, is not that the former feels and exhibits love for his individual charge, but that he *uses* the idea of such a relationship and everything else to better advantage. 'The pedant and the teacher say much the same; but the former says it at random, and the latter only when he is sure of its effect' (*E* p. 284). In short, for Rousseau in the final analysis, the science of pedagogy is the art of timing, rather than the art of loving.[8]

CHAPTER 3

A Critical Look at
Certain Themes in Rousseau

FREEDOM

One point, appreciation of which is vital to a proper understanding of Rousseau, should by now be evident: he is not a champion of freedom in any normal everyday sense. He is not, politically, a non-interventionist. And he is not advocating a *laissez-faire* theory of education.

The teacher guides, controls and manipulates. There are passages where Rousseau seems to write as if he merely holds the balance – like a man who doesn't kill you, but who stops somebody else preventing a third person from killing you. For example, he asks himself this rhetorical question, 'Have I retarded the progress of nature?' He answers it: 'No, I have only prevented the imagination from hastening it.... When Emile is carried away by the flood of existing customs and I draw him in the opposite direction by means of other customs, that is not to remove him from his place but to keep him in it' (*E* p. 280). But properly understood, this means that Rousseau, the tutor, is developing habits in Emile. He may say that 'the only habit the child should be allowed to contract is that of having no habits', but that very remark is made in a context where minute instructions are given for creating and regulating Emile's responses to animals by controlling his initial contacts with them (*E* p. 30). This 'natural' child does not await his first chance encounter with a frog. No more does this tutor who would 'develop no habits' in him refrain from ensuring that some habits rather than others are developed. 'I would have him accustomed to see fresh things, ugly, repulsive and strange beasts, but little by little and far off till he is used to them, and till, having seen others handle them he handles them himself.'

It is true that Rousseau asserts that he will 'not take pains to prevent Emile hurting himself' (*E* p. 41), which is always a good test of whether somebody really intends to give freedom to children. But Rousseau fails the test, first because his reason for adopting this policy is not that it involves giving Emile his rightful freedom, but that 'I should be vexed ... if he grew up unacquainted with pain.' The teacher has decided that the child should experience pain; the teacher ensures that he does. Second, the freedom granted is strictly limited anyway. Emile will do himself no real harm because the situation is quite literally a controlled situation – more like an experimental laboratory than the natural environment. Emile will not be 'left on a high place, alone near the fire, or within reach of dangerous weapons'. In much the same way, though he will run about with bare feet, since that is more natural than wearing shoes, such things as broken glass will first have been removed (*E* p. 104) – by the tutor, who looks as if he is going to be a busy man. All this may be very sensible, but it should not be interpreted to mean that Rousseau wants children to have unlimited freedom.

It is explicitly stated that Emile 'must not obey', but the context, which also includes the assertion that 'he must be dependent' on the tutor, indicates that this means not that he must not do what is required of him, but that he must never be expected to do something simply because he is ordered to (*E* p. 48). Rousseau explains that 'he is only subject to others because of his needs', which they are better placed to determine than he is; but the stark fact remains that 'it is the business of those who have charge of the child to keep him in his place'. He is not to have something just because he wants it, asks for it or has an interest in it (*E* pp. 49, 53). More than once Rousseau returns to the statement that he shall have what he needs – and always we must remember that, as far as Rousseau is concerned, what a child needs is a matter of more or less objective fact to be determined by the adult. We are now in a position to see that, when it is said that Emile 'must never act from obedience, but from necessity', this means not that Emile should act only when action is forced upon him, but that he must see the necessity for an action before he should be expected to do it (*E* p. 53). Thus necessity becomes practically synonymous with reason. The tutor's task is to create the conditions in which the child will see the necessity or reason for whatever action the tutor wants him to perform.

Rousseau bluntly tells us to 'use force with children', for that is one way of making the necessity of something apparent to them; one fact of nature, one necessity, one good reason for them doing something to suit you is your vastly superior strength. He makes it plain that a presupposition of granting even such limited freedom is that 'anything he can spoil' and anything that could spoil him is out of reach (*E* p. 64). The teacher is seen as ever-present, ever-active in Emile's education. 'You make children copy' your virtuous example (*E* p. 68). 'In everything you must show clearly the use' (*E* p. 153). Rousseau does not go back on the strong claim made for interest as a motive force. The tutor is still expected to follow closely 'what [children] perceive to be of real and present value, either for use or enjoyment' (*E* p. 81), since Rousseau apparently cannot conceive of any other form of motivation. But he still holds to the distinction between the child's perception and reality, and to the assumption that the teacher is better placed to grasp reality. He controls affairs in the interests of reality in two ways: first he *sometimes* lets the children proceed according to their inclinations so that they discover for themselves that their perceptions as to what is of value are not always accurate; that is good, Rousseau rather glibly asserts, because if they had accepted that judgement on the authority of the teacher they would have become intellectually moribund (*E* p. 153). Secondly, he manipulates the overall situation in such a way that he has some considerable control over what the child does perceive as being of real and present value in the first place. It is this that particularly distinguishes Rousseau from many latter-day child-centred theorists: they write and proceed as if what interests the child is a sacred given. Rousseau appreciates that there is nothing sacred about it and that it is seldom an inevitable and unalterable given.

As teachers we should have been concerned with 'what we can do for our pupil through our choice of the circumstances in which he shall be placed', Rousseau frankly admits (*E* p. 181). All that we 'have gained has been won by force or guile . . . Emile's obedience was gained by constraint and deceit' (*E* p. 281). As Rousseau sees it, self-interest, which at first is unconscious but is none the less there, initially prompts the child to follow the tutor's lead – for the tutor, standing in for the parents, has been from the beginning a provider of food, security and love. Then, since he delivers the goods, the tutor seems to prove the child's instinctive self-interested judgement to have been correct. In time habit takes the place of instinct, and the child is easily controlled because he is ignorant; finally the tutor relinquishes control to Emile himself once he has developed the rational ability that, through the medium of the tutor, has actually been in control all along.

Clearly Rousseau advocates not freedom (absence of restraint) but a structured environment – structured in such a way that the child will come to recognise what is appropriate, and what is right. This he thinks will lead to what he understands by freedom, for in his view 'that man is truly free who desires what he is able to perform and does what he desires' (*E* p. 48). That is Rousseau's promise. Not absence of restraint, but absence of conflict between individual and social constraints. He is not subscribing to the absurd thesis that if children are left alone they will inevitably discover everything of importance of their own accord. Nor therefore is he open to the charge of inconsistently veering between demands for freedom (absence of restraint) and demands that it be limited. He is arguing, in practical terms, that we should be prepared to proceed very slowly in education, particularly during the first fifteen years, and that we must find ways of making the child perceive for himself that whatever is real and valuable *is* real and valuable.

NATURE

Rousseau's argument gains a considerable degree of plausibility from the use of the term 'nature'. It does so because in one sense 'natural' means nothing more than what is right, fitting or appropriate. In this sense we should, by definition, behave naturally, seek to bring people up naturally and avoid the unnatural. To deny it would amount to saying that we should do what is wrong, inappropriate and not fitting, which would be absurd. It is because the word can have this meaning that Rousseau's insistence that education should be according to nature is persuasive. Equally, what some take to be the essence of Rousseau's thesis, namely that we should do what is natural, would obviously be true in this sense of 'natural'. No less obviously the thesis would be trivial and uninformative, because it would leave open the question of what conduct *is* natural. It would amount to the suggestion that we should do what is right, behave as we ought and act in a fitting manner. Certainly the claim that 'the first impulses of nature are always right' (*E* p. 56) must be meant to mean more than that the first intimations of what is right are right, if it is to have any significance. It is evident then that, though Rousseau may gain something in terms of persuasive force from the favourable connotations of this sense of 'natural', it is not the sense of natural that he has in mind when he argues for natural education. Let us therefore consider some other possible meanings of the word.

1. In some contexts 'natural' may be used as a synonym for 'familiar' or 'usual'. That seems to be the sense of such remarks as 'that is his natural expression' or the command 'behave naturally'. 'Naturally' here is to be contrasted with 'unnatural' in the sense of strange, unusual or unexpected, as in a remark like 'what an unnatural thing for him to do'.

2. Sometimes the word 'natural' implies something semi-automatic and practically unavoidable, as when we say of somebody provoked beyond endurance that 'it was only natural for him to react like that'.

3. A third sense is implied by such remarks as 'breathing is natural' or 'smoking is an acquired rather than a natural habit'. In this sort of context 'natural' suggests reference to certain physical or biological norms. 'The migratory instinct is natural in certain birds' implies that it is the norm for the birds in question to have such instincts.

4. The last remark might also be taken to mean that the migratory instinct is innate, which gives us a fourth possible sense of 'natural'. We refer to natural talents and characteristics in this sense.

5. 'Natural' may imply genuineness, authenticity or reality and be contrasted with 'artificial', as in advertisements for natural butter.

6. It may mean something like spontaneous. In this sense natural behaviour is unpremeditated and unreflective, while unnatural behaviour might be calculated. Closely connected is natural behaviour in the sense of easy and graceful behaviour contrasted with unnatural in the sense of clumsy or awkward.

7. One may use 'natural' as a term to contrast with civilised or sophisticated. It is not precisely the opposite of either of them, for

one would not equate 'unnatural' with 'civilised' or 'sophisticated', or 'unsophisticated' with 'natural'. But the word does none the less carry the force of primitive in some contexts. For example, 'The way of life of the American Indians used to be more natural than it is now'.

8. The previous sense may perhaps be an offshoot of that sense of 'natural' that is applied to non-artefacts and suggests something of 'as it turns out' or 'as it occurs'. Thus 'I am letting my hair grow naturally'. Rock and wood are natural in this sense, in a way that ashtrays and chairs are not.

The preceding list is not supposed to be definitive, nor is it being suggested that the word should be or is usually or necessarily used in precisely one such sense alone. Often the word in a particular context carries overtones of many different meanings. But there *are* such different shades of meaning available, such senses that sometimes need to be distinguished, and in order to assess claims involving the word 'natural' one needs to be alert to these and similar nuances. Whether, for example, it is or is not human nature to be friendly depends partly on whether by 'human nature' we mean 'whatever humans do spontaneously', 'whatever was characteristic of human behaviour prior to the advance of civilisation', 'whatever is typical of human beings' or something else.

Rousseau's use of the term 'nature' fluctuates; what is important is to sort out the different senses appropriate to the different claims he makes using the word. When he refers to 'the inner growth of our organs and faculties' as 'the education of nature' it is evident that he is thinking of 'natural' in the sense of conforming to some biological norm (*E* p. 6). In this sense certain stages of maturation and development are natural, and Rousseau's claim amounts to the assertion that we must wait upon the occurrence of such stages of development. This claim seems uncontentious and not very helpful or informative. It amounts to saying that there are certain stages and details of physical development that must necessarily have been reached before certain paths are open to one, and to that extent they have primacy. Thus nature determines that we cannot walk without a certain kind of prior limb development.

But when Rousseau announces that 'the law of nature bids the woman obey the man' he means something quite different by the word 'nature', and is plainly mistaken in his claim (*E* p. 370). There are laws of nature in the sense of regularities that are inevitable –

it is a law of nature that animate matter dies – but female obedience is quite obviously not a law of nature in that sense. Such a role for women was however a feature or norm of Rousseau's world, as a result of which fact he may have regarded it as natural in the sense of usual. He may also have regarded it as natural in the sense of fitting or right, but there is no reason given why we should agree with him or be misled into thinking that some kind of objective truth is being revealed as a consequence of his use of the authoritative term 'law'. Obviously what Rousseau is trying to suggest is that this kind of role for woman is inevitable and right; but there is no reason for us to accept this, and, more to the immediate point, this introduces without warning a different sense of 'natural' to that used in the first quotation.

When Rousseau first begins to depict what he sees as a natural mother he effectively retains only the normative aspects of the term 'natural' and therefore begs the question. What he has to say amounts to his personal view of the ideal mother coupled with his insistence that this is natural in the sense of right. When however he parenthetically remarks that 'there are still a few young women of good natural disposition who refuse to be slaves of fashion' (*E* p. 14), he must surely mean by 'natural disposition' 'innate disposition' (notwithstanding the fact that any disposition is innate). When he proclaims that 'prudence is unnatural' he might mean any number of things (*E* p. 46). Probably he wants to convey the idea that it is a habit evolved by civilised communities, that it is not spontaneous, and that it is bad. But the fact that he may, by the use of one term, be hinting at various different claims cannot alter the need for each distinct claim implied to be separately substantiated. The fact that prudence is unnatural in one sense does not necessitate that it is in another.

When Rousseau writes, 'I have discarded as artificial what belonged to one nature and not to another, to one rank and not to another; I have regarded as proper to mankind what was common to all' (*E* p. 217), he seems to be suggesting that whatever is common to all men is natural and is therefore good. But why should this be so? Why is what is observed to be typical or characteristic of man presumed to be good? Again, we are told that 'no doubt in a state of nature man would find the most palatable food the most wholesome' (*E* p. 115). He regards the like of Cordon Bleu cookery as unnatural in the sense of the product of man's contrivance and therefore worse than more down-to-earth cooking or natural foods such as fruit. But why is what exists prior to man's shaping and interference presumed to be necessarily superior? It looks very much as if in both passages Rousseau is guilty of what is sometimes called the naturalistic fallacy. The fallacy basically involves confusing questions of fact and value and seeking to deduce a value judgement from purely factual premises. In its starkest form it involves moving from some example of the factual 'this is the case' directly to the conclusion that 'therefore this is good'. Rousseau seems to have no more reason for his judgement that natural food and whatever is common to all men are good than that they are there! Clearly, the mere fact that something exists, occurs, happens or is there is not in itself sufficient to show that it is good that it is or does.[1]

The above examples illustrate some of the different senses in which Rousseau uses the word 'natural'. The considerations raised render a large part of his argument vague to the point of vacuity. Is it true that 'the first impulses of nature are always right'? In the context of *Emile* as a whole this must mean that spontaneous intuitive insights and reactions are always correct. But that claim is plainly false, unless it is made true by definition. It is only certainly true if it is stipulated that we will only call virtuous qualities such as kindness, generosity or integrity natural impulses while corresponding vices or defects (meanness, selfishness, deceitfulness) are to be by definition unnatural. But, if the statement is made true in this way by defining 'natural' and 'right' or 'morally good' so that they coincide, we are being told nothing of interest. The claim *is* interesting however if it means that, as a matter of empirical fact, people's first intuitive responses tend towards the kind, generous and good rather than to the mean, selfish and bad. The trouble is that it is manifestly the case that this is by no means always so. The only remaining option is to argue that people's actual intuitive responses are not wholly good as things are, but that that is because people have been corrupted by circumstances. In an ideal situation immoral responses would never have developed. But to argue thus is to transpose a sensible argument to the realm of the likely story. There is no evidence for (or against) the thesis; no way of verifying or falsifying it.

There seems no obvious reason, then, to accept that people will of their own accord always pursue the good. Rousseau now asks his readers whether they think that 'any man can find true happiness elsewhere than in his natural state; and when you try to spare him all suffering are you not taking him out of his natural state?' (*E* p. 51). Precisely what is meant by 'his natural state' is obscure, as is the contention that true happiness can be found only there. All that is clear is that the meaning of 'natural' has changed again. And so it goes on. Although reference is elsewhere made to 'our natural passions' (*E* p. 173) in the plural, we are told at one point that 'the only natural passion is selfishness' (*E* p. 56). In what sense it is natural we are not clearly told. Is it innate in each individual? common to all men? unavoidable? Similarly, why is Emile 'naturally indifferent' to other people? Is the claim that human beings are constitutionally indifferent? Is this just another way of saying that Emile *is* indifferent, or what? At one point it looks very much as if Rousseau wants to identify 'natural' with 'instinctive' and thereby to demean rational and planned behaviour. Finally, we should note a point that will crop up again in subsequent chapters of this book. Some of Rousseau's uses of the word 'nature', as for example the passage where he decides that in manipulating Emile he has not retarded the progress of nature, strongly imply a view of static, innate human characteristics.

What can be made of all this? That Rousseau uses the term 'nature' in a variety of ways is indisputable. The variety of uses he employs does not perhaps lead to any real inconsistency or incoherence in his argument. On the other hand, it is important to recognise how thin and lacking in argument much of the text is, and can be seen to be, if the word natural is removed. Quite unconsciously, Rousseau has traded on its many meanings and varying associative ideas. Again and again the reader is implicitly invited to say to himself 'that is natural and therefore it is good'. But it should by now be clear that this won't do at all: aggression is natural in some sense of the word, but it does not follow that we want it or that it is a good thing.

Overall, whatever in his view need not be and should not be, gets labelled 'unnatural' by Rousseau. Whatever should be and would be but for man's mistakes, he calls 'natural'. Once we appreciate that, two major problems arise: first, where is the evidence or argument for the correctness of his view of what is and is not natural in this sense? We need some evidence that what Rousseau says should and would be, but for man's corrupt state, indeed should and would be. Second, Rousseau conveniently forgets that we, and the ways in which we behave, are also part of nature. So if all of nature is good, what has gone wrong? We know what, according to Rousseau, goes wrong now: it is what *Emile* is about – our society corrupts people from birth. But what initially went wrong? How did natural people in a natural world become unnatural? If Rousseau's thesis were correct it is logically inconceivable that a fall from grace should ever have come about. It is a major weakness in Rousseau's analysis of the human condition that he fails to see that what is conceived of as natural changes. This is true not only of the normative sense, where clearly people's views as to what is natural (right, fitting, appropriate) change, but also of the other senses. Many things that are natural now, in a number of different senses of 'natural', were not natural in precisely the same senses at an earlier stage of history or evolution. Recognition of this point should remove any lingering tendency to see the natural as somehow necessarily desirable.

USEFUL KNOWLEDGE

Rousseau thinks that what is worth learning is what is useful, and that a cardinal defect of the education system is that it teaches useless knowledge. This emphasis on useful knowledge, coupled with attacks on most of the typical school curriculum as being remote, useless or irrelevant, is predominant in contemporary radical literature as well. Rousseau's treatment of the theme is superior to that of others in at least one respect: he does recognise the need to indicate what knowledge is supposed to be useful for, and he does give some specific examples of allegedly useful and useless knowledge to consider. The point that it is no good talking about useful knowledge *in vacuo*, obvious though it is, is generally overlooked. Yet it is crucial. Indeed, it is a surprising thing that those who object to talk of knowledge as if it were some permanent static given, as most of the radicals do, none the less talk of the useful (the relevant, the pertinent) as if there was a list of useful things that had remained unchanged since time immemorial. But nothing is useful or useless without some kind of qualification; nothing has a purpose or lacks it except in some context; nothing is relevant or irrelevant until it is considered in relation to other specific goals, wants or purposes. The idea, for instance, that engineering is somehow innately useful while Latin is useless is preposterous: for those of us who do not care about the products of mechanical engineering and want to be able to read the poems of Catullus in the original tongue the situation is reversed.

Rousseau's plan of education is designed to fit the individual in particular ways for life in a particular kind of community, and it is in the light of that broad aim that judgements as to usefulness in the context of his thought first have to be made. Subsequently, we can if we wish challenge his aim and the usefulness for our different purposes of what may obviously be useful to him. For example, it clearly is useful, given Rousseau's overall position, for Emile to travel the world, just as, in a different context, it was useful for Spartan children to be left to forage for their food as best they might. But it does not follow that either practice would be particularly useful for the typical child in this country today. Rousseau holds the straightforward general view that what is useful 'is that small store [of knowledge] which really contributes to our welfare' (*E* p. 129). But what does contribute to our welfare? Even assuming that we share something of Rousseau's ideals, it is at this juncture that reference to the useful is likely to become useless as a criterion for giving us practical help in discerning what ought to be done. Rousseau suffers from a weakness shared by all the radicals: while priding himself on his vision, he has too facile and unimaginative an idea of the possibilities of use – of the myriad ways in which things may be useful, long-term, short-term, direct, indirect, to hundreds of goals which may in themselves also function as useful steps towards other goals. The radical mind is in danger of focusing on a few hitherto neglected goals and then confining the term useful to a select list of the most obvious and immediate paths leading to each goal. It is this simplistic vision that no doubt partly accounts for the sense of impatient exasperation that one detects in some of their work: how could anyone seriously doubt, they seem to be saying, that it is more useful to apprentice yourself to a plumber, if that is what you are thinking of becoming, than to perfect your English grammar? The answer to such a question is that it unwarrantably presupposes that the question of what it is useful for children to learn can be reduced to what are the most immediately efficacious ways of picking up trades currently judged to be necessary by society.

Rousseau objects to 'heraldry, geography, chronology, languages, etc., studies so remote from man, and even more remote from the child, that it is a wonder if he can ever make any use of any part of them' (*E* p. 73). Now of course such studies are likely to be 'remote' from a good many children in the specific sense of 'not obviously and immediately part of their everyday life and thoughts'. But from the fact that something is initially remote in this sense of unfamiliar it does not follow that it will remain so. Initiation into some remote subject may quite literally transform one's everyday life and thoughts, so that what was previously remote becomes immediate and important, and vice versa. Again, from the fact that something is initially remote it does not follow that it would be surprising if any use were ever made of it: reading and writing are initially every bit as remote from the child as geography, but it would be a wonder if the typical child did not come to make considerable use of them. (What the claim that such studies as these are 'remote from man' is supposed to mean, I confess I do not know.)

Rousseau seeks to show us that children ought not to study such things as heraldry, geography, chronology and languages, and he hopes to do this by peppering them with put-you-down epithets such as 'irrelevant', 'remote', 'useless'. Very obviously they are not relevant, immediate and useful in the way that the skill of typing is to the role of the secretary; equally, they are not likely to seem to be immediately pertinent to the child. The basic fallacy in this kind of argument however lies in assuming that, if we concede that children should study what is useful, we thereby necessarily concede that (1) what they study should immediately be seen by them to be useful; (2) what is useful is synonymous with what is immediately and directly useful to some end; (3) what is useful must be calculated by reference to currently held aims or goals; (4) what is useful must specifically be related to what is useful to man in his wage-earning capacity. No argument has been presented to show that points (1)–(4) are implicit in the concept of useful or that we should accept them. One might consistently agree with Rousseau that we should teach useful knowledge and reject points (1)–(4).

What is taught should of course be useful rather than useless. But in practical terms that bland vague statement needs to be interpreted with reference to a number of important variable factors. We have to consider the immediate and long-term use of something; things that it may be directly and indirectly used for; whether its specific usefulness in some respects is offset by disadvantages in other respects; and whether while having no immediate use itself it might not be a necessary condition of certain other useful things. We have also to take account of whether ultimately we assess usefulness in terms of being a source of pleasure, a means to further sources of pleasure, a means of acquiring wealth, fame, advancement, a means of improving society or some other one or combination of many possibilities. We have to clarify also whether we assess usefulness in terms of the use that we *think* something *could* be put to, the use that we *think* it *will* be put to, or the use that it *will* be put to. Consequently, when Rousseau asserts that children should study their own town rather than Pekin in geography on the grounds that the former study is more useful, he is avoiding all the important and interesting questions about education (*E* p. 134). Of course, the study of our town seems more pertinent to the child, and has a more immediate and obvious use. But it is another question as to whether it is more useful that children should pursue such study than the study of Pekin. That question cannot be answered by appeal to the concept of usefulness alone.

The question of what knowledge is of most worth is crucial, but any answer couched in terms only of 'useful' is useless. At one extreme such an answer is a tautology, because 'useful' and 'worthwhile' are regarded as synonymous; at the other it is certainly highly contentious and probably false (what is useful in the sense of having obvious and immediate use is not necessarily the most worthwhile knowledge). The more serious problem is that the term obscures rather than clarifies argument, since its denotation may, and often does, vary. Rousseau has not shown us that the examples of activities and studies that he regards as useful are so in any significant sense; he has therefore not produced an adequate argument to support his specific claims about which studies are useful and which useless. That being so, we do not have a clear or satisfactory answer to the question of what is worth learning. Consequently it cannot at this stage be assumed that Rousseau's methods will produce desirable results.

LEARNING

'Give your scholar no verbal lessons; he should be taught by experience alone' (*E* p. 56).[2] The teacher should present problems to the student and let him solve them himself; this will serve to arouse the child's curiosity, develop his ability to solve problems and help him learn how to find things out for himself.

Rousseau thinks that, provided we do not fill the child's mind with irrelevant flotsam and jetsam, which we wrongly assume to be important, and provided we ensure that he is placed in a stimulating and intriguing environment, the child will learn from experience both various truths and bits of information and also how to learn.[3] In time he will come to master knowledge and his world. Behind this belief lie two further ideas: first the idea that 'sense experiences are the raw material of thought' (*E* p. 31), which is to say, in outline, that all knowledge is based upon what we can see, hear, touch, smell and taste, though Rousseau probably understands the term 'sense' more widely to include such things as instinctive reactions and feelings. Second, there is the idea that, generally speaking, adults overlay naked perceptions with a host of assumptions and that these unnatural accretions must be kept away from the child. Thus I say that I see John bullying James. But what I actually see might more properly be described as John's first landing repeatedly on James's face. That it is an instance of bullying is something that I can appreciate only if I know certain things about the situation that I am not directly perceiving. If we do not quite literally keep our mouths shut, then children will grow up seeing the world through our eyes. In appreciating this point Rousseau would seem to have grasped most of what is important in contemporary sociology of knowledge: to a considerable extent what is out there depends on how you look at it. Rousseau's suggestion is that one might in principle look at it naturally (without any preconceptions) and hence see only what is there. (The more foolish of contemporary sociologists deny that anything is there and thereby, besides rendering themselves foolish, make a nonsense of the political complaint that many of them also espouse. If there *is* only how one looks at it or perceives it, the world cannot do otherwise than present to its children what it sees – see Chapter 7 below.)

On the face of it this theory seems straightforward with regard to physical objects but absurd with regard to abstract ideas. In what way is sense experience the basis of the idea of justice, for instance? Rousseau is well aware of this problem and thinks that he has the answer in his distinction between images, which 'are merely the picture of external objects', and ideas, which are 'notions about those objects determined by their relations' (*E* p. 71). The claim is that 'from the comparison of many successive or simultaneous sensations and the judgement arrived at with regard to them, there springs a sort of mixed or complex sensation which I call an idea' (*E* p. 165), and Rousseau emphasises that the ideas, though dependent on sensations, are not really themselves sensations, and that it is the individual himself who produces the idea, although again he can only do this when he receives an impression from things. In the early years the child only receives impressions or images, but gradually he develops the capacity to produce ideas. Always, however, 'everything that comes into the human mind enters through the gates of sense', which leads Rousseau to say that 'man's first reason is a reason of sense experience. It is this that serves as a foundation for the reason of the intelligence: our first teachers in natural philosophy are our feet, hands and eyes' (*E* p. 90).

Has Rousseau given us a satisfactory answer to the problem he recognised? His use of the word 'reason' in the last quotation is confusing. It would be better replaced in the first statement ('a reason of sense expression') by something like 'awareness' or 'perception', since naked sense experience is precisely not reason in any normal sense of that word. In itself perception involves no reason (despite the fact that in practice we may modify our perceptions by the use of reason) and is to be distinguished from it. So what we are being told in straightforward terms is that awareness or perception precedes reasoning. Rousseau wants to persuade us that abstract and speculative reasoning is tied to perception, but the important question is what the nature of, and how strong, such a tie-up is supposed to be. He implies that the relationship is immediate, direct and strong. But it is quite plain that that is not so: atomic theory is as certainly not obviously, directly and strongly linked and related to everyday perceptual experience, as it certainly is related in some way. Once one realises that it is not disputed that there is some kind of link between direct perception and abstract reasoning, and that what Rousseau needs and wants to establish is that the link is of a particular strong and immediate kind, it becomes doubtful whether he has actually produced any argument at all for his case. He appears to have done little more than assert that the human mind has the ability to produce abstract ideas and to think in abstract terms, but that it can only do so when prompted by sense impressions or images. That doesn't tell us very much – it tells us, indeed, precisely nothing about the mysterious process whereby this happens, which is presumably what we are interested in. We want to understand how Emile will make the transition from an observer of isolated scenes to an abstract thinker, because, until we know *how*, it must remain an open question whether he *can* or whether he *will*, in the circumstances proposed by Rousseau.

It may be true that all our knowledge is based on sense experience, if we take that to mean that all our knowledge ultimately has to square with our sense experience, so that if our sense experiences were to alter radically this would necessitate a radical revision of what we took to be knowledge. This would be to say that, in so far as any proposition is true, it must either itself be or in principle be reducible to a number of other propositions that are directly verifiable by the senses. It is true also that as a matter of fact much of our knowledge is acquired by means of sense experience. But to say that some is, is not to say that all is; to say that all knowledge is *based on* sense experience, in the sense noted, is not to say that all knowledge is *acquired through* sense experience; and to say that all or any knowledge could be acquired in this way is not to say that it must or should be. One does not have to await experience of something or a chance encounter to gain knowledge of it. Even original advances in knowledge may be made as the result of an hypothesis. It is also important to distinguish two senses of learning: learning in the sense of acquiring knowledge, and learning in the sense of gaining practical experience of the application of knowledge. It seems more plausible to suggest that learning in the second sense can best take place through experience than learning in the first sense.

But whatever the epistemological relationship between knowledge and experience, it is clear that there are some things that cannot, and many more that will not, be learnt through experience in the sense of learnt as a result of having experiences that reveal them. One may learn that flowers bloom and that trees shed leaves by direct perception; but one cannot or will not learn that God exists, that justice demands impartial treatment, the square root of four, or atomic theory simply by perception. (Nor is it necessary to have experience of atomic theory in all its ramifications to have learnt it.) The truth is that most of the knowledge that schools typically teach and that societies typically want and feel a need to hand on is precisely knowledge or understanding of the unperceived workings that lie behind perceived events. As Rousseau himself admits when distinguishing between images and ideas, all that the individual perceives is a tadpole and then a frog. The individual does not see or perceive an example of biological development. He does not even have to interpret what he sees in this way. He may interpret it as a substitution, magic, the work of God or any number of things. The so-called perception that the tadpole becomes the frog is something that is ordinarily not perceived at all; to see it that way is to add a particular understanding to the naked perception. Again, it is all very well for Rousseau to aver that Emile, faced with the need to move an object far heavier than himself, will learn which lever to use to move it through experience (which here must mean trial and error), but even if that is true he will still not necessarily have acquired understanding of what he is doing (*E* p. 97). Hitting upon the lever that works does not in itself tell you what it is about it that makes it work. Emile might manage to abstract some formula, but it is by no means certain that he will.

Not only are there some things that could not and some that would not be learnt from experience, but the above comments must surely also lead us to wonder whether this is not a very inefficient way of learning. It will certainly be slow; it will probably be very limited. Rousseau, perhaps trying to forestall such a criticism, tries to draw an analogy with a desert island (*E* p. 130), where, he suggests, exploring the island itself would be a good deal more important than speculating on more *recherché* matters with the aid of scientific instruments. But why accept the analogy? We do not live in circumstances anywhere near approaching a desert island, so why act as if we did? Why confine ourselves to our immediate surroundings?

Rousseau's objections to instruction are not very strong either. It will be remembered that Emile finally has to visit other states, to compensate for the insularity of his previous experience. Perhaps such experience of politics will be more vivid for him than reading about it would be. As against that, this approach will give him a very narrow view of politics and it is quite false to imagine that it must reveal the naked truth whereas a book would involve distortion and idiosyncratic interpretation. An outsider studying Parliament through books might have no more idiosyncratic a view than Enoch Powell, whose knowledge is gained predominantly through experience. Rousseau believes that books and instruction *must* stultify the child's interest and imagination; but for that view, which a thousand personal experiences can falsify, he offers no argument, just as he offers none for his insistence that curiosity alone provides a motive for learning. He also suggests that if children learn to respect the teacher's judgement they may cease to think for themselves. But sometimes teachers do know better, and the lesson that sometimes one ought to take note of those better informed than oneself might itself be worth learning. Rousseau himself later observes that Emile should have a confidence in his tutor which 'should rest on the authority of reason, and on superior knowledge' (*E* p. 209).

Finally, there is the question of whether Rousseau's suggestion that he is teaching Emile how to learn has any mileage in it. If the claim were merely that he is bringing up the child in such a way that he will retain a natural curiosity, then we could let it pass, noting only that no case has been given for asserting that more traditional teaching methods must stifle curiosity. But Rousseau, in common with many contemporary radicals, seems to feel that he is saying more than this. The suggestion seems to be that Emile is actually learning the way to learn, so that he will subsequently be able to learn anything he wants for himself. This way of talking is to be strongly resisted for the excellent reason that there is no such thing as the way to learn and no such thing as the faculty of learning or talent to learn. This is not simply the empirical point that there is no real evidence for the phenomenon known as transfer of training; there is also the logical point that the idea that there could be some general ability that allowed the individual to switch from field to field is absurd, in view of the logically distinct nature of different kinds of inquiry. If the notion of knowing how to learn is to mean anything it must refer to a variety of characteristics and dispositions such as curiosity, determination, and being systematic. But in addition to these qualities, in order to learn anything it is necessary to understand the nature of the area of inquiry.

The upshot of this section is damaging for Rousseau's thesis. One of the points that he wishes to make is that instruction is a bad thing because it is unnatural. It is of course unnatural in the sense that it is an organised man-construct, but in that sense unnatural things are not necessarily bad. The suggestion that children inevitably, successfully and efficiently acquire all worthwhile knowledge and get inside all allegedly important disciplines is untrue, as is the converse assumption that instruction must dampen enthusiasm.

MORAL EDUCATION

Rousseau believes that in their innermost nature people are prompted and guided by self-love, not as a matter of contingent fact but as a necessary part of being human; but he also believes that they come to feel pity as a sentiment, and can be brought, given the right circumstances, to recognise a community of interest between themselves and others. On these characteristics of man, amoral though they may seem, a moral edifice can be created. He believes that the child is born like a *tabula rasa* in respect of moral values. Some of his remarks may suggest otherwise, and he has sometimes been interpreted as saying that the child is born good and all we have to do is let the innate goodness thrive. But in no recognisable sense is the child born good, and Rousseau did not suppose that he was. The doctrines of original goodness and its counterpart original sin are both in a straightforward sense absurd. They are absurd because being good or bad presupposes some degree of cognitive awareness and choice. Just as I am not morally responsible for what I do in my sleep, so the newborn baby is not a moral agent. Rousseau is well aware of this point (he makes it himself when he talks of the inappropriateness of punishment).

Of course you can interpret the claim that the child is born good in such a way as to *make* it make sense. You might mean that the child will inevitably become good, in which case the claim is intelligible and false. Or you might mean that it will become good given certain conditions, which is what Rousseau is claiming; but the question then is whether, once the conditions have been specified, the claim is true. If that is what you mean, then the statement that he is born good does not add anything to the argument about whether he is likely to grow up good. Whichever way we look at it therefore we are stuck with the notion of original vacuity (a *tabula rasa*) rather than original sin or goodness. We have a creature of flesh and blood, concerning which Rousseau is saying not 'Do not corrupt this innocent', but 'Do not do as is usually done or you will produce evil consequences; do as I suggest and the consequences will be good.' He is offering a specific prescription – demanding a positive course of action.

His claim is that, if the adult world holds itself back and is not over-eager to correct and reprimand, expecting results too early; if it creates habits by means of example and other little twists, in particular by creating consequences so that the child pays for what the adult has classified as his mistakes – in time a certain kind of character will be developed in the child, namely one that holds appropriate moral values.[4] 'The only natural [innate – R.B.] passion is selfishness': we are born with an instinctual self-preservation order and that 'becomes good or bad by the use made of it and the relations established by its means'.

It is not denied that the child may do mischief, cause trouble or harm, even do wrong things, but he will not be immoral because he will lack malicious intention. Before a certain age, then, it is true by definition that the child will not be a wrongdoer. But Rousseau also assumes that the child could not develop malicious intentions. To the observation that he clearly could, since some do, Rousseau will reply that of course some children do as things are. But in the better circumstances that he envisages they won't. Malice, ill-will, and exploitation of others are thus seen as entirely the product of environment. Whenever the child does do a wrong act the teacher must arrange for 'the natural consequences of [the] fault' to be visited on him, so that, in addition to having no ill-will or malicious intent, the child develops a prudent dislike for wrong acts. 'Thus you will arrange that all the ill effects of lying ... should fall on' his head, notwithstanding the fact that in telling a lie he is not strictly speaking a wrongdoer (*E* p. 65).

There is not a great deal of room for argument over the central claim that malicious intention is solely the consequence of environmental factors, since it is a 'likely story'. There is no way, in practice, of determining its truth or falsity. Rousseau may be correct in asserting that no individual would ever take up bullying, lying or stealing in the first place if he were not put into situations in which it seemed to him advantageous to do so or if he were not frustrated by circumstances. But it seems quite as reasonable to imagine that even in ideal circumstances some individuals might just want more for themselves, might just happen to dislike certain other people, and so forth. Two things are certain: the matter cannot be proven one way or the other; and anyway, in practice, the ideal circumstances on which so much is made to depend cannot be realised. Emile *will* be subjected to environmental influence. Any realistic proposal for moral upbringing must start by facing up to that fact of life.

The argument about natural consequences is another matter. The problem here is not that one doubts the truth of the claim; it is well enough attested that you can modify behaviour by systematic deployment of such things as praise, blame, gratification and pain. The problem is not whether such a procedure would be efficacious in achieving desired behaviour, but whether it is morally acceptable.

Rousseau employs our old friend 'natural' to disarm the reader; the consequences arranged by the tutor are 'natural' ones, which suggests to the unwary that they are somehow all right and deservedly introduced. But the only sense in which the consequences that Rousseau has in mind actually are natural is that they bear some relation to the act originally performed. (In one important sense they are obviously unnatural, since they have to be arranged by the tutor.) We must not be misled into assuming that forming habits by means of fixing the consequences must be legitimate since the consequences are natural. Appreciation of that point takes some of the attraction out of the doctrine of natural consequences and leads us on to a second point: what consequences does one arrange; how does one determine what they should be? What, for example, should the tutor judge to be the natural consequences of rape, theft or arson? If those examples seem a little extreme in relation to children, we may ask the same question of bullying or telling lies. Estimating what the appropriate natural consequences should be itself involves making value judgements: being despised, for example, will be a consequence of bullying other people in some groups and not in others, depending upon their values. If any consequences involving value judgements are left out of it, then estimating natural consequences seems to amount to predicting inevitable consequences. But are there any inevitable consequences of rape or bullying? Talk of arranging for natural consequences to befall the agent, therefore, obscures the point that in practice such a policy involves choosing which types of behaviour to reinforce with pleasing consequences and which to discourage with unpleasant consequences. This in turn leads on to a third and crucial point, the question of whether this type of up-bringing should be regarded as truly moral at all. In as much as freely choosing to act in a particular way rather than another is regarded as essential to truly moral conduct, the kind of upbringing here envisaged must tend in the opposite direction to that of producing a moral adult; it tends rather towards producing conditioned responses. Furthermore, it is at a variance with Rousseau's own arguments about punishment and wrongdoing, where he puts considerable emphasis on motive in determining moral responsibility. His plan of moral upbringing, by contrast, amounts to a plan for training children to behave in certain predetermined ways. In effect, he proposes a more systematic and efficient way of openly doing what most people do unconsciously, not very openly and rather badly.

However, there is not much room for doubt that in the long digression in Book IV of *Emile* in which the Savoyard priest is introduced, Rousseau invokes the idea of innate good. The priest is made to introduce the concept of conscience. He emphatically insists that conscience is not the product of the environment; indeed, it is described as withstanding the pressures of environment: 'Conscience persists in following the order of nature in spite of all the laws of man' (*E* p. 229). He is claiming quite plainly that there is within each one of us an innate sense of justice and virtue. This sense 'is to the soul what instinct is to the body' (*E* p. 252). There are, he points out, quite obviously instinctive feelings in animals such as dogs and, in a similar way, there are in man intuitive moral sentiments (*E* p. 249). Mankind spontaneously senses the goodness and evil of certain things. Conscience is the name Rousseau gives to that sense.

That men do have moral sentiments is true (though where they come from is another matter), and Rousseau's case appears the stronger because what he regards as moral values are closely related to intuitive and instinctive feelings such as self-love, fear, pain and dread of death (*E* p. 253). It is more plausible to regard self-love as innate than, say, charity. But the problems remain.

First, what is it that we are being asked to believe in? 'An innate moral faculty' is a useful turn of phrase, but it should not bind us to any notion of a discernable element in the human body; it need only refer to a tendency to do some things rather than others. If Rousseau's references to the conscience are supposed to imply some actual element in the make-up of a human being that necessarily and inevitably impels him towards right conduct, where is there the least trace of an argument or reason for accepting that there is such a faculty? Nowhere in his writings. Second, assuming that we accept that we do all have such a faculty, that is to say something that obviously, necessarily and insistently drives us towards certain types of conduct and away from others, how do we know that the conduct it impels us towards is indeed right conduct? How do I know that my instinctive moral sentiment is correct? If the answer given is that such is the nature of the moral faculty that it cannot but prescribe right conduct, then how do I know how to distinguish between the promptings of my conscience and the promptings of my selfishness, fear or any other faculties that it seems no less reasonable to suppose I have? Whichever way we choose to look at it, it is indisputable that people can feel 'drawn towards' different courses of action. There seems to be no warrant at all for saying that the 'moral pull' is clearly distinguishable from any other. Third, how does Rousseau's view of conscience square with his general thesis on moral up-bringing? If every individual has this conscience which cannot err, then there is no obvious need for the teacher to do anything at all. Conversely, if we need to promote it by means of arranging natural consequences, then we are not dealing with an innate faculty. The truth is that Rousseau is trying to have it all ways: the moral faculty is there and can do no wrong; it will inevitably grow; but you must stop it being uprooted or destroyed. But for none of this is there any evidence at all. It involves treating moral development as if it were a species of physical development and, furthermore, a species of physical development strictly analogous to certain forms of plant life. One may say that an acorn will grow into an oak tree in certain specifiable conditions, that it certainly will not grow into anything else, and that if we do not ensure the appropriate conditions it will not grow at all. In broad terms one might say something similar of the physical development of a human being. But no reason at all has been given for accepting the wildly improbable thesis that there is, so to speak, an acorn of the tree of moral virtue embedded in each human embryo.

One of Rousseau's particular concerns is to emphasise something other than man's rationality. He is not anti-reason but he is anti the stereotype ideal of the rational man that is so often, though quite unnecessarily, depicted entirely in terms of reason. He wants feeling and passion to be given their due. 'It is one of the faults of our age to rely too much on cold reason, as if men were all mind' (*E* p. 286) – another theme currently enjoying much favour. Hence central to his picture of the moral man is conscience, which is as much feeling and commitment as judgement. But heartwarming and well-intentioned as all that may be, his view of moral growth remains vitiated by a central contradiction: either there is within man an unfailing ability to see the good, or there is not.

CHICKEN AND EGG[5]

Rousseau alleges that *Emile* cannot be dismissed as mere speculation or Utopian dreaming. Furthermore, although the phrase 'noble savage' is often misleadingly quoted, it is explicitly said that Emile is not a 'savage' to be sent 'back to the woods' (*E* p. 217). This education is designed to produce a man fit to take his place and play an active part in civilised society, and as the book progresses Rousseau grows more confident that Emile could actually go back into society and cope with it successfully both on its terms and his own (derived from his peculiar education). 'Living in the whirl of social life it is enough that he should not let himself be carried away by the passions and prejudices of men. Let him see with his eye and feel with his heart. Let him own no sway but that of reason' (*E* p. 217).

But can the new-style education take place in society as it is? Only if Emile can somehow be removed from the evil influence of that society. A tall order in realistic terms. As Rousseau himself admits, 'here we have a real and sensible objection' to his proposals (*E* p. 58). In a nutshell: the perfect education demands getting away from the imperfect society. As we have seen, meeting the objection involves Rousseau in insisting on total isolation for Emile (which of course amounts to total control for the tutor) until the fourth and final stage, when, suitably strengthened against temptation, he can be led into society. But to the pressing practical question, 'is this possible?' Rousseau has only the astonishing reply: 'I fancy I could easily answer that objection, but why should I answer every objection?' (*E* p. 82).

The trouble is that by the nature of the problem, this cannot be a matter of degree. It would show a complete lack of understanding of Rousseau to say that in practical terms his theory demands *as little* influence on the child *as possible*. What his theory actually demands is the all-embracing and exclusive influence of his point of view; and, given what that point of view is, it is implausible in the extreme to imagine that such an education could take place in society either as it was in Rousseau's day or as it is today. But according to Rousseau himself society (the chicken) cannot change until education (the egg) is changed.

CHAPTER 4

A. S. NEILL
1883-1973

EDUCATIONAL THEORY

Neill professed to be hostile to theory and theoretical work, which at first blush seems rather odd in a man who devoted the first half of his life to picking up psychological theories and the second half to writing general books about education. Something of the explanation, however, lies in what Neill understands by the word 'theory'. At best, for him, 'theory' is 'talk': it may be true, it may be sharp and to the point, but talking isn't doing, talking isn't proving, and for the most part it's empty air. Usually, in his hands, 'theory' is a pejorative term, meaning something like 'unsuitably abstract' or 'idle speculation'. Very often he uses the term to suggest a contrast with truth or reality as implied in remarks such as 'This isn't theory, it's fact'; or, to take an example from Neill himself, 'I am not theorising, I know that . . .' (*S* p. 115). When he asserts aggressively that 'theory bores' children (*S* p. 55), the context makes it clear that 'theory' here is equivalent to 'abstraction' and is to be contrasted with the practical and concrete. When he says 'I have not spent the last forty years writing down theories about children. Most of what I have written has been based on observing children [and] living with them' (*S* p. 89), 'theory' suggests 'speculative rumination', to be contrasted with scientific inquiry.

But the word 'theory' does not have to imply vague, unfounded and unstructured talk. Scientific theory, for example, is highly systematised and precise talk. And although the theoretical and the practical are to be distinguished, they are not necessarily opposed to one another or in conflict. It is very much to be hoped, for instance, that the theory that lies behind bridge-building or medical practice is both sound and in close harmony with those particular activities. What is meant by educational theory is the product of disciplined thought about and inquiry into educational practice: an amalgam of information, research, hypothesis and ideas, which will probably owe something to the findings of sociology and psychology and other empirical investigations, something to studies of specifically class-room or school situations, and something to philosophical examination of the meaning and logic of crucial concepts, ideas and arguments. Theory in this sense may be good or bad, depending on the quality and accuracy of what is fed in and the use subsequently made of that data in an attempt to synthesise and draw conclusions. Theory in this sense is an inevitable adjunct of practice, although it may not be consciously articulated by the practitioner himself. We do things for reasons. Some teachers may do anything that they are told to do; others, only and precisely what they grew up to assume a teacher should do. But by and large we recognise that changed circumstances may demand changes in practice, and we try to adapt, while remaining consistent in principle and trying to meet certain broad objectives, so that we can continue to believe in ourselves and have some faith in what we are doing. All of this, which might be summarised as a tendency towards rational, purposive activity, presupposes, involves and demands theory. For we do what we do because we believe it to be best (or best in the circumstances), and reasoning towards that conclusion or attempting to substantiate it is to engage in educational theorising. Even when we do not overtly engage in such reasoning, our actions, in so far as we choose them, implicitly reveal that we subscribe to one view rather than another. It is true that a theoretical weakness is not necessarily a practical one. One might consistently hold the view that, although Rousseau's theoretical writings are fundamentally contradictory and incoherent, what he actually proposes to do represents an excellent course of action. But that is only to say that something might be true, even if a particular argument for its truth is unsound. That is certainly so, but we could only ever know that this was the case in a particular instance if we had some other argument, another piece of theorising, to show us that the thing in question was true.

Furthermore, whatever he may say, Neill indulges in theory no less than any of the other educationalists referred to in this book. For that is merely to say that his books like theirs are concerned with and involve abstract arguments and ideas about what we should do with children and why, drawing heavily upon such disciplines as psychology and dipping not a little into the realm of philosophy. Whether Neill's attempts at educational theorising are any good is another question. But that he is constantly making the attempt cannot be doubted. Nor should we tolerate a situation in which his theorising is removed beyond possibility of searching criticism by dint of pretending that it is not theory at all and that theory is just a vain pursuit for pedantic academics (see Appendix, p. 185).

It is also surely reasonable to insist that the theoretical pre-suppositions of particular practices should be articulated whenever and wherever possible. We must distinguish the question of whether theory and practice are necessarily divorced (to which the answer is clearly no) from the question of whether particular flights into theory are coherent and practical. The latter question must be pursued, if we are to arrive at sound reasons for adopting particular practices. Nor should it mistakenly be supposed that whether a theory is any good can only be decided by seeing whether it works, so that educational practice is the necessary and sufficient testing ground of all educational ideas. In the first place you cannot judge whether a particular system of education is working simply by looking at it in practice. The idea does not make sense, since whether it is judged to be working well or not must depend not only on what we see but also on long-term consequences that we cannot see, on inferences about how such an approach would affect other children in other circumstances that we cannot see, and above all on judgements as to what ought to be achieved out of the thousands of objectives that might be pursued. This means that judgements as to whether a school is working in practice presuppose some theoretical stance, and the less thought has gone into the theoretical stance, the more misgivings others may have about our judgement as to how well a particular school works in practice. Second, it is necessary to distinguish between the view that the final test of whether an idea, at any rate in relation to matters of fact, is true is to see whether it works (which is at least plausible) and the view that what makes a claim true or an idea valid is that it works and is seen to work (which is not even sensible). Even if we were all to agree that Summerhill works in practice, it would not be that fact that made it a good school. What would make it a good school would be that it was very successful in achieving whatever we thought ought to be achieved, which indicates yet again (1) that to determine whether it is a good school we must have examined our aims and objectives and alternative sets of means for achieving them; and (2) that that kind of theoretical inquiry, besides being necessary, might be sufficient to allow us to reach a conclusion. The practical business of setting up a school in accordance with our ideas cannot in itself prove the wisdom of our ideas. At best it can confirm that what we believed would happen does happen and to that extent it can show our theorising to have been sound. (For a further note on Neill's style of argument, see Appendix, p. 185.)

NEILL, ROUSSEAU AND HAPPINESS

Neill doesn't like the world as it is any more than Rousseau liked his world, to some extent for the same kind of reason: 'our veneered civilisation' is full of 'sham and shoddy' (*S* p. 176) and we need to be rid of it. We must break down 'the conflict between conscience and human nature' (*S* p. 263), the former term being used in a sense almost the opposite of Rousseau's to mean social and artificial feelings of value. There is also a new emphasis. Neill's main objection is not to triviality, hypocrisy or artificiality but to hate, which he sees as the source and symptom of all our troubles – a sort of all-pervasive scourge. Nor does he think it likely that the world will be saved by political means, for so much of what is nominally good in politics is actually founded on hate. 'Too many are socialists because they hate the rich instead of loving the poor' (*S* p. 92).

But he is less concerned about reforming society than Rousseau. It is not that he thinks such reform unimportant, but he does not see it as his particular province. To be sure, he sees the root cause of the sick and unhappy civilisation that we have as being a lack of freedom for children, as a consequence of which they are de-humanised, 'trained to say nay to life ... yea to all that is negative' (*S* p. 101). None the less, he will leave the world as it is. 'I have to compromise ... realising that my primary job is not the reformation of society, but the bringing of happiness to some few children' (*S* p. 35). Summerhill, then is not designed to contribute to the maintenance of society by bringing children up to keep it going –

indeed, the hope is that in time the nature of society will change, but the immediate objective is to allow particular children happiness now and to equip them to survive happily in the world as it is. More than once Neill asserts that happiness is 'the aim of life' (*S* p. 36). Although, characteristically, he does not recognise any particular problem about what happiness is or indulge in any close analysis of the concept, it is clear that he interprets it in substantially the same way as Rousseau to mean something akin to contentment. 'If the word happiness means anything, it means an inner feeling of well-being, a sense of balance, a feeling of being contented with life' (*S* p. 308). He claims that 'all crimes, all hatreds, can be reduced to unhappiness. This book is an attempt to show how unhappiness arises, how it ruins human lives, and how children can be reared so that much of this unhappiness will never arise' (*S* p. 15). But Neill nowhere entertains the idea that ultimate happiness might demand a present sacrifice: his task, as he sees it, is to give children happiness now, as a result of which, he seems to think, the future will take care of itself.

A basic difference now emerges between Neill and Rousseau.[1] The latter, as we have seen, for all the references to freedom in his writing, has an image of man as he would like him to be and proposes a system of education designed to produce man in that image. Emile is constantly subject to the tutor's control. Neill on the other hand means what he says when he proposes that children, once placed in a particular environment, should for the most part be left alone to do what they want. He believes that if they are left alone they will rapidly become happy and social persons. Rousseau will introduce Emile to history and physics when the time is ripe, ensure that he visits foreign states to gain an understanding of politics, prevent him reading to begin with and then give him *Robinson Crusoe*. Neill will have none of this. Both men place children in the playground rather than the classroom. But whereas Rousseau will get them to play the games that he wants them to play, Neill will let them play what they like. He does not want them to learn through doing or playing so much as to play and enjoy themselves (*S* p. 40).

Neill's view is that if the child is given freedom and love he will be happy and will grow up 'naturally' (here 'appropriately') so that he continues to be happy; that is all he wants or claims for children in his care. He is not concerned about academic success (or even competence), sporting prowess, cultivated manners or cultural goals.

'My own criterion of success', he openly avows, 'is the ability to work joyfully and live positively' (*S* p. 41). In common with most of the radicals, he thinks too much emphasis has been placed on reason, knowledge and intellect, and not enough on feeling and emotion. His basic tenet is that happiness can be bestowed by abolishing authority and letting the child be himself, surrounded only by love. He claims that Summerhill 'demonstrates that freedom works', which is to say that it produces happiness; whereas 'all the Greek and maths and history in the world will not help to make the home more loving, the child free from inhibitions, the parent free from neurosis' (*S* p. 20), and what that means is that the traditional school curriculum makes no contribution to the happiness of the individual. Whether it is true is another matter.

SUMMERHILL

Summerhill is a school that brings children up on what Neill calls the self-regulation principle. Ideally, since the object of self-regulation is that the individual should at no stage be subject to external regulation, children should be in such an environment from birth, as Neill admits. But they cannot be. Furthermore, the children whom Neill received at Summerhill in his lifetime tended to be misfits from moderately well-off middle-class backgrounds (the school is fee-paying). They were therefore very much the product of a particular background and, Neill observes, 'most [of them] required psychological attention' (*S* p. 45).

The children arrive at a place where certain decisions affecting them have already been made: the teachers are appointed, the catering has been arranged. But most decisions have not yet been taken. 'My view', says Neill firmly, 'is that a child is innately wise and realistic. If left to himself without adult suggestion of any kind, he will develop as far as he is capable of developing' (*S* p. 20). In line with this view the children are left to themselves, cut off from any traces of adult suggestion. Thus of classical music Neill remarks 'we make no attempt to lead them to higher tastes – whatever that may mean' (*S* p. 75), and the point can be generalised. No attempt is made to lead and steer them towards preconceived objectives.

(Even happiness is seen as something that will occur rather than as something to be striven for.) Neill, like Rousseau before him, shows an awareness of the hidden curriculum when he observes that 'our whole education system is full of lies. Our schools hand on the lie that obedience and industry are virtues and that history and French are education' (*S* p. 137). Whether these are in fact lies we may for the moment ignore; the much more important point is the observation that the typical school preaches such a message by deed even if not by word. Summerhill, it is hoped, preaches no message except the gospel that we should 'let people lead their own lives'. 'We are leading the children along the way of being tolerant by showing them tolerance' (*S* p. 119). Most schools, according to Neill, create fear and hate through their overt values and the covert influence of the means they employ to run the institution. 'Safety first expresses man's leading concern' in such schools – but not at Summerhill, where, within broad limits, there is no 'thought for the morrow' (*S* p. 119) (echoes of Rousseau's attitude to prudence).

The children board in single-sex dormitories. There are lessons in traditional subjects, but children only go to them if and when they want to, as, we are told, they usually do after a short while at the school. 'We have no new methods of teaching, because we do not consider that teaching in itself matters very much' (*S* p. 20). That remark is in line with the wider thesis that people learn what interests them and not what does not. 'The child who wants to learn long division will learn it no matter how it is taught' (*S* p. 21). And to that empirical claim about method Neill adds a value judgement: 'Long division is of no importance except to those who want to learn it.'

Countless other activities are available to the children, such as gardening, playing cowboys, carpentry, riding bikes and football. There is a general prohibition on unsafe activities (although it does not seem to extend to the handling of chisels and saws, as we shall see). A significant feature of the school was the opportunity for PLs (private lessons) with Neill himself. These consisted of children coming to see him either individually or in small groups for talks on such topics as 'The Inferiority Complex, The Psychology of Stealing, The Psychology of the Gangster, The Psychology of Humour, Why did man become a moralist? Masturbation, Crowd Psychology'. 'It is obvious', adds Neill, that children who have had the benefit of such PLs 'will go out into life with a broad clear knowledge of themselves and others' (*S* p. 26). To which one might reasonably reply: 'No doubt, if what they were told was true and comprehensive, if they understood it, and if they are able to apply the (theoretical?) knowledge that they have acquired.' Finally, so far as what we may loosely call the curriculum is concerned (and in addition to the rich variety of quite informal and unstructured activity that will fill the usual day), our attention is drawn to the theatre which, 'performing only original homegrown plays', is generally productive and therapeutic (*S* p. 74).

There is also the democratic government itself. With the exception of a few matters such as those mentioned above everything at Summerhill is decided by a majority vote, every individual from youngest to oldest counting for one vote alone. They make rules about things like bedtime; they decide what punishments to give individuals for particular offences (generally, and where appropriate, advocating some kind of reparation) (*S* p. 54). In outline Neill's view is that the experience of conducting affairs for themselves in this way is invaluable training in the only way of conducting affairs that a civilised and free people should entertain. If Neill himself wants something done he must ask for it and get a majority vote for it, the same way as anybody else. But we do the school an injustice if we emphasise too much the mechanics of its government and do not stress again that this community is full of love. 'At Summerhill it is love that cures; it is approval and the freedom to be true to oneself' that achieves results (*S* p. 50).

'The function of the child is to live his own life', and that he can more or less do at Summerhill (*S* p. 27). Success, for Neill, is measured in terms of whether children manage to live out their excesses and overcome their anti-social tendencies and then go out into the world happy and well-mannered in the sense of 'thinking of and feeling for others' (*S* p. 175). 'Education should produce children who are at once individuals and community persons and self-government without doubt does this' (*S* p. 11).

EDUCATION, SELF-REGULATION AND PUNISHMENT

Some may feel inclined to say 'This is all very fine and admirable in its own way, but it isn't education.' A lot of Neill's own remarks suggest that it is not meant to be education as such that he is providing. He is dealing for the most part, as he says, with problem children, and he frequently makes reference to his curative role, the therapeutic value of activities, the need to remove fear from children's minds, and the dangers of guilt feelings about sexual matters in general and masturbation in particular (e.g. *S* pp. 50, 139). And certainly therefore what he is concerned with is *not* education in some people's sense of the word.

To treat this observation as an objection, however, is surely to miss the point of Neill's challenge, which is that, call it what you will, this is what we ought to be doing with our children. Despite the fact that he does see himself more in the role of a psychiatrist than a teacher, he sees this kind of provision as ideal for all children and not just for a minority of troubled or troublesome individuals. Nor is it, as it is with Rousseau and some contemporary educationalists, a case of thinking that schools should not push forward certain studies or worry about specific skills until the child has acquired an interest in them. Neill is serious in his suggestion that nobody should ever be expected to learn to read, write, study a foreign language, do carpentry, study English literature or anything else, however old they are, unless they want to.

One of Neill's objections to the normal or traditional conception of education is that it incorporates a great deal of knowledge or learning that he, like Rousseau before him, sees as useless or irrelevant. 'What', asks Neill, 'is the use of teaching quadratic equations to boys who are going to repair cars or sell stockings?' (*S* p. 325). 'Our great tragedy is that school learning has little contact with life after leaving school. How many old pupils read Milton or Hardy or Shaw? How many listen to Beethoven or Bach?' (*S* p. 10).

One might reasonably observe in reply that it is not always evident in advance who is going to sell stockings. One might also draw the sting of the impassioned 'How many' by replying 'Quite a few. How many do you want?' Certainly there is no shortage of people – all old pupils of somewhere – who love Milton, Hardy, Shaw, Beethoven and Bach. Third, one might counter by asking Neill how many of his ex-pupils masturbate or discuss masturbation, which is one of the activities that he seems to expect his pupils to engage in and to want to talk about. Fourth (and here I pick up points already made above, Chapter 3), why is it assumed that relevance has to be of a direct and immediate kind, so that if you aren't actually reading Milton or working out quadratic equations 'contact' is lost and the use of these studies is shown to *have been* non-existent? There is no reason why we should accept Neill's simplistic view of and restrictive definition of 'relevance' or why, if we do understand the word in his sense, we should agree that relevance has any importance. The question of what is relevant may involve complicated long-term predictions and calculations and value judgements. What one sees as relevant, in contact with life and useful is obviously partially dependent on how one envisages the ideal social setting or way of life to which education is supposed to be making an apposite contribution. It is rather naive and confused to imagine that relevance is some kind of objective and discernible quality that things either have or lack.

Our attention is now drawn to the question of the way of life that Neill's education is designed to relate to. Rousseau proposed the impractical policy of total isolation in all seriousness, not least for the reason that as things are, the influence of other people and the ways of the world would corrupt Emile. Given the emphasis that Neill places on self-regulation, one might have expected him likewise to require total isolation. He does not. At Summerhill children, who in any case do not arrive before the age of five and who continue to spend their holidays in contact with the outside world, are in effect handed over to the random influence of their surroundings at the school – surroundings predominantly consisting of other children. But this practice makes a nonsense of the idea of self-regulation as conceived by Neill: for it transpires that the selves that do the regulating are themselves the product of their environment, formed by the influences of the outside world in their early years and still subject all the while to extraneous influence. This means that the self-hood of the Summerhill pupil is no more authentic than that of any other child. The distinction between the individual who is what circumstances made him and the individual who is what he made himself cannot be drawn.

In itself this does not invalidate Neill's style of education. Indeed, it is arguable that self-regulation as Neill tries to envisage it is an absurd idea anyway (since it does not make sense to talk of a newly born child regulating his own life) and one that is unnecessary to the thesis in question.[2] The real problem is this: properly understood, Neill's proposal amounts to leaving children to develop as they may in response to their surroundings, which include, to an unusually marked degree, the influence of various other children. If the world were already refashioned according to Neill's ideals the belief that children would grow up to match the ideals might have some plausibility. But if the world (and hence the background of these children and they themselves initially) is judged to be hopelessly corrupt, then surely a modern-day Emile in Neill's hands is quite literally being thrown into bad company: he is being left to develop in response to the already corrupt influence of other children. That being so, it must presumably be claimed that out of evil may come good or that, strange as it may seem, a group of corrupted children may and will influence each other for the good. That conclusion flatly contradicts the premiss on which the whole argument for this schooling rests: that the world is corrupt and we must get children out of it and away from the corrupt surroundings in order to allow them to develop uncorrupted.

From the conclusion that there is a contradiction in Neill's thesis here it does not follow that his claim that children will outgrow their corrupt background at Summerhill but not in the outside world is necessarily false. But what does follow is that, if the claim is true, it must be for some other reason than that they are left to develop as they may in response to their surroundings. It might be, for example, as Neill himself ultimately began to feel, that children live out and through their corrupt background at Summerhill, as they would not elsewhere, because of the loving atmosphere that surrounds them.

Given his enthusiasm for self-regulation, albeit misplaced, it is not surprising that Neill objects to systems of reward, competition and punishment. His claim that rewards and punishments cannot compel interest seems dubious, however (*S* p. 149). It may be that generally they don't; or, putting the emphasis on 'compel', it may be that they cannot 'compel' it in the sense of 'guarantee' it; or one might insist that only interests that arise spontaneously in the individual really count as interests and thus make it true by definition that one cannot compel (or cultivate) interest in another. (The last move is the one that Neill seems to be making.) But the important question is presumably whether, as a matter of empirical fact, the adult can deliberately and successfully engender interest or cause children to acquire an interest in something new. Neill gives us no reason to doubt that he can do that, for the excellent reason that without any doubt he can.

With regard to the more general thesis about punishment, the central question is what Neill means by his typically dogmatic and sweeping statement that 'he knows from experience that punishment is unnecessary' (*S* p. 151). Does this mean that he knows that it will always be unefficacious or unproductive to keep a child in, smack him, fine him or send him to detention? Efficacious in the long or short term? Productive or unproductive in respect of what? Like Rousseau, Neill correctly sees that it is a conceptual truth that a lot of what might loosely be called punishment is not strictly speaking punishment at all. Rousseau put the emphasis on the need for the child to have wittingly done wrong. Neill stresses the different but equally valid point that punishment, by definition, involves the idea of just retaliation for moral wrong. Hitting somebody in a temper is therefore not an instance of punishment. Neill gives the following example. Imagine, that the child borrows your saw and ruins its teeth by leaving it around or using it on a brick (*S* p. 152). Refusal to let that child have the saw again would not constitute punishment; it is simply a self-interested and understandable reaction. ('That was not punishment, for punishment always involves the idea of morality'.) Neill regards such retaliation as quite acceptable. Even hitting a boy, which as explained is not necessarily punishment, can be justified. 'Hitting a child gives him fear only when it is accompanied with a moral idea, with the idea of wrong' (*S* p. 154); then it is bad and becomes punishment. But when it is a question of spontaneous reaction or retaliation, then 'the boy had learned a necessary lesson of life'.

Remarks such as 'punishment is unnecessary' then do not mean that Neill thinks that spanking, refusing co-operation or preventing the child from having or doing something is unnecessary. What he is saying is that, when the occasion for such things arises, we should employ them unselfconsciously and without reference to moral or religious cant: if you stop the child riding his bike across your lawn, do it honestly – that is to say, because you don't want him to do it and have the strength to enforce your wish rather than the moral superiority to allow you the right to enforce it. Thus we are back, by a different route, at Rousseau's doctrine of learning morality by natural consequences: children will learn by this method what pays and what doesn't, what is acceptable and what is not, what social claims have to be upheld and what do not.

PSYCHOLOGY

Neill sees his work as related to the psychological domain in two ways. First, he relies on and argues his case by reference to various pronouncements about human, particularly child, psychology. Second, he claims to act as a psychiatrist to some of the children. (He also regards the teaching of psychology as important, as the emphasis that he gives to psychological issues in PLs indicates.) He is therefore committed to certain claims about human character and appropriate behaviour or treatment in the light of those claims. One would expect him therefore to have some knowledge of evidence for these various claims. I am not a psychologist simply because I commit myself to some aphorism about human nature such as 'everybody's good at heart' or 'all crime is really disease'. I begin to be one when I clarify, research and authenticate such remarks. So the first question must be whether Neill is in any sense a psychologist and, if so, whether he is a good one.

The psychologist has to draw inferences from his observations and that is where his troubles begin; for what he wants to draw inferences about (mind, motivation, etc.) and what he observes (behaviour) are not at all the same thing. But despite certain obvious problems that must beset anything attempting to be a science of human behaviour, there is naturally an important place in our pursuits for an attempt at the systematic study of man. The emphasis however must fall on 'systematic'. Good psychology draws inferences from evidence that has been systematically gathered; it tests hypotheses and, where possible, studies behaviour in controlled situations, always looking for, but only for, that degree of certainty that is appropriate to the matter in hand, which may be very far from complete. Marks of bad psychology would include an absence of systematic inquiry, an absence of evidence, an absence of due caution, and the confusion of what is typical with what is average (the last being an extraordinarily common mistake).

What does Neill do? How are his psychological conclusions derived? He conducts no systematic inquiry. He produces no evidence for his assertions. His psychological pronouncements are arrived at in one of two ways: either he takes fragmentary bleeding chunks from the tentative and certainly unproven theoretical frameworks of others and presents them as established truths, or else he offers his own unsystematic and unrepresentative intuitions. 'Psychiatry', he tells us, 'has proved that man's actions are controlled to a large extent by his unconscious' (*S* p. 219). The use of the word 'proved' is unhelpful and misleading; it would be more accurate to say that 'it has been hypothesised that . . .'. But still, out of context the remark may be allowed to pass, if only because it could mean practically anything, the concept of the unconscious mind being preternaturally obscure, 'to a large extent' showing signs of the Manfred Syndrome, and 'prove' not meaning much more than 'suggest'. The 'unconscious mind' is after all the name we give to what we cannot explain. It is observed that some human actions cannot be satisfactorily explained in terms of what we see; it is hypothesised that there may be reasons that are beyond recall and that would explain the actions; sometimes the hypothesis seems to be sensible and has explanatory force (though sometimes it does not). Understood in this way, the assertion that man's actions are to some extent controlled by his unconscious mind is not implausible, may be helpful and may be true. But Neill's interest is rather different. He wants to argue that no one can help doing what they do, and he refers to the notion of the unconscious mind to support that contention. But *this* assertion (no one can help doing what they do), at least in most of its possible senses, is highly implausible and very far from obviously true; and similarly, any interpretation of the notion of an unconscious mind that is such as to establish automatically the truth of the theory that no one can help what they do (in all but a few uninformative and trivial senses) must be extremely suspect. Certainly, psychiatry has not proved anything that amounts to evidence that, for example, when Crippen murders or Johnny steals there must be subconscious reasons for the actions, which if discovered could perhaps be cured, but which while undiscovered are irresistible.

Again and again Neill presents us with glib examples of his home-spun philosophy under the guise of the fruits of scientific inquiry. 'Psychiatry has demonstrated and proved that an unfulfilled wish lives on in the unconscious' (*S* p. 221). It may, in some sense, be the case that an unfulfilled wish does this, but it has not been *proven* to be the case in any significant sense. It is curious that Neill, who spends so much of his time denying the idea of expertise in any sphere, should show an almost slave-like devotion to the ideas of men such as Freud and Reich. 'Freud showed that every neurosis is founded on sex repression' (*S* p. 257), and for those who dare to doubt it a traditional trap is brought into play whereby the denial is simply construed as further evidence for the truth of the original assertion. Thus, 'the very people who rail against Freud because he sees sex in everything are the very ones' (*S* p. 183) who are obsessed and fascinated by sex, and their denial that this is so shows only that Freud was right and that they have repressed their sexual eagerness. (This trap has the effect of rendering the claim in question a 'likely story', for it is apparent that no evidence is going to be allowed to count against it.) Sometimes Neill's assertions are trivial truisms: 'kleptomania in the last analysis signifies a wish to find happiness' (*S* p. 222), we are told. This is only true in the sense that *everything* is, 'in the last analysis', a wish to find happiness. But if everything is, then, whatever we are being told, we are not being told anything very revealing about kleptomania. To be significant or interesting the remark would have to mean that, if we could make kleptomaniacs happy in an everyday sense of the word, in the sort of way and to the same degree that people typically are happy, they would not steal. But it is almost precisely the fact that this is not so that makes a kleptomaniac what he is: somebody who has a compulsion to steal although he has no need to and may, in all other respects, be perfectly normal and happy. It is at this stage that one appreciates the price that people like Neill pay for scorning theory in the specific sense of precise and logical thought. They talk nonsense.

Neill's writing consists to a very large extent of a string of such disconnected and dubious pronouncements. He does not know their worth (or lack of same) and he seems unaware of their meaning. In addition, he acts on the strength of such aphorisms as a psychiatrist. But how important is all this? Don't all schoolmasters have to work on certain psychological assumptions, and do we not have to act as if they were certain, even if we know that they are not? Probably we do, although one could wish that more emphasis were placed on the conjectural and tentative nature of most psychological findings, not to mention the grave danger of distorting truth by looking at complex educational problems too much from the psychological perspective alone. But to admit that we must very often act in accordance with unproven beliefs is not to say that any belief is as good as another, or that we should not be rigorously examining the credentials of all our beliefs. We certainly and obviously should be doing just that, if we want to assure ourselves that we are doing what seems to be the most reasonable thing. And when Neill stands at the bar of critical inquiry with his views on child psychology it is difficult to avoid the judgement that (1) some of his beliefs are highly questionable; (2) he has produced no good grounds for entertaining most of them (which are heavily dependent on a simplified understanding of Freud and Reich); (3) he certainly has no grounds for his dogmatic assurance that they represent obvious truths; and (4) he has even less warrant for assuming that he is in a position to provide psychiatric treatment.

But suppose he were to avoid statements such as 'bad manners always spring from a disordered psyche' (*S* p. 172), which is pretentious claptrap, and stick to claims such as 'I know that a problem child can come to my school and become a happy normal child' (*S* p. 115) and 'I generally do the right thing with a child because my long experience has shown me the right way' (*S* p. 256): would he not then be beyond reproach? Could it not be that his attempts to articulate publicly what he tries to do are inadequate but that what he is actually doing is not? Is he not entitled to point to his own experience and to refer to that as the proof of his psychological theory and competence? Certainly he is entitled to do that, and certainly he may merely have failed to explain what he is up to in a convincing manner. But the question is still there: are his claims in all that relates to child psychology true? And nobody can be in a position to answer that question until we have some understanding and agreement on what is meant by such words as 'problem', 'happy' and 'normal', some understanding of the various other claims that Neill wants us to accept as warranted by his practical experience, and some evidence that he does indeed 'generally do the right thing' and, specifically, that his problem children turn out not merely less problematic than they were, but less problematic than they would otherwise have been were it not for factors about Summerhill that can be isolated and pinpointed. Nobody disputes that Neill may have had an intuitive knack of getting on with children, or that many children gained something from Summerhill. What we need to know is that these children could not have gained more elsewhere, and on what grounds Neill is asserting that schools generally should imitate the pattern of Summerhill. We want a clear understanding of the aims of Summerhill and the methodology and the rationale behind it, and then we want some reasons for supposing that the approach is the best way to the desired result.

Neill *seems* to believe that every individual is born innately good and with more or less determined aptitudes. The former belief seems obviously implied by such remarks as 'children unconsciously realise that stealing is sickness' (*S* p. 216) and 'I believe that it is moral instruction that makes the child bad. I find that when I smash the moral instruction a boy has received, he becomes a good boy' (*S* p. 221), not to mention the straightforward statement that 'the child has been born good ... [and] will inevitably turn out to be a good human being if he is not crippled and thwarted in his natural development by interference' (*S* p. 224). The latter belief is not so obviously held by Neill, but is implicit in remarks such as that children should from the moment of birth 'live according to their own inner nature' (*S* p. 106) and the accompanying conviction that such 'faith in the child's personality' is quite justified – for example, 'we know that if Tommy wants to be a doctor, he will voluntarily study to pass the entrance examinations' (*S* p. 146), and although 'we cannot tell from a study of child psychology why one child is born with courage but another is born with a shrinking soul' (*S* p. 120), reading between the lines it would appear that we *can* tell that every child is born with some particular kind of soul. Neill also uses the word 'nature' in ways that make it synonymous with 'character', 'personality' or 'aptitude', but with the added implication that they are innate qualities. Unlike Rousseau, who was primarily wedded to the notion of natural man in the sense of the man who behaves in ways that Rousseau regards as instinctive and inevitable (were it not for the mumbo-jumbo and chains of civilised society), Neill's concept of 'natural' is closely tied up with the idea of 'normal' (biologically natural) processes of unfolding or growing – an idea that is characteristically associated with plants or the physical aspects of animal development. He believes in education according to nature in the sense of an education that allows and responds to, rather than controls, distorts or suffocates, the natural development of the individual in respect of physical, mental and moral development.

Given a suitable environment for such natural development, the individual's inherently good moral nature and his particular talents and abilities will blossom and shine through.

It has sometimes been suggested that Neill did not believe in original or innate goodness so much as in a neutral original state (original vacuity, as I have termed it). In other words, the emphasis goes on Neill's denial of the validity of the religious doctrine of original sin. According to this view, Neill saw the child as a *tabula rasa* at birth – a personality neither good nor bad, but which might turn out to be either depending on the type of upbringing provided. The objection to this interpretation is a double one: it doesn't square with the texts, which is to say that it is at a variance with most of what Neill actually writes; and it doesn't square with the overall thesis that Neill propounds: his argument that we should educate children in the manner he recommends depends upon the assumption that individuals are innately good if it is to get off the ground at all.[3]

We may accept that Neill does not deny the power of environment in this matter and that some of his remarks taken out of context stress environment, do not positively claim that the child is born good, and are compatible in themselves with a *tabula rasa* theory. But most of what he says is not. As he himself acknowledges, his commitment to the idea of 'self-regulation implies a belief in the goodness of human nature' (*S* p. 102), which clearly means more than a belief in a new-born infant who is by nature neither good nor bad. And the next quotation would seem to settle the issue: 'many psychologists believe that a child is born neither good nor bad, but with tendencies towards both beneficence and criminality. I believe that there is no instinct of criminality nor any natural tendency towards malevolence' (*S* p. 239). I take this to mean that the child *is* born with a tendency towards goodness which means that already he is potentially good just as already he is potentially red-haired and that therefore he inevitably will be good unless somebody, or more likely the community at large, obstructs him. In that sense, then, Neill means what he says when he writes that the child is born good, and that he misleads, probably without realising it, when he writes 'when we look at the infant we know there is no wickedness in him ... no more than there is wickedness in a cabbage or a young tiger' (*S* p. 220). The analogies here are incompatible with the general thesis: the child is not comparable to either cabbage or tiger, if I have interpreted Neill correctly, for neither of them is born good, naturally good, unconsciously good, instinctively good or anything similar in any conceivable sense.

Furthermore, Neill must hold some such view as that which I have attributed to him, if his position is to begin to make sense. If one sincerely believes in the *tabula rasa* or the idea that the individual is born either denuded of moral characteristics or, which comes to the same thing, possessing a potentiality for both good and ill, then in practice the environment that you provide for the individual to grow up and live in is the sole decisive factor in whether he turns out good or bad. One cannot consistently hold that view and claim that goodness is natural and evil unnatural. For on this view both goodness and evil are simply the product of circumstances; neither one is more natural than the other in any sense of 'natural' at all. If anything is clear, it is that Neill does not subscribe to the view that there is a variety of ways of living one's life between which there is nothing to choose so far as their inherent worth is concerned, and that the individual will 'opt' for that way of life into which he is conditioned. Certainly he is aware of the power of the environment to condition; none the less, he believes that there is some essential core in each individual at birth which is a tendency towards moral good – the development of that core he regards as a process of natural maturation: the emergence of the good adult is the triumph of the core and not the product of the environment.

Neill's point then is not that the method of upbringing that he advocates produces certain consequences that he approves of and values, but rather that this method allows the consequential appearance of what is innate – what is there waiting to be allowed to flower, what is a natural development – and that is why it is supposed to be good, because the result is the emergence of the natural. Now what can this mean? First, it might mean that there is something physically innate in the child, in which case either it should be discernible or we should be able to discern the elements that might generate it. But that is surely not the case. There is no moral organ there like the liver or potentially there like the wisdom tooth. Second, the reference to an innate embryonic goodness might be a way of saying that there is a potentiality, in the sense that it *may* come about that the individual will be good when adult. In this sense the claim is clearly true. We know that men are capable of being good and we may say, if we like, that therefore they had the potentiality to be so from birth, since all we would mean by that is that it is possible for some infants to grow up to be good. This interpretation is obviously inapposite, since the point is supposed to be rather more than that man can turn out morally good. Third, one might construe the claim as analogous to the interpretation that posits a physical element, but one substituting an incorporeal 'something' that causes good behaviour. Apart from its inherent improbability and absurdity, this view has the demerit of being a 'likely story'. Besides, this reference to a 'something' that is precisely not some thing, since it is 'incorporeal', is surely no more than an attempt at reification of what is altogether better expressed in the fourth possible interpretation.

The fourth interpretation is the view that given certain conditions the child must inevitably turn out to be good. Establishing the truth of this claim is all that Neill needs for his overall thesis, and it seems clear that this is what must be meant. Talk of nature and innate tendencies merely obfuscates the issue. But is this straightforward claim true? To answer that question we need to have the conditions specified (which Neill has made some attempt to do); we need a precise specification of what constitutes goodness (which is less well done); but then above all we need some evidence that the specific conditions do promote goodness as specified. And the trouble is that there is none. There is not a shred of evidence that Summerhill conditions necessarily produce goodness (however defined), or that the conditions in traditional or more typical schools necessarily do not (or do it less, or worse).

But is this quite fair? Granted that the claim may not be susceptible of incontrovertible proof, may we not say, indeed do we not in practical terms have to say, something a little more down to earth such as that by and large children brought up in this sort of way can be seen to turn into relatively good adults? Is the proof of the pudding not in the eating? Perhaps – provided that enough pudding is eaten by a wide enough cross-section of judges. One would not object to some cautious summary such as the following: 'Judging from pupils who have been to Summerhill, where education is natural in the sense of being delimited only by the actual instinctive feelings and wishes of the community, it would seem clear that goodness is innate in some children in the specific sense that they grow up to be good people.'

But how far does that get us? As has already been said, in order to verify it to our satisfaction we need to agree on what constitutes goodness. But suppose we bypass that problem by taking goodness very crudely to consist in not hating Jews and Negroes. Neill's remark that he 'knows from experience that children brought up with self-government and freedom will never hate Jews or negroes' (*S* p. 12) can then be taken as the specific statement of the general point. When we reflect on this statement we must surely see that Neill has not shown and cannot claim to know what he asserts. At best he knows and has evidence that none of the children who have been to Summerhill in the past did hate Jews or Negroes. He does not know (at any rate there is no evidence that he does) that self-government and freedom were the cause of this fact; that these same children would not have shown the same lack of hatred if brought up in different schools; that these same individuals might not yet betray such hatred if faced with the kind of circumstances that have turned other unlikely people into racists in the past; that other children in other schools are not equally antipathetic to such hatred. We would be quite unwarranted in drawing the conclusion that if we want to minimise racial hatred we must adopt a Summerhill style of schooling. And that point can now be generalised again: all in all, at the very best, a not-proven verdict must be given on the claim that 'there is no need whatsoever to teach children how to behave. A child will learn what is right and what is wrong in good time' (*S* p. 224). It is by no means established that the sort of upbringing embodied in the arrangements at Summerhill is necessary (or even sufficient, though that is a more plausible inference) for the development of morally good individuals.

Now we have to turn to the other, less often remarked, half of Neill's view of human nature. There is sufficient evidence to show that he committed himself to the thesis that character and intelligence are also innate. 'The child is innately wise and realistic' (*S* p. 20), we are told; he will be a doctor if he wants to be, like a child named Tommy; like another he will become a non-bed-wetter when he's ready to be; like Mervyn an instrument-maker should he feel the urge to be (*S* p. 289). In none of these examples is it said in so many words that the individual in question was born to be a doctor, an instrument-maker or a non-bed-wetter; but the implication must be that, for it is clearly not *true* that John will be an X when he's ready to be unless you hold some such thesis. The more that emphasis is placed on people being what circumstances make of them, the less sense it makes to talk of readiness, wants and suchlike as if they were static rather than dynamic. Conversely, the more you refer to them as static givens, as Neill and all the radicals except Rousseau do, the more you push yourself into the position of seeing individual human natures as static rather than as the product of their environment. That Neill does have this view of static human natures is clear from this remark: 'If left to himself without adult suggestion of any kind, he will develop as far as he is capable of developing. Logically, Summerhill is a place in which people who have the innate ability and wish to be scholars will be scholars; while those who are only fit to sweep the streets will sweep the streets. But we have not produced a street-cleaner so far' (*S* p. 20). Here is the clear implication that one is born to be king or carpenter. Neill's writing may not usually reveal that view. Indeed, most of the time he puts the stress not on Tommy's inner drive towards some predetermined objective but on what Tommy happens to want, as if that might be anything and might change from day to day in response to whatever circumstances he encounters. None the less, as we have seen, he believes that at birth little Tommy is already an embryonic doctor – or, if that is too absurdly specific, an embryonic academic with a potential leaning (which might conceivably be thwarted) towards medicine. And he must believe that Tommy is born to be something, if he is to maintain his overall educational theory; because the more he moves towards the alternative thesis that man is essentially the product of his environment, the more meaningless becomes his justification of Summerhill in terms of natural development.

Sadly, it is a matter of but a few more lines to point out that such a justification is meaningless anyway. For whatever Neill happens to have believed, it is beyond serious question that the doctrine of innate characteristics, in the extreme form implied here, is without foundation. There are obviously limits, both physical and mental, to an individual's capacities, so it would be false to state that anybody could become anything given the appropriate surroundings and conditions from birth. But there are no recognisable grounds at all for suggesting that such things as one's feeling for Negroes, one's desire and competence in respect of medicine or one's taste for academics is innate in the individual from the beginning. In fact, it is difficult to conceive of a more self-evidently preposterous theory. Consequently the practice of Summerhill cannot be justified (or even explained) in terms of arguing that individual natures are there given the opportunity to develop themselves to the full. There is no such thing as a static state of fulfilment for an individual nature: the individual nature is dynamic.

Summerhill, then, cannot sensibly be regarded as the neutral territory on which truth and innate nature will flower and finally out. It must be recognised for what it is: a particular environment which may or may not lead, more or less efficiently, to certain specific consequences.

Freedom

Neill does not believe that freedom is in itself a good thing or that what matters is not so much what you do as that you should be free to do what you feel like doing. He is not subscribing to the view that sincerity is all or that spontaneity is of surpassing value. The fact that there are passages that suggest that he is saying just that is to be explained in terms of his wider theory: Neill thinks not that spontaneity and freedom are good, but that what is done spontaneously and freely will be good, since men are innately good.

Despite careless remarks such as that 'the child should not do anything until he comes to the opinion, his own opinion, that it should be done' (S p. 111) and 'self-regulation means the right of the baby to live freely, without outside authority' (S p. 104), and despite emotive tirades such as 'the curse of humanity is the external compulsion' which, whatever its source, 'is fascism in toto' (S p. 111), nobody who reads Neill widely could be in any serious doubt that, as he says elsewhere, under his regime 'a child is not allowed to do as he pleases' (S p. 303). As a report of HMIs who visited the school (and who wrongly saw freedom as 'the main principle on which the school is run') put it, 'this freedom is not quite unqualified'.

Neill therefore faces the problem that we all do of deciding how one should qualify freedom. By what criteria does one decide whether particular freedoms should be curtailed or not? Neill tries several answers (often in the course of a single page, without apparently realising that they are different). More than once he refers vaguely to common sense: 'At Summerhill ... freedom does not mean the abrogation of common sense. We take every precaution for the safety of the pupils' (*S* p. 34); for example, no child under the age of eleven is allowed to cycle on his own. Referring to common sense, however, does not constitute an answer to the problem at all, since the dispute is precisely about what it is and what it is not sensible to do. What passes for sense is very seldom a matter of common agreement. As if aware of this, Neill also gives a lot of particular examples of things he would restrict and things he would not. In themselves, the examples are useful and help us to gain a clearer picture of Neill's attitudes. But naturally they tend to be either obvious or contentious. What we need is the principle whereby Neill selects his examples, especially since some of his examples are on the face of it contradictory. The child should be free to interrupt my work by playing with my glasses when it feels like it, but not apparently by banging on my door (*S* p. 132). Neill forbids jumping on the sofa, presumably because he doesn't think that children should be free to damage valuable property, but counsels us to allow the child to play with our valuable breakable ornaments. He asserts that there should be bars on windows, and that no child under a certain age should be allowed to swim without the presence of an instructor, both on grounds of safety. But then why does he place no restriction on the use of dangerous tools? As a matter of fact, the saga of the tool shed, though a little difficult to understand, provides further food for thought as Neill veers uncertainly between a decision to open the shed to all comers and risk losing his valuable tools (as happened before) and jealously guarding them for himself. As he dimly intuits but fails to articulate, specific rules about freedom and restriction are not easy to work out precisely because people are different in their interests and inclinations. In a revealing passage Neill confesses that his treasured tools mean nothing to his wife, while her valued books mean nothing to him. He seems not to see the significance of this observation, however, in relation to the very real practical problems about freedom: for all Neill's touching faith in a natural community of interest, people will keep being different – and that means that they tend to get in each other's way.

Another attempt to sort out the problem is Neill's appeal (also made by Rousseau) to a distinction between liberty and licence.[4] This, like the appeal to common sense, is of no practical use because it is purely formal: it tells us that some freedoms are undeserved and should therefore be classified as licence and not granted. But it does not tell us which they are or how to recognise them. He then tries the classic liberal formula: 'Each individual is free to do what he likes as long as he is not trespassing on the freedom of others' (*S* p. 143). Finally, there is the utilitarian position which probably represents the nearest we can get to his considered opinion: the view that in things that affect himself alone the individual should be completely free; otherwise 'the test is always this: is what Mr X is doing really harmful to anyone else?' (*S* pp. 299, 303). By reference to this test liberty and licence may be distinguished, the demands of common sense may be defined, and the limits of freedom established.

There are problems in this last formula, as in any other, but it is at any rate clear and comprehensible, and practical use can be made of it. But taking this position in relation to freedom implies that something like happiness is one's ultimate aim and that freedom is to be valued only as a means. Considerations of happiness may, where necessary, legitimately curb freedom. In other words, children are given self-government not because it is their birthright, although Neill is capable of talking in such terms, but because there is no warrant for denying it to them unless it can be shown to be harmful, and Neill thinks that as a matter of empirical fact it will benefit them. When he says that 'we have proved that self-government works' (*S* p. 59) he must be understood to be saying that life at Summerhill (and afterwards) is happy for these individuals and that that is the school's justification. If children do not attend any lessons, that is not good because they freely chose not to; it is shown to be an acceptable state of affairs in so far as life is none the worse for it. If there were reason to believe that individuals were suffering for this non-attendance the logic of Neill's position, whether he realised it or not, would demand that they should start to attend.

Even those who accept Neill's assumption that happiness is the supreme consideration might object that that does not lead to the consequence that children's freedom should be restricted only by reference to considerations of *their immediate* happiness. They might argue that freedom should be restricted by reference to the long-term greater happiness of the community as a whole, which might materially alter some of the specific recommendations one wished to make. Others will challenge Neill's empirical assumptions. Is there in fact any reason at all to suppose that children at Summerhill, as a direct result of the freedom they are given, will be happier than they would otherwise have been? If Neill's views on human nature were sound, he would have a case for arguing that the answer must be yes. If human nature is to a significant degree innate, then coercion and restraint will, in so far as they curb that innate spirit, be 'crippling' and 'thwarting' as Neill emotively suggests. But, since we see no reason to accept a view of static innate natures, we see no reason to accept the thesis that restraint must necessarily irk, cripple and thwart, or consequently that it must militate against happiness even in the short term, let alone the long term. Neill himself has depicted happiness as being essentially a feeling of contentment. No reason at all has been given for supposing that children must necessarily be more contented in a Summerhill environment than they would be elsewhere, still less for supposing that this kind of upbringing would necessarily be most suitable for preparing individuals to lead happy adult lives in a community such as ours.

INTEREST

Nobody is obliged to study anything at Summerhill. To the often-asked question, 'Won't the child turn round and blame the school for not making him learn arithmetic or music?' (*S* p. 27), Neill replies that 'young Freddy Beethoven and young Tommy Einstein will refuse to be kept away from their respective spheres'. Besides being further confirmation of Neill's belief in innate aptitudes, this remark directs us to the belief that interest is the mainspring of learning.

In common with Rousseau and subsequent radicals he sets great store by the possibilities of learning through experience (*S* p. 134). In addition he emphasises the importance in education of 'real doing, real self-expression' (*S* p. 37), and writes occasionally as if the wants of the child should determine what he learns. The predominant assertion, however, is that the child's interest should be the main determinant of what learning takes place. But whereas Rousseau saw interest only as a crucial source of motivation, and therefore something that might itself profitably be created and manipulated by the teacher, Neill sees interest in more exalted terms. In his view, 'true interest is the life force of the whole personality, and such interest is completely spontaneous' (*S* p. 149), which suggests that it cannot be created, implanted or fanned into flame by the teacher.

Neill maintains that 'one can compel attention, one cannot compel interest' and that 'no man can force me to be interested in, say collecting stamps; nor can I compel myself' (*S* p. 149). This is possibly true, but only if the emphasis is placed on 'compel' and 'force': you cannot force someone to be interested against their will or inclination, because part of the meaning of interest is that one is inclined towards something. It does not follow that interests cannot be *generated* by the individual himself or by others. Neill's assumption that it does seems to rest on two mistakes: first, his tendency to see interests no less than the rest of the individual's nature as part of a set of baggage he is born with and carries through life, and second a confusion between compulsion and cause which no doubt arises from (or is compounded by) the ambiguity of the word 'make'. I may not be able to compel interest but I can certainly cause it. In that sense I can make people more or less interested in a variety of things. It must be failure to see this point that accounts for Neill's otherwise bizarre lack of concern for teaching methods. Superficially it is odd to see such an emphasis on interest as his go hand in hand with a total lack of concern for methods. On the face of it, if you believe that children should be interested, you will welcome novel methods of teaching. But of course there is nothing odd if Neill sees an interest as some kind of innate and indestructible characteristic; you either are Freddy Beethoven or you are not. You either have an interest in music or you do not. If you do, you do not need to have interest provoked. If you don't, you can't.

This involves a serious error. No doubt there are Freddy Beethovens, but there is far too much evidence that interests can be both created and destroyed to make Neill's way of looking at it remotely sensible. Once that is admitted, little of what he has to say about interests remains significant. He makes certain specific observations about what in his experience does or does not interest children. In general he informs us they 'are eminently practical and theory bores them. They like concreteness, not abstraction' (*S* p. 55). This may very well be true for most young children; but, because of his way of looking at the matter, it does not occur to Neill that if it remains true of children as they grow older this could be a consequence of the type of schooling they have had. There is also the danger that what actually doesn't interest them is hard work. I mention that possibility because abstract thinking is hard work, and because Neill also records that 'they are not much interested in elaborate joints of the dovetail variety; even the older boys do not care for difficult carpentry' (*S* p. 29). This seems most surprising, and on Neill's analysis it would have to mean that there are far fewer Charlie Carpenters about in Summerhill than certain other schools. Many would prefer to draw the inference that nobody is helping them to get interested in the challenge of difficult carpentry.

Whereas most educationalists confine the use of the word 'interest' to describe what fascinates a child, Neill extends it to cover what the individual sees as being to his advantage. He tells the story of how the children would not help to build a new infirmary, because they could not see such hard work as being in their interests (*S* p. 65). But they built a bike shed quickly enough when they saw the need for one. This extended usage of the word 'interest' confuses the issue somewhat, inasmuch as one might have an interest in either of the two senses without having it in the other. But it also raises the question of why we should be governed by children's 'interests' in this new sense of their 'perceptions of relevance'. In the first place, their perceptions may be faulty, particularly if we take a long-term view. (Their perception about the infirmary was obviously faulty.) In the second place it is no more true that one cannot learn except where one has an interest in the second sense than it was true in the first sense (see pp. 111–15 below).

CHAPTER 5

PAUL GOODMAN
1911-73

SOCIAL CRITICISM (*Growing Up Absurd*)

Paul Goodman's *Growing Up Absurd* expresses a sense of hollowness and purposelessness in society. Goodman hates the materialism, the preoccupation with status and the advertising ethos that he feels engulfing him. He fears the pervading sense of alienation and frustration that he detects about him.[1] His overriding wish is for fulfilment, more accurately a sense of fulfilment, for every individual on whatever terms suit him, provided that his terms don't involve preventing other people fulfilling themselves. His indictment of society is more or less that 'we live increasingly ... in a system in which little direct attention is paid to the object, the function, the program, the task, the need [of anything]; but immense attention to the role, procedure, prestige and profit' (*GA* p. xiii).

Goodman does not hold any strong views to the effect that knowledge is relative, as some of the radicals appear to do. He is aware that different cultures see things differently and may have differing values; he does not think that what is right for us now is necessarily right for others now or would necessarily be right for us at another time. But he does not accept the idea that everything is relative or that the truth depends entirely on how you see it. He specifically resists Wright Mills' view that the definition of man must vary from culture to culture and place to place so that in the last analysis man is 'what suits a particular type of society in a particular historical stage' (*GA* p. 4). By contrast, Goodman regards any suggestion that such values as personal freedom may be rooted in the particular stage of social evolution we have reached as on a par with the suggestion that 'mathematics was "rooted" in the Greek way of life' (*GA* p. 226). Not surprisingly, he thus comes to the position of stating a commitment to the notion of innate human nature – something that is there, though it may be only 'a developing potentiality, not yet cultured, and yet not blank' (*GA* p. 6), and that can be brought to light or revealed.

No less than Rousseau and Neill before him, Goodman runs into a certain amount of trouble with this elusive word 'nature' and the specific notion of human nature. But he makes the quite reasonable point that, while defining 'nature' is not at all easy, it is still possible to pinpoint the sort of thing that offends against human nature. And his belief in something called human nature allows him to ask a question that those who do not believe in any such thing cannot meaningfully ask – namely, whether or not contemporary society in its various aspects suits our nature as human beings or whether rebels and outsiders might not be right in rejecting society as a whole. Could it be that the difficulty that some people evidently experience in the business of growing up is not the result of their shortcomings but the result of the fact that 'the harmonious organisation to which the young are inadequately socialised [is] against human nature or not worthy' of it? (*GA* p. 11).

Goodman thinks that the answer is yes; in his view what is wrong or contrary to human nature in contemporary Western society or culture is that there are no 'manly jobs' for people any more. There are no jobs that can be readily and widely seen to be vital and valuable and in which, consequently, a man can take unashamed pride. You may think that your job as a clerk in a big firm is important, because you believe in the firm and your place in it. But others do not see why we have to live in a world dominated by your firm, still less do they see you as irreplaceable. It therefore requires effort on your part to sustain the fiction that you really are doing something crucial – and you don't really believe it yourself, hence your deep-rooted anxieties and sense of hopelessness. Such a job is not 'necessary or unquestionably useful' (*GA* p. 17) in the way that the cavalry's role in taming the West was. Such a job is not of the sort 'that require energy and draw on some of one's best capacities, and that can be done keeping one's honour and dignity' (*GA* p. 17). There is no longer scope for us to devote our lives to such manly jobs as hunting the food we need or providing shelter to protect our families. We have to work in enterprises such as advertising where the very reverse holds: not only do we not do anything for which there is a clear unsolicited need; we create a feeling of need for things that are not needed. The car mechanic symbolises the whole picture of decay (*GA* pp. 19ff): in the truly Golden Days he would have tamed rapids and not been a mechanic at all; even in the recent past he would have had a reasonable and respectable job in which he could take pride, caring for, understanding, maintaining and prolonging the life of something that had become necessary to our way of life. Now that is gone, because manufacturers build cars deliberately in such a way as to make it practically impossible to maintain them for any appreciable length of time. The attitude of society to cars has become one in which the normal assumption is that you get rid of them after a few years: the mechanic mends punctures and fills petrol tanks. His job is not necessary, useful, demanding of talent or preservative of dignity. Nor, by and large, does Goodman feel that the position is appreciably different in the professions: the same pattern of misleading appearances and fundamental hollowness recurs.[2]

Much of the time Goodman is remarkably moderate both in tone and in interpretation, given that he is offering a wholesale condemnation of a way of life. He does not subscribe to a conspiracy theory and thereby dissociates himself from many who might otherwise share his view of what society is like (*GA* p. 39). We are not where we are because it suits some minority group that we should be: we are where we are because nobody realises that we are here. Society quite unconsciously anaesthetises a great deal of opposition to itself, the more so as it quite sincerely liberalises its attitudes. It is not the machiavellian machinations of capitalist newspaper bosses that manipulate and censor information; the criterion of being newsworthy is not a cynical excuse they hide behind: it is the real criterion of what gets published, the real censor of what we read. Goodman does not subscribe to the extreme view that delinquency is something that we have defined into existence or even that it is solely the product of exploitation and deprived environment. He makes the more startling suggestion that, although many delinquents are indeed delinquent, they may have some very reasonable demands: in sum, 'a manly job'.

But Goodman does give vent to his feelings when his hostility to the horrors of urban life bursts forth. There is more than a slight affinity with Rousseau in his romantic and nostalgic view of life as it used to be – the 'natural' non-industrial era, as they like to term it, without giving any reason for the assumption that tilling the earth with a wooden plough and oxen is more natural than manufacturing steel ploughs. None the less, a point is made: 'concealed technology, family mobility, loss of the country, loss of neighbourhood tradition, and eating up of the play space have taken away' (*GA* p. 86, Ch. 5) something, even if one questions Goodman's right to call what is taken away 'the real environment'. He argues that our environment today is positively dehumanising. In addition, he draws our attention to the extent to which we are subject to the influence of the hidden curriculum. Giving wider application to the idea than Rousseau and Neill, his point is that all the time, every day, we are learning things that nobody intended us to learn, that nobody recognises that we are learning and that nobody desires that we should learn. For example, every time the family television set breaks down and the repair man is called, we learn the lesson that we are incompetent to cope with such aspects of our own lives (*GA* p. 87).

We thus face 'a crisis of boredom, a lack of personal engagement, cultural irrelevance and ineptitude in mass industry and education' (*GA* p. 80). What are we going to do about this widespread spirit of alienation? Although *Growing Up Absurd* is not particularly concerned with education, Goodman already senses that the only way to change matters at the root is to change the nature of education. But at this date he contents himself with broad ideas and suggestions only. The culmination of his argument consists in a spitting and indignant denunciation of the ugliness of life, rather than its injustice, and a call for some return to the rather unprogressive-sounding ideals of patriotism and pride. If we give our children pride, *a fortiori* we give them something to believe and something to be proud of. The kind of thing we have to sweep away is 'the lack of bona fides about our liberties, the dishonourable politics in the universities, the irresponsible press, the disillusioning handling of adventure in space, the inferior and place-seeking high officers of the State, the shameful neglect of our landscape and the disregard of the community' (*GA* p. 113). We have to fight ugliness, social injustice, stupid laws. As things are – 'our society weakens the conviction that there is a Creation of six days, a real world rather than a system of social rules that indeed are often arbitrary' (*GA* p. 143). We need to have faith in the idea of soul and absolutes to keep us going. Above all we need creative individuals such as we are not likely to get from our present system of education, particularly if that system becomes more rather than less involved with such things as multiple-choice questions and programmed learning (*GA* p. 148). The sad truth is that 'balked, not take seriously, deprived of great objects and available opportunities, and in an atmosphere that does not encourage service – it is hard to have faith' (*GA* p. 154).

According to Goodman, then, we have produced a society that is horrible and debilitating to live in. What is more, increasingly people recognise this fact and that is why, in one way or another, they cop or drop out. Given the premiss, who can blame them? Good ideas have been forthcoming over the years which, if adopted and acted upon, might have improved things substantially. But for the most part these ideas, when put into practice, have been truncated, reduced or modified; they have gone off at half-cock, generally doing more harm than good. Progressive methods in education are a case in point: they were never given a real chance, which would involve subordinating everything to them rather than trying to gear them to the traditional apparatus of exams, diplomas and so on. 'The actual result [of their deployment in limited contexts] has been to weaken the academic curriculum and to foster adjustment to society as it is' (*GA* p. 225). More generally, 'permissiveness', which as an attitude has potential, in practice has led to 'anxiety and weakness instead of confidence and strength'. Turning to more material matters: our physical environment has not been improved, despite the creation of such things as Garden Cities and more conscious attention (not to mention money) being paid to such people as architects. There have been economic and social gains – wages, for instance, are by and large a great deal better than they were at the turn of the century and more equitably distributed – but in isolation they have not achieved a great deal. As if to offset what material gains we may have made, we are faced with increasing frustration and alienation. Despite well intentioned advances in the direction of greater democracy, we seem to face ever more incompetent government and a greater loss of individuality. (Despite?) Popular culture turns out not to resemble the dreams of Utopian socialists like William Morris: it is commercial rather than the inspired work of craftsmen. Job satisfaction is minimal. Few people have any alternative faith to compensate for the inevitable lack of faith in this world.

EDUCATIONAL CRITICISM (*Compulsory Miseducation*)

In *Compulsory Miseducation* Goodman argues that the public system of education, while sucking up an enormous quantity of money, survives and expands because it is the subject of a mass superstition. The schools claim to achieve and are generally assumed to achieve a number of distinct things, including 'preparation ... for a complicated world, ... [a] haven for unemployed youth, ... [the equalisation] of opportunity for the underprivileged, [the administration of] research', as well as being 'the indispensable mentor for creativity, business practice, social work, mental hygiene [and] genuine literacy' (*CM* p. 11). Goodman has various objections to this. First, he thinks that the claim is false: schools do not achieve these various objectives. Second, as a result of trying to do too much they lose their image as centres of scholarship and then fall between two stools: they are not very effective in terms of their avowed practical aims nor are they prosperous Groves of Academe. Third, he doesn't think that they ought to have some of these objectives anyway, for he clings to his intuition that education is about truth, beauty, learning and culture. Fourth, which follows from the previous point, he is appalled at the extent to which the schools *have* been successful in their task and have consequently failed to foster a spirit of love of beauty and truth for their own sakes (*CM* p. 31); instead they have succeeded in 'socialising to national norms and regimenting to national needs' (*CM* p. 23). To the question, 'But is not some such concern for national norms and needs necessary and justifiable?', Goodman replies that we must seek a degree of homogeneity and he advises us not to despise 'middle-class values', but none the less, he adds, we must cherish and foster individuality (*CM* p. 24; cf. *GA* p. 161). (We are becoming involved in the Manfred Syndrome again here.)

He is worried in a general way by the increasing devaluation of language, which involves words losing their sharpness and precision as a result of their pervasive misuse or unsubtle exaggerated use in advertising and the media. He sees language becoming uniform and essentially meaningless, which leads him to reopen his attack on programmed learning and teaching machines. Never one to mince his words, he sees education based on such technological artefacts as tantamount to brainwashing and bound to create anxiety (*CM*

p. 59). Goodman would like to reverse what he sees as a movement in that direction and to return to a quest to develop the independence, curiosity, scientific attitude, scholarly habits, poetic speech, sense of identity, initiative and productive enterprise that he feels can never be the outcome of current practice (*CM* p. 61). The trouble is that, although according to some research children are consciously in attendance for only ten minutes a day at school, they have to be there physically for a good many years (*CM* p. 76). And all the time the child is there, what does he do? Does he think of things to do? No. He has to do assignments. Can he browse in the library, get on with his hobbies, get a job, travel the world? No. He sits in a room that is 'too crowded, facing front, doing lessons predetermined by a distant administration at the state capital and that have no relation to his own intellectual, social or animal interests and not much ... to his economic interest' in the long term. He is being shaped overtly and covertly. No wonder that people no longer show initiative.

Notwithstanding his predilection for the arts, Goodman also has a particular interest in science. His concern at the time of writing *Compulsory Miseducation* is to enable people to feel at home in the new technological era and so to diminish the sense of alienation (*CM* p. 40). Not surprisingly, therefore, he advocates the learning of science on the job and through experience. Science education is more a question of coming to see the need for and benefits of science, of learning to control it, of becoming familiar with it and being able to make use of it, than of being in receipt of various laws and parcels of information.

He tends to favour discovery methods in relation to all subject matter and is sarcastic in the extreme about what he regards as compromise measures whereby the child discovers what it has been ordained he shall discover. By being allowed and enabled to find things out for himself, the child may develop confidence in himself as a source of initiation (*CM* pp. 42, 73), which is one necessary precondition of being creative and self-sufficient. However, Goodman is careful to say that he does not advocate a uniformity of teaching technique. Different styles may suit different people in different situations. But he does think that 'there is a case for a uniform standard of achievement' (*CM* p. 34).

Judged purely as the author of this and preceding works, there is nothing very exceptional or remarkable in Goodman. He would

appear to be a free- rather than a de-schooler and he quite specifically allies himself with people like Dewey and Neill; indeed, his
qualified conclusion that 'on the whole, the education must be
voluntary rather than compulsory, for no growth to freedom occurs
except by intrinsic motivation' (*CM* p. 56), might, word for word,
have been written by Neill with its vague and somewhat obscure
phrasing, its touch of the Manfreds and its gross overstatement. But
already there are some ambiguities: on one page Goodman quite
emphatically talks of using education to change the world; on another
he emphasises the need for people not to learn to change society
but 'to learn to live in a high technology' society. His final position
on certain matters about which he has a lot to say, such as
various kinds of competence tests, is hard to determine, as is his
position on the vexed issue of heredity and environment. His anarchic
lapses fit ill alongside his Dewey-like vision of a greater democratic
tomorrow. These and other specific obscurities and apparent con-
tradictions however should be seen as merely aspects of the central
problem running through his argument, and that is the question of
what he understands by 'education'.

He says that we must stop using the word 'education' honorific-
ally to give a veneer of respectability to activities such as keeping
children off the streets or training them in some skill (*CM* p. 51).
In addition, he has a personal commitment to the arts and intellectual
activity and regards them as valuable in themselves. That suggests
that he has a normative conception of education that regards it
as closely connected with traditional curriculum fare. On the other
hand, he very strongly suggests that the child's upbringing, whether
we call it education or not, should be centrally preoccupied with
jobs. His objection is not that schools provide vocational training,
which is not truly education, but that schools constitute an in-
sufficient means for effective vocational training, which is what
children should be getting.

MINI-SCHOOLS AND APPRENTICESHIPS

The pessimistic conclusion of *Compulsory Miseducation* was that
our values are awry and consequently our society intolerable and

our children ineducable. A final chapter depicts the plight of the typical teenager: he has never initiated anything of his own accord; he has no enthusiasm for the academic fare that is set before him; and he cannot relate to any of it. When something does interest or provoke him the physical circumstances in which he is situated stand in the way of his taking the point up, discussing it or arguing about it. Not surprisingly, he has little or no feeling for culture, by which Goodman means in Arnold's phrase 'the best that has been spoken and thought'. He is not interested in abstraction; he is solitary and lonely.

On the assumption that our present system of schooling will inevitably continue to produce such typical cases, Goodman offered two proposals: first, rather than seek to vary the schooling pattern and to increase flexibility within the schools themselves, 'structure all of society and the whole environment as educative' (whatever that means) 'with the schools playing the much more particular and traditional role of giving intensive training when it is needed and sought or of being havens for those scholarly by disposition' (*CM* p. 106). In other words, schools as institutions for the promulgation of general worthwhile learning cease to exist and are replaced by schools in a sense akin to that implied when we refer to schools of driving or dancing. Second, he proposes that we abolish grading in all its various shapes and forms.

Those two proposals supply the essence of Goodman's proposed alternative education, which is elaborated in two subsequent articles, 'Freedom and Learning' and 'Mini-Schools'. In those papers Goodman proposes a two-part plan to meet the ills of the world as he sees them and has previously described them. The first part relates to children up to the age of twelve and is strictly speaking a free-schooling proposal. For he concedes that, if only to protect children from bad parents and unattractive homes, 'there should be some kind of school', and so he suggests what he terms the 'mini-school' (FL p. 109).

The essential administrative and institutional features of the mini-school are that it should be small, containing about twenty-eight children, and run by four adults: 'a licensed teacher, a housewife who can cook, a college senior, and a teenage school drop-out' (FL p. 109). He calculates that at a ratio of one to twenty-eight there are already enough licensed teachers available (in America, at any rate), and claims that for the sort of school he envisages there would be no lack of willing graduates and literate housewives eager to be involved at a moderate salary (MS p. 35). A slight mystery hangs over the question of why Goodman, who at one point remarks that 'the only profitable training for teachers is a group therapy and, perhaps, a course in child development' (FL p. 108), requires any kind of *licensed* teacher at all. It is also unclear, to say the least, why the proposal that the fourth member of the team should be 'a literate, willing, and intelligent high school graduate' (MS p. 35) should have been modified in the course of the two months that separate these articles to a demand for a drop-out. However, the general picture is clear enough: small groups of children should be entrusted to the care of a varied band of committed persons rather than to trained professionals.

Physical surroundings are of little significance to Goodman, and he may well be right that recent stress on the allegedly demoralising effect of Victorian buildings and the corresponding emphasis on the delights of plate glass and the educational value of open-plan has been grossly exaggerated and extremely costly. At any rate, perhaps because he wishes to emphasise the practicality of his proposals, he stresses that 'the setting is especially indifferent since a major part of activity occurs outside the school house' (MS p. 35). He requires a base or centre for operations in a real situation, 'real' being defined in terms of current neighbourhood practice and way of life, so all that is needed are a couple of rooms in some local building, which might or might not be the existing school. Many mini-schools might occupy the same building, but even if they did they would remain quite autonomous units; that is why they are mini-schools rather than classes or sets; one of the main objects of the exercise is to decentralise education and to replace allegiance to authorities with allegiance to persons arising out of shared interests. The school must be located near the children's homes, partly to reinforce the sense of its being part of the real world, but also 'so that children can escape from it to home, and from home to it' (FL p. 109). For although Goodman envisages a situation in which children under the age of twelve are obliged to attend such schools, he evidently does not envisage any particular rules about attendance, probably because he does not envisage any serious desire on the part of children not to join in the fun.

As at Summerhill, children would have a large say in what goes on and in what they do. But whereas Neill always gives the impression that he has no wish to extend this freedom to parents and that he would rather they steered clear of the place, Goodman wants parents involved as well, for this is a neighbourhood school – one, furthermore, that ideally is not to be seen as a school at all. Although 'the school should be supported by public money' and although compulsory attendance may be demanded, that does not give the state any rights over the institution as far as Goodman is concerned. The school should be 'administered entirely by its own teachers, children and parents' (MS p. 35). What is being proposed, once the state has put up the money, is a free market situation in which, though the people may not always get all and precisely what they want, they none the less want what they get.

In *Compulsory Miseducation* Goodman had asserted straightforwardly that primary schooling for the most part 'is, and should be, mainly baby-sitting. It has the great mission of democratic socialisation – it certainly must not be segregated by race and income; it should be happy, interesting, not damaging' (*CM* p. 52). His views have not changed on this issue: the mini-schools are devised as a way of achieving these objectives. However, unless something is done to change society and people's living patterns first, the idea of a neighbourhood school, particularly on the small scale proposed by Goodman, is quite obviously incompatible with the ideal of no segregation by race and income. It is true that the mini-school would not itself segregate by these or any other criteria. But Goodman's ideal involves avoiding the spirit of discrimination and not merely the letter of it: he presumably wants people of all colours, backgrounds and incomes to mix unthinkingly as equals. They won't in a mini-school in Harlem. So it is hard to see how it will perform its 'great mission' any more than an English Public School does.

The mini-school proposal was first put forward as a means of getting children to read and write. Goodman draws a highly dubious analogy between learning to speak and learning to read, and the mini-school is envisaged as a means of promoting and nurturing rather than choking or killing the spontaneous inherent interest in and impetus towards reading which Goodman believes children have (MS p. 34). It would be a mistake to infer that he is particularly concerned about whether or not children can read and write. Over the years Goodman consistently maintained that the value of functional literacy was overplayed. According to him, one can live a fulfilled life without being literate as easily today as one could in medieval times. What he values is literature, and for him literacy has value only as a means to reading or writing literature or to some other academic pursuit. But since he does not think that literature, science or anything else ought to be or will be valued by the majority, he is not driven to the conclusion that all children should necessarily become literate as a means to those ends. He seems unaware of the obvious objection that we do not know in advance of the fact who will value literature, or any other pursuit depending on literacy, and who will not. Likewise, he seems not to have entertained the thought that teaching literacy may be a productive means of teaching certain elements of rational thought. He offers no reasons in support of his assumption that it is easy for the illiterate to live a fulfilled life or for the very unlikely view that acquiring the capacity to read and write is comparable to what is in so many respects plainly different, namely acquiring the habit of speech.

It is not only the development of literacy but also all other specifiable aspects of the traditional school curriculum that are to be expunged from the timetable of the mini-school. 'I am assuming', Goodman writes, 'that for the first five years of school, there is no merit in the standard curriculum.... Up to the age of twelve, there is no point to formal subjects or a pre-arranged curriculum' (FL p. 108). This does not only mean that the content should not be organised in any way by the teacher; it also means that the teacher should not have any prior idea of content or what ought to be learned. 'It seems stupid to decide *a priori* what the young ought to know and then to try to motivate them, instead of letting the initiative come from them and putting information and relevant equipment at their service' (FL p. 107). In other words, the adults involved with the mini-schools should have no pre-ordained goals or objectives (which suggests that they will need an implausibly wide range of 'relevant equipment' or resources at their disposal).

But can Goodman really mean this? Suppose a child has an interest in torturing cats. Shall I put information, sharp knives and a cat at his disposal? The question is whether such a view as this is based on the belief that if something interests somebody at a particular time it is for that reason a good thing for him to be doing it, or on the very different belief that in ideal surroundings people are not interested in evil acts like torturing cats. Goodman inclines to the latter view, though he does not clearly and consistently proclaim it. In any case there is serious trouble with either viewpoint: it is not true that what we mean by 'good' is such that a thing is always good when someone is interested in it, and it is not true that people are never interested in doing things that are not good. Whether they would cease to be in ideal surroundings is an issue that has all the hallmarks of a 'likely story' stamped upon it.

Goodman, like Neill, is really left with no option but to align himself with the rather vague view that, by and large, within broad limits, children, if brought up in pleasant surroundings, tend to be interested in some of a wide variety of acceptable pastimes. Should a child prove exceptional and display interest in positively evil behaviour he may have to be forcibly restrained. But generally the children's enthusiasms and interest are themselves more to be valued than anybody else's views as to the merit and importance of what they're interested in and enthusiastic about. So the emphasis falls on providing children with love, security and respect, especially by catering for their enthusiasms as evoked by their everyday environment.[3]

After the age of twelve no child will receive schooling as the term is currently understood. Nobody, that is to say, compulsorily attends an institution explicitly set up or administered for the purpose of teaching or educating. This is not to say that teaching, training and education do not take place on Goodman's proposals, or that the present school curriculum or aspects of it do not exist. But education is no longer the province of the schools; it is the province of the whole environment in which the individual moves, while teaching and training are the responsibilities of the appropriate professionals in any sphere. Basically, therefore, Goodman envisages an unparalleled extension of an apprenticeship system.

He observes that what he himself regarded as the entirely proper function of the primary school as a baby-sitter becomes, when transferred to the secondary level, 'policing' and as such totally undesirable (*CM* p. 52). So what we have to do in the adolescent years is 'open as many diverse paths as possible, with plenty of opportunity to backtrack and change' (FL p. 109). In line with this, he offers us a rather simplistic picture of life as a series of avenues one might follow or options one might take up. It appears that there is nothing to choose between these options except in so far as the individual has a personal preference; the preconditions of embarking on them are minimal or non-existent; and the consequences of sticking with them or changing one's mind and rejecting them are immaterial to oneself and everybody else. Goodman uses the old-fashioned term 'apprenticeship' in a free and all-embracing way; he does not confine the idea to trades and sees the possibility of an individual becoming apprenticed to practically anything from the Sea Scouts to philosophy. The individual might apprentice himself to academia and thus to all appearances still go to school. That would be the new role of schools and schoolmasters: just places and people whose trade is academics, to which and to whom you go, if that is what you want to do with yourself. You do not go there to qualify for anything else. If you want to become a doctor, a lawyer or a dustbinman then you go and apprentice yourself directly to one of those trades. All you qualify for at the school is the trade of academics: if you are good, you may become a teacher of academics.

Goodman evidently hopes that some people would choose to pursue offbeat and uncommon pursuits, and he is insistent that there must always be the opportunity to drop what one is doing and start something else (*CM* p. 57). Thus a twelve-year-old might apprentice himself to the local paper for a while, decide it's not for him, and then, because he misses some of his friends who went in for academics, apprentice himself to the school. Perhaps that doesn't work out either, so he apprentices himself to doing nothing for a bit, then to travel, then back to the paper. And so on. Finance is, by Goodman's calculation, catered for by the simple expedient of dividing up the current educational resources among those of secondary school age. They can use that money to pay for 'any plausible self-chosen educational proposals, such as purposeful travel or individual enterprise' (*CM* p. 57). (Why, given Goodman's perspective, does he slip in the word 'purposeful'; who decides what is purposeful, and how? The Manfred Syndrome from another angle. And still one wonders what makes a proposal 'educational' according to Goodman). Apparently by adopting this simple expedient, we solve at a stroke all the problems that Goodman has previously analysed: people are no longer alienated; they feel constructive; they do useful and interesting things; and the non-academic are not broken on the wheel of academia.

SLIPS AND FALLACIES

On what grounds does Goodman assume that such means will eradicate the ills of society? Sadly, much of what passes for argument is the mixture of assertion and rhetoric that is becoming disturbingly familiar. A significant proportion of what he writes is simply the statement of a faith. As is the way with faith, there is a certain amount of deep-sounding but possibly quite empty intoning going on in the background. There is, for instance, talk, reminiscent of Rousseau, of freedom being 'the only way towards authentic citizenship and real ... philosophy' (FL p. 108), but what, if anything, this actually means and the evidence that it is so (assuming that it does mean something) I am unable to discover. And it really will not do to avoid the challenge by uttering such lofty pronouncements as 'It is not necessary to argue for freedom as a metaphysical proposition; it is what is indicated by present conditions' (FL p. 108), since that amounts merely to a reassertion of the faith. What freedom? Why so? What does 'what is indicated by' mean, and what is the difference between arguing for freedom and arguing for it as 'a metaphysical proposition'? The emperor is wearing no clothes. Behind the verbiage it seems that we are being told that Goodman thinks that we should give the young freedom (unspecified) and he sees no need to defend that view even when confronted by alternative points of view or requests for further explanation.

Again, the bland assertion that schools now 'rigidify class stratification' (FL p. 108) cannot be left to stand without question. Does he mean that a system of schooling perpetuates the phenomenon of class stratification or does he mean that the system serves to keep the individual in the class into which he was born? If he means the latter, then he will need to explain away quite a lot of evidence about social mobility; granted that education has not proved as effective a source of mobility as it was once dreamed it might, it is clear that many who would not otherwise have done so do move from social class to social class as a consequence of the effects of schooling. If he means the former, he needs to explain how deschooling is going to improve things. This is particularly a problem for Goodman, since he, like the other radicals, believes in innate aptitudes and characteristics. For despite the emphasis on the need for the individual to have the opportunity to make frequent changes in his work while an adolescent, from which it might be inferred that Goodman sees people's talents and interests as fluid, it is clear from his habit of referring to the academic and the non-academic as if they are distinguishable from early childhood, and from his heavy reliance on Conant's view that 'fifteen per cent learn well by books and study in an academic setting' as if it were holy writ, that he does believe in innate qualities.[4] Whatever the explanation of the state of affairs, he accepts that there will be ineluctable differences between children by the age of twelve. Given that far-from-unreasonable belief, deschooling society seems calculated to increase class divisions and to perpetuate the phenomenon of class stratification, while perhaps changing the composition of classes to some extent. A significant part of what constitutes an identifiable class is a particular shared way of life and outlook. A compulsory schooling system with some kind of common curriculum, even if hidden, is at least one way of trying to provide a common way of life and outlook for all. Schooling *can* contribute to breaking down class stratification, whether it does or not. Deschooling cannot but leave things as they are.

A common curriculum may also contain elements that it would benefit all to be acquainted with or cognisant of. In his earlier works, Goodman himself stressed such an idea when he argued that all need to be familiar with science in a technological era. But his proposal of mini-schools followed by apprenticeships makes no provision for this at all. And at no stage does he entertain the possibility that there might be certain other things that we should, as a community and as individuals, benefit from all persons having some awareness and understanding of – for example, politics, race relations, the law. The deschooled society makes no effort to ensure such common understanding. It offers a job here, and a job there: fragmented and narrow skills and bits of knowledge, with never a thought for communal points of reference.

Drawing once again on the research of Conant, Goodman makes the announcement that 'it has been shown that whatever is useful in the present eight-year curriculum can be learned in four months by a normal child of twelve' (FL p. 109). But this could only be said to have been 'shown' given the following four conditions: first, that we define and agree on what is 'useful' in the present cur-riculum; second, that such children as are going to be cited as evidence that the claim is true are agreed to be 'normal'; third, that these 'normal' children be 'abnormal' to the extent of being taught nothing prior to the experiment (otherwise they can hardly be cited as evidence); and finally, that these particular children are taught for four months and seen at the end of that time to have learned all that the typical child learns in eight years. To expect such conditions to be met in practice would be absurd, and they have not been met. What Goodman might more accurately have said is that 'as a result of their observations and work with a limited number of children many years ago, certain people such as Conant surmised that what we take eight years to teach could be taught in four months, and I agree'. But why should we?

The further claim, that 'if left alone' the normal child will have learned most of what is useful by himself anyway, is if anything even more clumsy and absurd. To make such a crude generalisation is to ignore a mass of evidence that different home backgrounds may make a material difference to what a 'normal' child will or will not achieve. The child of unconcerned, brutal and poor parents in a slum area is not likely to learn as much of whatever is useful as the child of concerned, perhaps capable, parents who have time and money to spare.

It is unfortunate that Goodman cannot offer us a precise account of what he means by 'useful', since, when it comes to the question of what kind of knowledge he would most like children to acquire, he cannot advance much beyond the vague idea that we should reverse the present trend of cramming 'the young with what they do not want at the time and what most of them will never use' (FL p. 111). He seems unaware of the various counter-objections to this creed that spring to mind: he implies that wants are static, given and common to all, whereas they are plainly dynamic, can be created or generated and vary from individual to individual. Apart from assuming that future use is the all-important criterion, he implies that 'useful' is to be located by reference to what is necessary for social life as it is now. It is also apparent (though not from this quotation alone) that Goodman finds it hard to recognise usefulness except where it stares him in the face: finding a book in the street is only useful as far as he is concerned if he wants to read that book. It does not occur to him that he might sell it, exercise a charitable act in returning it or a philanthropic act in giving it away, or that the book is useful to those ends. It is perhaps this paucity of imagination in the radicals that explains why, without exception, they see themselves as having uncovered some dark secret when they lay stress on the 'hidden curriculum'. The truth is that what is labelled the hidden curriculum is to some extent a deliberate and conscious contrivance. Thus one possible defence of teaching history might be that it is useful (indirectly to the aim of a better society) not because of what is overtly learned but because of such things as a sense of a common heritage, a sense of human folly, concern for evidence, awareness of others and appreciation of how interpretations can vary, which are covertly put across and unconsciously taken in. All in all, it is very difficult to see how, by reference to his chosen words 'useful' and 'educative', one could ever in practice determine whether or not a child was doing something of which Goodman would approve.

Finally, three examples of fallacious reasoning are worth noting.

1. Goodman commits the fallacy of regarding the fact that something is the case as sufficient reason for concluding that it ought to be the case. That is the implication of his claim that freedom doesn't need arguing for, since 'it is what is indicated by present conditions'. It is also implied by the curious assertion that 'the best young people resist authority' (FL p. 108), since one must presume that Goodman's point is that we should admire and follow their example. But even if it were so, it would not follow that they were right to resist authority. Even the best do not always do what is right. (An alternative explanation of this remark is that Goodman observes many young people resisting authority, considers that that is right and appropriate behaviour, and therefore concludes that these are among the best young people.) That it *is* fallacious to regard the fact that something is the case as sufficient reason for concluding that it ought to be the case is self-evident. If it were not so, the mere existence of concentration camps would justify their existence.

2. Second, there is what one might call the fallacy of the faulty football manager. This is to make the mistake of thinking that, if something fails to work or to achieve its object, that is sufficient reason to conclude that the thing in question is no good. But of course, the fact that a football manager can be shown to have failed in a manager's task does not in itself show that he is a failure as a manager. Other factors might explain the particular failure in question. Goodman's writing to a large extent consists of painting an

impressionistic picture of the failure of the current schooling system. But even if it were clear and agreed how we are to define success and failure, which it is not, and even if the evidence for failure were of a higher order than remarks such as 'I have heard James Coleman ... express the opinion' (*CM* p. 66), still one could not deduce from the fact that schooling has failed that it ought to be done away with. Goodman never raises the question of whether such failures as he detects might not be removed and replaced by such achievement as he wants within the present system. (On this issue Goodman cannot be compared with other deschoolers, whose thesis is such that they could not coherently accept the present system, whatever it achieved. That is not true of Goodman.)

3. Third, there is the fallacy of confusing definitional points with substantive factual claims. No doubt the assertion that 'with guidance anything a child experiences is educational' (FL p. 108), or that 'for a small child everything in the environment is educative, if he attends to it with guidance' (MS p. 36), can be made true by definition. One might mean by 'educative' no more than 'interesting' or 'having some effect', in either of which cases it would be true that watching torture or cleaning the drains could be educative. Similarly 'with guidance' is a pretty vague phrase, and by interpreting it in various ways one could ensure that the above remarks were true. But in order to use the claim as an argument for deschooling it is necessary to interpret it to mean something like this: 'Whatever the child sees, does or experiences, provided that it is accompanied by the sort of guidance that committed but largely untrained people, who may know nothing about the experience in question, can give, is not only educative in the sense of improving, good or valuable, but is also sufficient in itself to constitute education.' Interpreted in this way, it is palpable nonsense. The point about the school is not so much that it does special things and that only those special things can be educative, but that things can be educative only when treated in certain ways and that schools have the wherewithal to treat things in an educative manner. That is the basic point that deschooling theory seeks and seems to challenge, but never in fact faces up to at all. Granted that the schools have failed in many identifiable respects, none the less there is a strong *prima facie* case for saying that treating experience or activities in an educative manner is easier in a controlled situation than outside.

THREE CRUCIAL ISSUES

Learning

When we turn to questions of learning and motivation we focus on a crucial aspect of radical theory. James Herndon states starkly that 'nobody learns anything in school' (*D* p. 6). Only slightly less abruptly, Illich insists that 'an illusion on which the school system rests is that most learning is the result of teaching', whereas in point of fact 'most learning is not the result of instruction. It is rather the result of unhampered participation in a meaningful setting. Most people learn best by being "with it", yet school makes them identify their personal cognitive growth with elaborate planning and manipulation' (*D* p. 6). One must concede that many of us tend to talk and think as if most learning takes place as a result of instruction in schools, which is probably quite untrue. But surely we are not primarily interested in arguments about *quantity* of learning. Whatever we may say, what we presumably mean when we tie learning and schools closely together is that many things that are worth learning are more likely to be more effectively learnt by more people via the school system than outside it. It is some such view as *that* that the deschoolers have to debunk rather than the Aunt Sally that only professional teachers can enable anyone to learn anything.

It will be remembered that according to Goodman whatever is useful or worth learning in the current curriculum could be learned in four months. Unless the term 'useful' is redefined to exclude anything that might take more than four months to learn, that assertion is false. Pure physics, understanding of English literature and mathematics – which are not regarded as worthless by Goodman – are not things that can be picked up in four months by most people, especially if they want to pick up all three, perhaps in some depth. Nor for that matter can be the wisdom and skills of the gardener, the proficiency of the dancer, the techniques of the artist or the knowledge of the pop enthusiast. *Prima facie*, a more plausible claim is that technological know-how has to be learnt 'in actual practice in offices and factories' (FL p. 110) and that this often involves unlearning what has been learnt at school; similarly, it is suggested, the technical competence of skilled workmen can be better and more rapidly acquired on the job. But further thought reveals the limitations of this view. The notion that school learning has to be unlearnt when it comes to doing the real thing seems to be a vague conflation of three different ideas none of which are very significant or threatening when distinguished and considered in isolation as they should be. First, there is the view that a great deal of school learning is irrelevant to particular jobs. That may be true in many instances, but it does not follow that school learning has to be unlearnt; to suppose that it does is to commit oneself to an implausible picture of the mind as something comparable to a suitcase that can only hold so much, so that a head must be emptied of what is irrelevant to the job in hand before it can take in what is relevant. Second, there is the view that what one learns in school about, say, electricity is incorrect and misleading. If that were so the practising electrician would indeed be well advised to unlearn or forget his school learning on the subject. But if this were the case, it would follow only that what was being taught in the schools should be corrected to square with the truth of the matter. Third, there is the view that the school cannot teach one various tricks of the trade which are important and have to be learnt on the job. This too may very well be true, but once again it does not follow that one needs to unlearn what one learnt at school, only that there is still more to learn on the job.

The further point, that technological know-how and competence has to be acquired on the job, obviously has something in it: there are some things that can only be picked up on the job, some jobs that can be thoroughly mastered by practice alone, and some aspects of some jobs that are best mastered in this way. But it is not true that everything has to be acquired or is best acquired in this way, and still less is it true that schooling cannot contribute, directly or indirectly, to the acquisition of know-how and competence. It depends very much what kind of activity we are talking about. The best way to learn to dig a ditch is probably to dig it. But it by no means follows that the best way to learn to become a doctor is to try and pick it up on the job, rigorously avoiding anything that might be taught in schools or universities.

A third claim is that one cannot teach social sciences or literary criticism to 'youngsters who have had no responsible experience in life and society' (FL p. 110). Social science and the critical study of literature *are* likely to mean less to those who have no real experience of the subject matter than to those who have. But that is hardly sufficient to show that schools should not be concerned with them. Literature in particular is precisely a way of introducing people vicariously to experiences that they would not otherwise come across: Othello's jealousy may possibly mean more to the adult who has suffered agonies of jealousy than to those who have not, but on the other hand coming to understand Othello (being brought or helped to understand Othello) is one good way of coming to understand a certain kind of jealousy. Furthermore, we know – from experience – that 'youngsters who have had no responsible experience in life' can be successfully taught the social sciences and literary criticism at least to the extent that, later on in life, what they have learnt can be recalled and drawn upon and otherwise made use of to inform their reading, their professional work and other aspects of their daily lives.

The claim that people 'learn more about the theory and practice of government by resisting the draft' (FL p. 113) than from lessons in political science is revealing. For it is at once apparent that what you learn from resisting the draft is not necessarily more but is decidedly different, and this is a timely reminder that at the back of all the radicals' talk about more efficient learning lies a particular schema of values. The real point is that by resisting the draft you learn something about the politics of daily life. You learn nothing at all about political theory and a very very limited amount about the practice of one particular government. Consequently Goodman's conviction that you learn more indicates only that he holds the somewhat bizarre view that wide-ranging knowledge of political and comparative government practice is an insignificant part of the theory and practice of government compared with experience of draft-dodging.

The deschoolers are on stronger ground when they make limited empirical claims about the actual failings of the schooling system than they are when they try to glorify these failures into manifestations of eternal laws. It is impossible to deny Lister's generalisation that 'in mass systems ... majorities clearly do not learn what the school pretends to teach' (*D* p. 6) (though 'pretends' seems uncalled for). It is certainly true that to some extent schools devalue learning that takes place outside the school, that a great deal of profitable learning could go on outside the school, and that a lot of school organisation is done for reasons of administrative convenience rather than for educational reasons and, as such, may impede rather than promote learning. One must therefore accept that schools are far from perfect on their own terms, and that even if they were perfect they should still not be thought of as the sole source of wisdom, the necessary means of acquiring all knowledge. But of course it does not follow from this that the schools should be disbanded. To draw that conclusion one would need to show, as Goodman evidently realised, that such is the nature of learning that it is foolish to expect it to take place in a school setting, or at least that the school constitutes a most inappropriate setting for it. There are two ways in which one might try to establish that, and Goodman attempts both. First, one can take the line that what people are to learn should not be pre-arranged or planned for (e.g. FL p. 107). If that were agreed it would strike a severe blow at the idea of schooling, which is closely tied up with the idea of organised knowledge. But whether we will agree must depend on whether we think that the individual on his own initiative will want to learn everything or most of what we deem to be of importance. Goodman for example wants children to develop into adults ready for authentic citizenship and responsive to the needs of society. If we accepted those objectives as necessary and sufficient, and if we saw reason to believe that children would learn whatever is necessary to authentic citizenship and responsiveness to the needs of society, then indeed we should be unlikely to insist on the necessity of a system of schooling (though we might still try to defend the system on the grounds of efficiency). But we have been given no convincing reason to accept any of that. Consequently it is the second line of argument that becomes crucial to Goodman's thesis and this is the claim that 'nothing can be ... learnt at all ... unless it meets need, desire, curiosity or fantasy' (FL p. 107).

We must distinguish here between the thesis that the school *does not* motivate and the thesis that it *cannot*. Many people take the view that in practice schools diminish natural curiosity and debase self-motivation. Goodman himself hints at this view when he writes that we must cut out 'top-down direction' such as is implicit in instruction 'in order to maintain human initiative' (FL p. 108), and when he says that 'schooling is too impersonal, standardised and academic' to allow learning to become self-motivated and second nature. And indeed it may well be as Becker maintains that 'most people learn better when they can pursue their own interests at their own pace' (*D* p. 17). But such empirical generalisations are quite different in kind to what Goodman generally appears to be saying and needs to be saying in order to justify deschooling. He needs to show that no learning at all *can* take place, or at least that no *worthwhile* learning can take place.

Goodman rightly insists that by definition learning involves some degree of knowledge and understanding. The man who is hypnotised into reciting some chemical formula of which he has no understanding has not learnt that formula, although he may be able to recite it accurately whenever prompted to do so. To learn something is to acquire some information, skill or knowledge that one did not have before and that one understands and can make appropriate use of.[5]

But once we clear our minds as to what we mean by the crucial terms, Goodman's claim is clearly absurd. While we may concede that usually or often people do *not* learn what does not interest them, none the less it remains true that one *can* learn what does not interest one. One can acquire some new skill or information with understanding and in such a way as to be able to make appropriate use of it without having been (or now being) curious, interested or self-motivated. The only way to deny this is to render the initial proposition trivially true and to insist that one must have 'needed' or been 'curious' about what one learnt, if one learnt it. But the important point is that schools can (and often do) cause learning to take place both by creating interest, arousing curiosity and provoking fantasy on the one hand and where there is no curiosity or interest on the other.

Examination and assessment

There are so many issues and dimensions involved in what may loosely be called the question of assessment that I shall start by listing, without argument, certain objections that I accept, not as decisive reasons for discontinuing practices such as examining, but as valid points to which due weight must be given. First, although I see no reason to imagine that the mere abolition of certification, grading and examination would eradicate the influence and control of the educational system, I do not see how one can reasonably deny Lister's point that to a large extent 'the social power of the educational system ... lies in its power to print its own money'

(*D* p. 88), by which he means the fact that it controls the busi-ness of certification. That is the source of much of the system's power, and for that reason alone, if for no other, the business of certification demands very careful scrutiny. Second, I accept what in the present state of knowledge seems to be the reasonable view that there is a negative correlation between certification and job performance. But from that I conclude only that, if one of the purposes of certification is to predict subsequent job performance levels, it is in that respect not very successful. It might serve other purposes, and it might none the less be the best pointer that we have and at present can devise for predicting such things. Third, how could one deny that the pervasiveness of centralised examinations in a qualification-conscious society limits and governs syllabus con-tent regardless of individual teacher or child interest, and hence in-creases the likelihood of irrelevance? There is enough truth in Good-man's assertion that 'the galloping increase of national tests guaran-tees that the classwork will become nothing but preparation for these same tests' (*CM* p. 59) to allow us to forgive the exaggeration. Similarly, and fourth, it is difficult to deny that the seriousness or worthiness of a subject tends to be assessed, by children and parents alike, with respect to whether and how it is examined: carpentry is regarded as inferior to Latin at least to some extent because the school does not demand that children take O-level in the former. Finally, one could say that all these points come to a head in a fifth point put most succinctly by Illich: 'In school we are taught ... that value [of learning] can be measured and documented by grades and certificates' (*D* p. 65) to the point where in Hutchins' words 'we do not ask what a graduate knows but whether he has his diploma' (*D* p. 58).

All that is conceded, as is Goodman's observation that those who have passed tests with distinction may not 'have necessarily learned anything relevant to their further progress or careers; or of advantage to the body politic' (*CM* p. 72). What is not conceded is that an accumulation of such observations leads to any such fatuous conclusion as that 'we must make discrimination by education illegal' (*D* p. 16; cf. *SD* p. 145), as Buckman demands, or, more soberly, that examinations are necessarily more harmful than useful. To justify a system of tests it is not imperative to show that success in a test *necessarily* indicates that one has learned something of advantage.

In an attempt to throw some light on this issue, let us distinguish between four distinct elements. First, there is the practice, regardless of what form or shape it may take, of grading people in respect of specific abilities, skills or knowledge; the practice, in other words, of distinguishing between people's competence in any matter by any means. I shall use the word 'grading' to refer to this practice. Second, there is the business of making one's grading public by use of diplomas, degrees or other forms of qualification. I will call this 'certification'. Third, there is the use of examinations as one means of assessing grades and hence determining certification; and fourth, there are other means of assessment such as continuous assessment or the intuitive judgement of teachers. I shall use the word 'assessment' as the generic term which includes 'examining' as one species. It seems far from obvious that, because one has reservations about one of these four practices, it necessarily follows that one will have reservations about any of the others: one might well favour assessment, but not by examination, for example, or accept the necessity for grading, but object to certification.

It should be noted that, although the attack on assessment or aspects of it is introduced by the deschoolers as a stick with which to beat the formal schooling system, it has no necessary connection with it. Not only is it possible to have a schooling system without assessment; it is also possible, and quite common, to have assessment where there are no schools. Football clubs, for example, practice grading, have mechanisms such as transfer fees for certification or making grading public, and obviously have many types of assessment – so do things as disparate as orchestras and large businesses. In fact, only political clubs and political parties seem obviously not to concern themselves with assessment, and that is because they are not interested in competence so much as in faith and loyalty to an ideology. In practice, any area of life or pursuit that involves the idea of trying to attain to a certain degree of competence has a system, however informal, of assessment and grading associated with it. The importance of this point is that it indicates that deschooling would not necessarily get rid of the alleged evil, and that getting rid of this alleged evil, besides being extremely difficult, would not necessarily require deschooling.

Goodman repeatedly confuses the question of assessment with the question of academic study. It is as if he had made the double mistake, first of assuming that all assessment must take the form of examinations, and then of assuming that examinations necessarily imply academic subject matter. But that is clearly not so. Assessment is not inextricably bound up with academic study. A diving competition in which the performances of a number of individuals are judged and ranked in order certainly involves assessment as much as an examination in Latin; one might even say that it is itself a type of examination. The consequence of Goodman's confusion on this point is faulty argument such as the following. Having said that 'school methods are simply not competent to teach all ... the school establishment pretends to teach' (FL p. 110), he immediately proceeds to explain and support this by saying that 'for some professions – e.g. social work, architecture, pedagogy – trying to earn academic credits is probably harmful because it is an irrelevant and damaging obstacle course.' This would seem to mean that one cannot teach architecture in an institutional or classroom setting because earning credits is detrimental to that end. The implicit assumptions appear to be, first, that all teaching must involve assessment; second, that assessment must involve grading; third, that that must be counter-productive; and fourth, that all of this makes the teaching of architecture unsuited to school methods, if not impossible to teach in schools. However the last, concluding, point does not follow from the previous three, and would not even if they were well-founded; rather, it involves the quite separate issue of the nature of the relationship between theory and practice. I need not add to what I have already said on that topic above: certainly there is more to being an architect than theorising, but initiation into various theoretical studies may still be a most useful, perhaps necessary, element in training an architect. As to the first three assumptions noted, they are certainly not well-founded. To be sure, the business of grading may put some people off and dampen their enthusiasm; but conversely it may galvanise otherwise lazy people into action. Equally, you do not have to conduct examinations in architecture, or anything else, just because you are teaching it in schools. You do not even have to assess. Goodman has therefore not actually produced any argument at all to support either of two quite separate contentions: that some conventional school subjects cannot be taught in the conditions of a school, and that on balance the business of certification does more harm than good in such spheres as social work and pedagogy.

The basic question is surely whether or not there is good reason to accept the practice of assessment (which necessarily implies grading). And the answer is surely that there is good reason. Education involves a concern for standards and for progress. That is not necessarily to say that there are determinate, objectively valid standards and criteria of progress in all or any spheres, and that education must show concern for standards in that sense. We might, for example, only be concerned to measure progress by an individual from his point of view on his terms; we might be interested only in trying to help him achieve standards that he had set himself. But in some way or another in education we are certainly concerned that people should make some kind of progress and achieve some standard of competence in some matters. How could one begin to justify the role of teacher, even as conceived by the deschoolers, without reference to ideas such as improvement and progress? How could one begin an argument about the best way to enable children to learn without being prepared to make reference to the idea of seeing how well people are doing and what standard of competence they have achieved? Education just does involve seeking to promote progress of some kind, and consequently we need to have some way of measuring progress. Whether we are teaching French or bus-driving, we aim at developing competence and we need and want to know how successful we are being, which means that we need to assess.

Having said that, there are a number of further questions that can be raised. Does the school system have to do all the assessing itself, and does it have to do all or most of the certification itself? Does there have to be certification at all? What is the best form of assessment? Might it not be that examinations should be done away with? Are the certificates (i.e. degrees, diplomas, etc.) that are awarded fittingly distributed and properly understood by the outside world? Are the things for which we award certificates of one kind or another all relevant and worth certificating? I shall not attempt to answer all those questions. The important thing is to take the trouble to distinguish between these and other questions and to consider each one on its own merits. The question of examinations, for example, which I shall no longer pursue, is a question about whether or not on balance examinations are better than other possible ways of assessing and determining the appropriate certification. It must not be confused with the separate questions of the need for assessment and the desirability of certification.

In respect of the first question raised, Goodman, while accepting that we want competently qualified practitioners, at any rate in fields such as law and medicine, and hence that there must be some kind of grading, suggests that such grading should be done internally by the profession itself. No doubt there are arguments for that point of view. Equally, there are obviously arguments against it of which one of the strongest is probably the dull but forceful one that it is ludicrously impractical to expect every firm, business and profession to assess and grade all potential employees itself. This brings us to the nub of the matter, which is contained within the last question raised above. Goodman's central point is that certification of the type 'O-level pass in French' 'grade 7 pass' or 'third class honours degree in sociology' is irrelevant and not worth doing. What the firm, business or profession needs to know is whether the potential employee can count quickly in his head, flatter a customer or hoodwink a judge, and that kind of thing they had best find out for themselves. But this kind of argument could be convincingly upheld only by one who was willing to do the one thing that Goodman always shies away from – namely, make it absolutely clear how one determines what is valuable and relevant to what.

Certainly I do not wish to put myself in the position of claiming that the sort of certificates that we award are general certificates of competence – what one might call Rail Rover Certificates, that allow the bearer to do anything. We should guard against the assumption that a good degree in X means that one is in some general way competent. Nor do I wish to maintain that all certificates currently available have some value. The fact remains that, generally speaking, specific certification tells one something about the particular talents of individuals which is sometimes invaluable and very often useful. And to this should be added a point that deschoolers should not have missed: in many cases prospective employers take note of certification not because they believe French or mathematics directly relevant to the job in question, but because they take the certification as evidence that what the deschoolers call the hidden curriculum has had its effect: the employee with good grades in specific subjects thereby indicates that he has what it takes to get some good grades. The assumption that the prospective employer imagines that the particular good grades indicate some general intellectual superiority seems to be the gratuitous invention of certain educationalists. It is far more likely and entirely reasonable that he should take them as evidence of the individual's willingness to set his mind to a particular task.

One must concede to the deschoolers that certification has now got out of hand: we award certificates too easily, there is too little consistency between different institutions and certificating bodies, and we grossly overvalue certificates. One must also face up to the fact that assessment and certification are procedures that are very imperfect at the moment and need very careful scrutiny. None the less, it is difficult to see how we could hope to do without some forms of assessment. And since one of the functions of certificating is to help us all in choosing appropriate people for particular jobs, it is crucial that the business of certificating should be centrally organised and uniform. Goodman is right to insist that we must get rid of 'mandarin requirements' and 'diplomas for dustmen' (FL p. 112), but such points must be appreciated as the specific objections that they are, rather than construed as part of an argument for a general condemnation of assessment and certification. What is wrong with insisting on potential dustmen having diplomas is that no actual diplomas have any bearing on the qualities needed for that particular job. It is merely poor reasoning to see this as a vivid example of the general point that diplomas are irrelevant to practice.

Let me conclude this section by returning to Buckman's view that:

> we must make discrimination by education illegal. Employers should no longer be permitted to ask about an applicant's school record any more than they are allowed to ask about religion, politics or race. The only tests applied should strictly concern ability to perform the job available ... whether a doctor has attended school for two or twenty years doesn't matter in the least. The test is whether he or she can make you well. [*D* p. 16]

For sheer ingenuousness this passage takes some beating. Yes, indeed, 'the test *is* whether he or she can make you well', but I for one would like some idea of whether he or she is *likely* to make me well before I entrust my life to him or her. Certainly, the fact that he may have been at school for two, three, ten or twenty years does not in itself prove anything; but the fact that a doctor is qualified gives me some guidance, though by no means infallible, as to whether it is likely to be wise to entrust myself to him or not. In what way? What does his certificate show? Well, it is strong evidence that he has done some studying, that he has some interest in medicine, that he has satisfied some people with some medical expertise that he has some competence. But were the things that he studied relevant to his present task of being my doctor? Here we are again. Of course the radicals are correct to insist that what is certificated should be relevant to whatever the certificate qualifies a person to do, and of course 'the only tests applied [when appointing] should strictly concern ability to perform the job available'; and of course, in practice these demands are not always met. But the radicals seem at times quite incapable of appreciating that the questions of what is relevant and of what does strictly concern specific abilities that are important are usually highly contentious. They seem not to understand that none of us think that two A-levels (good grades) and a degree in medicine are irrelevant to being a doctor but are none the less qualifications that ought to be demanded; the point is that some of us think that by and large our doctors will be the better for having had such an education. It is in short difficult to think of anything more facile or misleading than to put the record of one's schooling on a par with one's racial characteristics: it just is the case that, whereas the fact that I am white and born of English parents is not likely to have any bearing on my capacity or lack of it to do most jobs, the fact that my schooling was such as it was and the fact that my certificates are such as they are certainly does have a bearing on that question.

Chicken, egg and choice

The tendency of the radicals to interpret usefulness and relevance in terms of whatever would immediately strike one of little imagination as obviously related leads them to a frighteningly narrow conception of education. And whatever its merits, it is clear that Goodman's substitution of learning through apprenticeships for schooling will in many individual cases lead to a very limited education. The empirical question of the likely efficacy of resorting to learning everything on the job will not be pursued here, although it is worth drawing attention to Becker, whose inquiries led him to the 'pessimistic conclusion . . . that on-the-job training does not do a very effective job' (*D* p. 128). But the possibility that many individuals would, in the end, have acquired only a limited number of specific competences and the element of pot-luck inherent in Goodman's system remain very worrying. It seems quite reasonable to presume that many people would know nothing of a variety of things that the current system of schooling promotes some acquaintanceship with and awareness of, and that some things would become unfamiliar to practically everybody. In particular, it seems likely that those pursuits that involve difficulty and demand perseverance at the beginning for the sake of a distant reward would for that reason alone be ignored by many. It is arguable that none of this matters very much. But it is also arguable that such a state of affairs could hardly be characterised as one in which *education* was taking place. What do we imagine education to be about? What do we conceive of it as being? Is it sufficient to say that, provided a fellow finds a job that really satisfies him, which is what Goodman clearly hopes to achieve, he has been educated?

Not, paradoxically, in Goodman's own view. But then, he would concede that *as things are* his approach might merely produce people who were satisfied with their jobs. What he envisages is a world in which the community as a whole is educative, so that the impetus towards developing other aspects of character and mind, currently the concern of the school, would be provided by the community itself. But that hope invites two urgent questions: (1) what comes first the chicken (a better world) or the egg (a better way of educating); and (2) what are the likely consequences in practice of embracing one in the absence of the other? If we lived in an ideal community of the sort envisaged by Goodman, one in which all activities had their place, were open to all and could be engaged in without fear or commitment, and one in which the theatre, the market place and the media were stimulating and encouraging, then he would have the beginnings of a case for arguing that the schooling system was unnecessary and possibly detrimental. But we do not live in such a community; as Goodman himself began by pointing out, we live in a world that is predominantly anti-educational on anybody's definition. So how, in the world as it is, if we follow his advice, do we ensure even such basic things as that understanding of technology and politics that at one stage he appeared to want? How do we open up a path towards culture for those who want it? How do we ensure any degree of familiarity with and tolerance for the range of diversity that seems likely to materialise? How do we help individuals to distinguish between the good and the pernicious in the society that is moulding and influencing them? Deschooling leaves children at the mercy of the media and to the prejudices of peers and parents. Far from bringing an end to conditioning and indoctrination, it substitutes the random control of the dominant attitudes of society as it is for something approaching a thought-out and arguably desirable direction of control. Consequently, we are left wondering on what possible grounds Goodman can suppose that 'it should be possible to find an interesting course [in the sense of pursuit in the wider context of society] for each individual youth' (FL p. 111). Crudely phrased, what he is after is satisfaction for all. Bringing people up in such a way that for the first twelve years of their life they are exclusively influenced by their immediate environment and then offering them the opportunity to try their hand at what they feel like gives no guarantee of satisfaction for anyone.

The second question, which is closely related to the first, is, in what way is individual choice supposed to become a reality that actually does open all doors, in the world as it is? One cannot choose that which one does not understand or is unaware of and, empirically, people are less likely to plump for things the more unfamiliar, new and foreign they seem. Consequently in the world as it is people are likely to bend to and be restrained by the limits placed on their imagination, experience and conceptual awareness by the neighbourhood in which they grow up. This point involves no necessary commitment to the view that some sub-cultures in a society are superior to others. It involves only the observation that there are different neighbourhood environments, that all are in themselves limited to some extent quantitatively, and that some are quantitatively more limited than others. Are we satisfied to proceed with Goodman's educational plans while the differences are as they are? Are we unconcerned by the obvious limitations in some areas? It is at this point that Goodman's emphasis on 'use' seems most frightening; for 'use', like most other things, is defined and characterised to some extent in terms of the nature of one's situation. What is useful for survival in a depressed slum area may not be useful in other contexts and may not have a lot to do with what most of us would understand by education. Surely we must make some attempt to distinguish between the trivial, the worthless and the slight and their opposites? An upbringing centred on the two criteria of neighbourhood and use is bound to be static, insular, limited and in some cases no education at all.

As if in reply to the suggestion that choice, far from being increased, is in many ways effectively limited by his proposals, Goodman asserts that 'voluntary adolescent choices are often random and foolish and usually transitory but they are the likeliest ways of growing up reasonably (FL p. 111). It is evident that to substantiate his thesis he has to believe something like that. But on what possible grounds could he defend the belief? (We are talking about individuals who will not even have had a normal primary schooling; they are not necessarily literate, numerate or used to making an initial effort for a longer-term gratification.) And on what conceivable grounds does he insist that random choices will cater satisfactorily for needs? There seems to be a belief in natural law implicit here to the effect that, though we may argue about what we need, ultimately the human mind unfailingly chooses what is needed. Alas, that is plainly not so, unless what is needed is defined as what is chosen. Illich is more cautious: his plans involve parents having control of funds until such time as the children are able to choose wisely for themselves. (*D* p. 54). But Goodman, untroubled by such worries, is now in full flight: 'Free choice is ... responsive to real situations'; by relying on it 'the needs of society will be adequately met' and people will become 'independent' and 'inventive'. 'It is not necessary to argue' for it. After attending the mini-schools and engaging in various apprenticeships, 'most adolescents would have a clearer notion of what they are after, and many would have found their vocation'. As a result of this style of education, individuals will gain from being taken seriously, will learn from their mistakes and will learn to learn. Schooling is dismissed as being counter-productive in that we turn against what we are offered in school and become subservient and broken-spirited creatures (FL pp. 108, 109).

Here we do have 'theory' in the sense of mere fancy, sheer speculation that owes practically nothing to reason or evidence. It is not necessarily true that the schooling system breaks us. No doubt it can do, but it clearly does not have to; Goodman himself stands proud witness to that. And in all probability a deschooled society would break another kind of personality. It *is* necessary to argue for this proposal to give absolute priority to free choice because, on the face of it, there is no reason at all to accept that it is responsive to needs and reality, even assuming that we were agreed on what was needed and realistic. That we learn from our mistakes is

true in the specific sense that they teach us a lesson; it is quite unwarranted and absurd to infer that one of the best or even a good
way of learning in general is by making mistakes – indeed, mistakes
usually teach us very little in themselves, except what not to do.
Leaving children alone to make their own decisions and to fend for
themselves is *not* the only way of showing that you take them
seriously, if it is a way of doing that at all; it is perhaps the only
way of showing that you really think they should fend for themselves. But perhaps we don't think that – certainly we still await a
reason for adopting that view. The references to independence, in-
ventiveness and learning to learn accumulate to the point at which
there is danger of their swamping our critical faculties. But the fact
remains that, to be inventive or to do something well while being
independent, one needs a lot else besides freedom to manoeuvre,
a lot else that is not obviously being catered for in Goodman's
scheme of things: one needs knowledge both in the sense of information (even if it is only information about where to get further
information) and in the sense of cognitive ability, conceptual clarity
and rationality. There is in fact no evidence at all to support Goodman's hope that children brought up in the way he advocates will
be more than usually inventive; and its plausibility would seem to
rest on a simplistic picture of human intellect whereby the opportunity to perform any intellectual activity is assumed to be both
necessary and sufficient to developing the capacity to do it. 'Learning to learn' does not mean anything more than becoming the sort
of person who can make something of a wide variety of situations.
It is a smart phrase to cover up an inadequate conception. But without doubt all the competent schooled scholars learned how to learn.

Basically it is the logic of choice that makes all this absurd: to
'choose' is to select for some reason or reasons, it involves having
reasons for preferring one thing to another, or it is not worth the
name of 'choice'. If you have no way of distinguishing between
various options then you 'choose blindly', which is a polite way of
saying that you do not 'choose' at all. Goodman's educational
proposals curtail, or are likely to curtail, knowledge of a wide range
of ideas, options and alternatives, even more than the present system
of schooling, and therefore in the long term they are likely to
restrict the individual's capacity for choice rather than to develop it.
(See p. 192, below for a further note on Goodman's values.)

CHAPTER 6

EVERETT REIMER (*b. 1922*) and IVAN ILLICH (*b. 1926*)

ILLICH, REIMER AND GOODMAN

Ivan Illich is often regarded as the guru of the deschooling movement. A prolific writer, he brings to ideas such as those of Goodman a more comprehensive framework and a more rigorous attempt at an explanatory thesis. He also pushes those ideas further in his attempt to locate the specific problems of schooling in the wider context of institutionalisation. But the quantity of his output is not matched by the lucidity of his writing. His style is opaque and pregnant with insistent significance at the expense of clarity. He relies so heavily on metaphor and comparative examples that one is sometimes unsure whether he is merely illustrating or actually extending his thesis. Fortunately, the essence of his views on schooling, which is contained in *Deschooling Society* and *Celebration of Awareness*, is presented also, in far more readable form, by Everett Reimer in *School is Dead*. According to Illich himself, Reimer's book and his own *Deschooling Society* represent a record and an account of precisely the same evolution of a single set of ideas. In this chapter I shall therefore treat the two as one, where they hold the same opinions, and generally shall quote from Reimer rather than Illich on the grounds that his language is more readily comprehensible.

Goodman saw the schools as having failed and not being worth resuscitating except in the limited shape of mini-schools. Reimer and Illich are concerned not only to argue that schools cannot hope to succeed in promoting learning and education, but also to stress that they do succeed in doing certain undesirable things. Hence they emphasise the hidden curriculum and the school's function as a teacher of societal values such as conformity and how to beat the system.[1] Whereas Goodman had entertained the idea of free schools, Reimer states that 'Summerhill still teaches dependence on school' (*D* p. 3) and thereby a variety of presumptions about society. Goodman resented the way in which schools alienated people and wasted opportunities, but Reimer and Illich have the positive intention of combating certain allegedly inevitable tendencies of schooling. They see the school as one type of institution and the crucial faults and shortcomings of schooling as being endemic to institutions. Reimer outlines what, according to him, is the typical cyclical pattern of institutional domination, and we are told without a blush that 'studies of prisons and asylums indicate how over-whelmingly such institutions produce the very behaviour they are designed to correct' (*SD* p. 25); the conclusion is drawn that in precisely the same way schools *make* children childlike, or render childlike those who in other situations would not be so. Therefore, 'a cure for student unrest would be to stop making children out of people old enough to have children, support them and fight for them'.

None the less, Reimer and Illich advocate alternatives that most of us would regard as schools of a sort, to an even greater extent than Goodman did with his mini-schools. These alternatives would not be schools by their definition, namely 'institutions which require full-time attendance of specific ages in teacher-supervised classrooms for the study of graded curricula' (*SD* p. 35). But that definition is very specific – far more specific than normal usage would warrant, for 'school' is one of those words that has a variety of defining criteria, and different people may put the stress on different combinations. Whereas to the man in the street it seems natural to distinguish between a school that demands attendance at classes and one that does not, by this definition the latter is not a school at all. The advantage of Reimer's and Illich's definition is that it allows them to use the resounding and emotive catch-call 'deschooling' to focus attention on alternatives that might otherwise be regarded in more humdrum fashion as merely different types of school.

Nor is this a purely verbal point, because behind it lies a real difference in attitude between Goodman and Reimer and Illich in respect of the secondary school. Goodman means what he says when he insists that we should do away with schools except as one available option; he means what the man in the street would mean if he said 'there's no point in children going to school if they don't want to'. As Reimer puts it, 'Goodman holds that people learn what they need to learn in the course of real-life encounters. Professions and trades are learned by practising them. Schools can only teach alienated knowledge: knowledge divorced from both its origins and its applications and therefore dead knowledge' (*SD* p. 167). The problem with that view, as we have seen, is that there is no obvious evidence for it. 'Dead knowledge' and 'alienated knowledge' are emotive phrases that either beg the question at issue or else are true by definition and quite unterrifying. But it is certainly what Goodman believes. By contrast, neither Reimer nor Illich believes that a reliance on real-life situations and encounters is either sufficient or necessary for the promotion of all the knowledge that ideally we would like all children to acquire.

Unlike Goodman, they accept (1) that confining oneself to knowledge acquired by first-hand experience of some matter is seriously limiting in that it is a slow, uncertain way of learning, and governed by the situations in which one finds oneself; (2) that in many cases the same knowledge can be acquired either in that way or without first-hand experience (e.g. knowledge of how a particular library classification system works); and (3) that in practice some important things can be learnt only other than by first-hand experience (e.g. the second law of thermodynamics). (The question of whether in principle some things could be learnt only in this way is not so important to the argument. Let us concede that, given the right circumstances, the individual might gain such knowledge for himself at first hand; still from the pedagogic point of view the important point is that that is not likely to happen.) Consequently, whereas Goodman's alternatives to school are all models of activities involving the opportunity to learn something at first hand on the job, the alternative proposals of Reimer and Illich include the provision of opportunities to acquire knowledge in situations divorced from any specific activity – 'off-the-job' centres, so to speak. Even where knowledge related to the performance of particular activities is concerned (knowledge how) they recognise a related dimension of theoretical knowledge and seek to provide for it. They recognise that there is such a thing as abstract learning and envisage creating appropriate settings in which to acquire it.

THREE OBJECTIONS TO SCHOOLING

Reimer and Illich have three closely related objections to the institution of schooling: (1) the multi-dimensional objection, (2) the graded curriculum objection, and (3) the hidden curriculum objection. To these some might add as a fourth the objection that schooling involves a wastage of resources. But though they more than once make the point that 'schools use up the resources available for education' (*SD* p. 68), we can hardly treat this as a separate objection. If it can be shown that schools cannot educate adequately or that they necessarily cause more harm than good, that is sufficient to discredit them; it would be otiose to add that they were expensive. If that cannot be shown, then no case against schooling has been established, and its cost, though it might be more than we could afford in some sense, could hardly be called wastage. The cost could constitute an objection to schooling in its own right only if the argument was that the same degree of the same kind of success could be achieved in some other way with less consumption of resources. That is not, and never has been, the deschooling argument. In the context of what the deschoolers *are* saying, to treat the wastage of resources argument as a distinct additional objection would be rather like treating the cost of one gramophone record as a separate factor over and above questions of quality of performance and recording. Admittedly, some advertisements try to encourage us to think in this way and to weigh incommensurables such as cost and quality against each other. None the less, it only makes sense to reject one record as not worth the extra cost over another, if it is not in some other respect appreciably better.

The multi-dimensional objection

Reimer and Illich both object that schools 'combine four distinct social functions: custodial care, social role selection, indoctrination and education as usually defined in terms of the development of skills and knowledge' (*SD* p. 24), and they see this combination as responsible for much of the expense of education and for the school being inefficient educationally and too effective in terms of social control. They claim that concern for custodial care, besides being expensive, is wholly inappropriate since it extends childhood beyond its natural term. It is this feature of the school more than any other that puts it 'well on the way to joining armies, prisons and insane asylums as one of society's total institutions' (*SD* p. 25). The use of the school to sort people out for different kinds of jobs and social roles they regard as 'wasteful and often disastrous' in its consequences, and they cite the number of people who drop out completely after 'long and expensive investments have been made'. Having to study medicine is a slower and more costly way of discovering that medicine is not for you than is becoming an hospital orderly. Furthermore, in a schooled society life chances are determined by school achievement level, and that in practice means by certification, so that 'even a garbage collector needs a diploma' (*SD* p. 26). If society is such that something tangible and important hangs on having the right qualifications, it is difficult to get people to accept what Reimer calls 'euphemisms about the transcendent importance of learning and doing your best'. Furthermore, in practice schools define merit (the 'meritorious' is he who does well at school), and what causes merit, or a lack of it, is 'principally the advantage of having literate parents, books in the home, the opportunity to travel, etc.'. Thus 'merit is a smoke-screen for the perpetuation of privilege' (*SD* p. 29).

While the school thus betrays the ideal of knowledge for its own sake because of the need for it to function as a sorter, it is succeeding only too well in another of its roles as an indoctrinator. This is closely connected with the hidden curriculum objection, since the word 'indoctrination' is used loosely to imply the covert and perhaps quite unconscious forming of attitudes and beliefs.

We must distinguish between the objection that the combination of these roles imposed on the school is disastrous and militates against successful education, and the objection that one, some or all of the elements here combined are in themselves pernicious. It is the former objection that is our immediate concern.

There is no necessary reason to assume that an institution could or should not at one and the same time be concerned with the individual's ultimate social role, custodial care and education. Indoctrination and education, on the other hand, as usually defined, are necessarily incompatible, because the former involves closing the mind, while the latter involves opening it. But the schooling system does not deliberately try to close the mind. It need not indoctrinate in any sense that is necessarily incompatible with education. It *does* indoctrinate in the looser sense of that word, but then in that sense there is no necessary incompatability between the two: you can educate while at the same time teaching various specific values, whether overtly or covertly. In any case, how by means of deschooling could one hope as a community to avoid indoctrination in this sense? Whatever one does and whatever one's intentions, people will pick up messages and acquire values from their surroundings. Even granting that the schools may be particularly prone to passing on such messages and values, they might also be the best place for teaching people to question the values they thus imbibe.

There is then no logical necessity for these different roles or functions of the school to get in each other's way, but does the combination tend to be disastrous as a matter of fact? We do no doubt sometimes kill enthusiasm because we are worrying about discipline and grading. It probably is reasonable to assume that a good home will give a good start in school, and that success in school terms leads to a good grade, which is a powerful advantage in securing influential and privileged jobs. And no doubt that state of affairs does not rest easily alongside the hope of schooling for its educational sake. None the less, it need not destroy that hope; it is not actually impossibly difficult to educate in an institution that admittedly has that further function. In short, there is no good reason for concluding either that in practice the four functions of the school inevitably militate against each other (still less destroy each other), or that in a deschooled society the situation would be markedly different.

Turning now to the acceptability or otherwise of the individual elements, one must concede that baby-minding contributes to the longevity of babyhood. This is not so much a matter of empirical as conceptual truth: treating people like babies or children forces them, by definition, to behave in certain ways that go towards forming the concept of babyhood or childhood. But to contribute to and to be wholly responsible for are two different things. There is a danger here of committing buggery in Bootle. It would be folly to deduce that but for schools there would not be a period of babyhood of any significant length, partly because it is not schools alone that contribute to this phenomenon, and partly because there just are certain stages of physical and mental development to be passed through between the embryonic state and adulthood.

As to the function of sorting people out, it is difficult to see how this could be avoided in any society that chooses to sort people and distinguish between the more and less suitable for specific activities. Even if one argued for a society based entirely on self-selection, so that the individual does whatever he thinks he's fit for, one would still need to have some means of knowing what other people were like: when a man offers himself to tutor my children, mend my gas fire or take out my appendix, at the very least I want a language whereby I can seek to elicit from him how competent he is. We need to label people and to distinguish between them, and it therefore does not seem inherently reprehensible of the schooling system to contribute towards that task.

The graded curriculum objection

Reimer and Illich, like Goodman, have a battery of claims to make about learning, but they are considerably more cautious. Reimer concedes the need for some kind of sequence in learning and adds that 'there must also be some correlation between different sequences of learning' (*SD* p. 40). But he objects that 'schools treat learning as if it were the product of teaching' (*SD* p. 37), which he thinks is not the case. There seems to be a simple confusion between necessary and sufficient conditions here. Of course, learning is not the product of teaching in the sense of being exclusively caused by it, so teaching is not necessary to it. On the other hand, teaching can produce learning or cause something to be learned and is often sufficient to do so. But what Reimer really objects to about the graded curriculum is the fact that the content, order and pace of the learning in schools, the way in which the curriculum is graded, is dictated by university requirements.

This is a common complaint of the radicals, but, at any rate as stated by Reimer, it is highly misleading; it is quite obvious that we cannot discuss the question of whether the universities should or should not call the tune until we understand what tune they do call and why. If schools are teaching what is not worth learning because of the pressure of universities, that is indeed deplorable. Conversely, it is something to be thankful for if the universities insist that the schools teach worthwhile and useful things. Yet again we come back to the crux of the matter: what is useful, what is worth while, and what have the deschoolers to say on that topic? But Reimer has the usual radical disinclination to answer that kind of question; he feels that 'how much required attendance, classroom teaching and curriculum is tolerable is not a matter for academic discussion. Free people, choosing freely as individuals and in voluntary groups among an ample array of alternatives can best make these decisions' (*SD* p. 39). And he seems content to accept the simplistic views of Goodman and Neill that, where academic subjects are concerned, 'students who are interested in these matters learn them and those who are not do not', asserting boldly but without a shred of supporting evidence that 'whether interest in them is stimulated by schools remains very doubtful' (*SD* p. 33).

Generally the argument is poor at this juncture. Consider that last assertion: apart from the absence of supporting evidence, note that, since it is undeniable that literally thousands of people have the interests in question and yet have been schooled, there is once again an unexamined presumption in favour of innate characteristics and tendencies implied. Note also that in any case the general thesis that Reimer is expounding requires that it be shown not that schools *do not* promote interests, but that they *cannot*. The radicals are fond of referring to isolated examples of genius such as Einstein (in fact it usually *is* Einstein) who had an unhappy and, according to him, unfruitful schooling. Does it need to be spelt out to them that, in the phrase of Aristotle, one swallow does not make a summer? – that Einstein might conceivably have been remarkable and atypical, and that even this exemplar of genius might have been mistaken in his judgement that he gained nothing from his schooldays? Here, besides, is another instance of the extraordinary way in which the radicals pride themselves on discovering the hidden curriculum, which they did not, and yet fail to appreciate the workings and the significance of the phenomenon: who is to say what Einstein did and did not pick up from his schooling *without being aware of it?* Not he, presumably.

Then there is a lamentable and outrageously badly argued attempt to show that schools fail to teach language skills. 'Literacy has always run ahead of schooling . . . there are always children attending school who do not learn to read' (*SD* p. 32). Faced with reasoning like that, one marvels at Lister's emphasis on the need for more empirical research to back up or confute the deschoolers. It is doubtful whether we need any empirical research at all at the moment. What we need first is some clarification of terminology and argument and some intelligent reasoning. The above quotation establishes nothing, except that literacy can be acquired outside the schools and is not always acquired within. The further observation that 'in general the children of literate parents learn to read even if they do not attend school, while the children of illiterate parents frequently fail to learn even in school' (*SD* p. 32) is astonishing in its naivety; it has no bearing at all on the question of whether schools do make a contribution towards developing literacy or could make a better one.

The essence of the graded curriculum objection is that, as a consequence of the assumption that learning presupposes teaching (an assumption, be it remembered, that schools do not need, in order to justify their existence), knowledge is seen as a product to be distributed. The graded curriculum, which is described as 'an ordered array of packets of knowledge each with its time and space assignment in proper sequence and juxtaposed with related packages' (*SD* p. 39), is regarded as the undesirable and inevitable outcome of this line of thought. Perhaps none of us would wish to deny that the packaging and departmentalising of knowledge can, and very often does, go too far in schools; but that is a very long way indeed from seeing schooling as the inevitable cause of something necessarily obnoxious. There is no reason why the realisation that some learning can be facilitated by teaching should lead to the idea that knowledge is a product in some pejorative sense. Even if we conceded that straight instruction necessarily gave that impression (and why should we?), we still would not have an argument against schooling as such. Nor is it at all clear what in principle is supposed to be wrong with a curriculum graded or organised in respect of logical sequence, suitability and difficulty. There is after all some truth in the observation that one needs to be able to walk before one can run; and indeed, on a more serious level, some of the confused and irate argument of the deschoolers themselves is itself further evidence of the horrible consequences of the habit of refusing to take one step at a time. School curricula may sometimes represent a quite nonsensical barrage of facts to be stored, but no case has been made for doing away with all kinds of graded curriculum on principle, and no necessary link has been shown between this issue and schooling. Schools do not have to have a graded curriculum;

Reimer's and Illich's image of a deschooled society does not preclude the possibility of graded curricula being on offer.

The hidden curriculum objection

Behind the talk of indoctrination lies the contention that schools, simply because they are institutions, have a logic of their own which impels them towards a certain type of propaganda. They may want or claim to teach this or that, and even succeed in doing so to some extent; but inevitably they are more consistently effective in teaching such things as 'the value of childhood, the value of competing for life prizes and ... the value of being taught' (*SD* p. 30), whether they recognise it or not. Such lessons are not consciously taught; they are implicit in procedures and organisation. It is suggested, for example, that the system perpetuates and validates what is in fact inequality by calling it equality and institutionalising it – which is to say by enshrining it in the daily setup of the school so that it comes to be taken for granted. In the same way, while 'the flickering lights of freedom are going out' (*SD* p. 48), we are seduced by the rituals and trappings of democratic elections and the exhibition of academic freedom into assuming that all is well in our free and freedom-loving country. Complaints that this is not so themselves lull us into security: is not the protest evidence of the freedom to protest? Progress in our situation is now non-existent, but 'the ritual or research fools us' (*SD* p. 49); progress must be being made, we foolishly think, because people keep looking into things and coming up with new ideas and answers – and research, of course, is wrongly equated with schooled research. The example of research can be generalised: by keeping some activity going, the myth of efficiency is perpetuated: doing something is confused with taking useful and appropriate steps. And schools 'learned long ago that the way to keep children from thinking is to keep them busy'. So the whole merry-go-round of degrees and diplomas, besides keeping people active and consequently under the misapprehension that they are doing something worthwhile, prepares people well 'to participate in the activity rites of the outside world: more committees, more projects, more campaigns, more products, more industries, more employment, more gross national product' (*SD* p. 52).

More precisely, according to Illich, 'in school we are taught that valuable learning is the result of attendance, that the value of learning increases with the amount of input' (i.e. that what you learn casually and easily is less worth learning than what you struggle over), 'and finally that this value can be measured and documented by grades and certificates' (*D* p. 65). Add, if you like, that 'the inflexible grade system [which] almost prevented Einstein from continuing his studies [and] probably encouraged others to march on, in step, towards Stalingrad and Auschwitz' teaches obedience and silence, 'the virtue of punctuality and of time dictated by the clock and not by the seasons', and the lesson that the children's role in life is 'to know their place and to sit still in it' (*D* p. 4).

Let us first, once for all, rid the discussion of emotive nonsense: if the grade system led to Auschwitz, it also led to Dunkirk; if it nearly hindered Einstein (and note that it did not), it was very likely the making of many others. Something that may lead to either good or ill cannot be dismissed as self-evidently reprehensible. Furthermore, we have here a classic instance of the *post hoc ergo propter hoc* fallacy – that is to say, the fallacious assumption that because something follows X it must have been caused by X. The Germans of tradition are stolid obedient things; they are known to have had a particular kind of schooling, so the inference is drawn that the schooling must have caused the alleged characteristics. Consider also the absurd Rousseau-like sneer at the poor unnatural clock (which, after all, only does what it is told), as if there was something more virtuous about downing tools at sunset than at six o'clock. The questions that need to be considered are: (1) Is there a hidden curriculum? (2) If so, does it contain the sort of elements or items listed? (3) If it does, is that objectionable? (4) Can one avoid a hidden curriculum of some sort or another?

1. It is sad that this issue should have been marked by so much preposterous overstatement since the fundamental insight is surely correct. There *is* a hidden curriculum. Schools undoubtedly do influence children in more ways than by overtly instructing them or otherwise consciously teaching them. But one of the oddities of this topic is that the deschoolers treat it as an highly significant discovery, since the idea has a recorded history since the time of Plato, and many would argue that schools are supposed to have and ought to have some kind of hidden curriculum. Many people have always assumed and expected that schools would implicitly teach such things as allegiance to the state or, to use a phrase of Illich's, celebration of the present.

Generalising, it is difficult to see how a society could do otherwise, since a society that did not to a large extent implicitly pass on that sort of value and idea would cease to function as a society. And it must be stressed that we are generalising. Just as we accept without argument the point that there is a hidden curriculum, so we reject the specific suggestion that we are taught this and that as if it admitted of no exception and every child must have imbibed the same cultural values. What however we surely must accept is that many people do come to hold certain views that the school intended them to hold, and some that it did not consciously intend to promote, and that the school played its part in forming both kinds.

2. Are the beliefs and values cited by the deschoolers the usual or predominant content of the hidden curriculum? Most of them are, particularly if some extreme phrases are toned down. Most of us do tend to value schooled learning and to assume that what is picked up casually is either less worth picking up or less well picked up; we do tend to believe that degrees mean something, whatever we say we think; we do tend to believe that we have a high degree of freedom and equality and that competition and differences between people are, if not good, at least inevitable. On the other hand, it simply isn't true, as many of us can testify from experience, that we treat all degrees as sacrosanct, that we are quite incapable of distinguishing between education and schooling, and that we have been lulled into thinking that all is for the best in the best of all possible worlds. This is important, because tendencies are altogether less threatening than inevitabilities. The difference of emphasis is not just a matter of degree: if we really did hold categorically to the extreme version of the various views, then there could be no hope of improving the situation.

3. The vulnerability of the radical thesis becomes most apparent on the question of whether the hidden curriculum is necessarily a bad thing, because one might argue that some of these covert messages embody true and valuable beliefs: we are, for example, freer than most countries (certainly than communist countries) and perhaps it is time we remembered that; we may concede the danger of drifting into complacency, but that is no reason for ridiculing what we have got, still less for refusing to acknowledge it. What is wrong with people learning to be punctual? What is wrong with seeing knowledge as divisible provided that the divisions are valid?[2]

4. Can and should we rid ourselves of the hidden curriculum? It might reasonably be argued that we should if we can, even if the

messages transmitted by it were not regarded as objectionable, on the grounds that ideally beliefs should not be unconsciously acquired, but should be adopted (or rejected) after rational reflection. But it does not seem to me that the question of whether it *should* be expunged arises at all, since I do not see how it *could* be. The deschoolers have not shown that schooling is both a necessary and a sufficient cause of there being a hidden curriculum. It seems very probable that it is sufficient. But it seems most implausible to regard schooling as necessary to the existence of the hidden curriculum. Schools are not the only institutions there are, and it is not only institutions that teach in this way. Surely it is the environment generally, certainly including the family. One may dream of a society that is not like that, a society in which people are in no way affected by their surroundings. But it is difficult to credit that anyone would seriously posit the idea of working towards a society of non-influenceable people. Our tendency to react to our surroundings and, in spiralling fashion, thus to develop is one of the things that makes us what we are. To get rid of schools, then, is not to get rid of the hidden curriculum.

It seems indisputable that schools have a hidden curriculum. As Freire puts it, 'education cannot be neutral' (*D* p. 4), and its values come out in both the overt and hidden curricula. Consequently Lister is correct to suggest that full-scale curriculum reform must also involve a change in the hidden curriculum (*D* p. 93). But the idea of some change that would do away with a hidden curriculum altogether is inconceivable, so deschooling cannot be defended on these grounds. All that can be done to combat the dangers of a hidden curriculum is, first, to take steps to control its content so that the messages it transmits are desirable, and second to take steps to offset the surreptitious nature of the transmission by bringing the values and beliefs imparted into the open and subjecting them to examination. One defeats insidious influence, as one does all forms of indoctrination, by enabling and encouraging people to examine and reflect. Deschooling, by contrast, would not remove all signs of the hidden curriculum; it would merely place it beyond immediate control and allow of no calculated steps to offset its effects.

ALTERNATIVE STRATEGY: NETWORKS AND WEBS

Broadly speaking, the new way proposed by Reimer and Illich involves as many cheap and non-competitive individual alternatives as possible, so that going to school is replaced by the opportunity to go practically anywhere, from a seminar course in nuclear physics to the local fish market. But there are also one or two other assumptions integral to their positive plans which must be commented on.

First, since naturally enough the alternatives are expected to avoid the pitfalls of schooling, they must not 'dominate', which is Reimer's term to cover and encapsulate the sort of influences that were referred to in the previous section. In his view it is hardly an exaggeration to say that the institution of school dominates children as Brazilian landlords dominate Brazilian peasants (*DS* p. 90): in just the same way the truth is withheld from our children in a thousand different respects by us and from us by vested interest groups. He seems to forget, however, that we ourselves form vested interest groups. It is true that it would not be in the interests of the mechanics' union that we should all be able to service our own cars, and it might therefore be to their advantage to peddle the myth that to handle cars you really need to be a properly trained, qualified and certified mechanic (i.e. a schooled mechanic). But then some of us are mechanics. Furthermore it is arguable not only that we and the schools do not dominate to the same extent and in the same way as any chosen political power group, but also that the idea that we should not dominate at all is incredibly naive in one sense and quite compatible with schooling in another. It would be impossible to achieve a complete absence of dominating influence, while a concerted attempt to avoid surreptitious influence and to draw attention to such influencing factors as there are is perfectly compatible with schooling.

A second presumption is that learning should not be separated from other activities and pursued as an activity in itself. Reimer sets the scene by saying that 'learning occurs only with great difficulty in the role of the classroom student', that it occurs 'naturally at work and at play, but must be artificially stimulated when separated from them', and that 'everything and every person in the world is a learning resource' (*DS* p. 105). These are dangerous slogans. As we have seen, they can be made true by definition, but very often at the price of triviality. In order to establish the conclusion that we ought to deschool they would have to be interpreted in such a way that what they claim would in fact be false. For example, if we take them as tantamount to the assertion that there is no point in learning, say, English literature and that one cannot do so in school anyway, that would constitute an argument against schooling, but it would not be true. The truth of the matter is quite obviously that one is certainly going to acquire some information, some skills and some reasoning facility anyway, without school, but that the extent and calibre of these will depend on one's surroundings, and that there is in practice a severe limit to what can be picked up in this way. The last two quotations seem particularly vacuous: what does Reimer understand by 'work and play'? To me the phrase suggests practically everything and, like Goodman, I would include academics or the trade of attending class as species of 'work and play'. But if 'work and play' is defined in contrast to the classroom, then the claim would seem to beg the very question at issue: why, and in what sense, is it maintained that I naturally learn things as I sit in my office or talk in the pub? And what things? And why is it denied that I can learn things naturally in the classroom? What is meant by 'artificially stimulated'? Would it matter if it were true that we need 'artificial stimulation' in the classroom? Is it something to be frightened of or embarrassed by? That everything is a 'learning resource' is true only if it means that there is something that can be learned about everything, which is not very helpful. The questions are: is it equally worth while learning about everything, and can one learn all that is to be learned just by coming face to face with things? The emphasis on on-the-job learning serves as a way of deflecting the question of whether there are not some things that should be mastered which are abstract. (This is all the more odd with Reimer, who actually mentions some abstract subjects, such as politics and psychology, and insists that they are important.) And it is not too much to say that until this issue is settled no case for deschooling can be satisfactory. Nobody has ever pretended that schools were the best or even a good way of teaching journalism or train-driving. What has been consistently maintained by educators in favour of schooling is that there are some abstract bodies of knowledge that have a value and can be (most) effectively taught in schools.

Little needs to be said about the other basic demands that Reimer and Illich would make of any alternatives to schooling. That teachers should do less is not a separate idea so much as an integral part of the deschooling faith and as such tied up inextricably with other ideas. That alternatives should be cheap is not in principle a consideration to be jeered at, but we need to know how cheap is cheap; and, as I have already suggested, whether and to what degree a thing is cheap depends to some extent on how valuable you think it is. Alternatives are not to be recommended just because they are cheap, and there can be no objection to spending money that is worth spending in some way. That alternatives should be non-competitive introduces another theme common to all the radicals, but one about which they say little beyond voicing their feelings, and one that I shall therefore not pursue. It will be sufficient to pose three questions. (1) What precisely do we mean by non-competitive, or what exactly is the nature of the competition that is regarded as self-evidently objectionable? Are we referring to competing against oneself, one's physical neighbour or some standard set by person or persons unknown to us? Would a ban on competition involve an end to races, games of tennis, attempts to produce the best homework or what? (2) Why is competition, in whatever sense we have in mind, deemed to be objectionable? Is there any good reason to condemn it? (3) Is the idea of competition inseparable from schooling? Would it be any easier to bring an end to competitive tendencies if there were no schools than it would be to do so within schools? This third question certainly seems to me to invite the answer no; as with much of deschooling theory, insights or values that we may accept do not seem to involve a deschooling conclusion at all. However, my point here is only to observe that these questions need to be answered before we can reasonably take a stand on the issue of competition, and they have not been answered by any of the radicals.

It is on not altogether strong premisses and presumptions, then, that Illich and Reimer base their alternative strategy. But the alternative itself is perhaps flimsy enough to stand on shaky support. Not to put too fine a point on it, all that is proposed is a national system of resource centres or what Reimer calls 'networks of things' and 'networks of people'. (Illich calls them 'learning webs', but they are in all important respects the same thing.)

Networks of things are collections of things, particularly (though not exclusively) record and filing systems, so that it is always possible for the individual to find out where to look for further information. Computers, which to some extent take the place of books, are seen as the gateway to knowledge. Access to these networks should be directly open to all with the minimum of fuss and bother, and, we are told, 'the quality of this education will depend only upon the quality and completeness of the records which are available' (*SD* p. 108).

This is really a quite extraordinary anticlimax to the huff and the puff of the message that school is dead, and no less extraordinary a proposal in its own right, for it is so naively bland and vague. After the attack on the way in which knowledge is controlled by means of the hidden curriculum, how can Reimer and Illich have failed to ask themselves who will supervise these networks and hence control knowledge? After the emphasis on motivation and interest, how can the question of whether and how individuals will be inclined to approach such resource centres be ignored? We have many such opportunities available as it is; is it entirely the fault of schooling that few people seem interested in taking advantage of facilities provided by local museums, local schools, adult education centres and the Open University, or that Open Day at the library, fire station or police station attracts a fraction of the local community? Above all, after the great to-do about the difference between schooling and education, and the attack on the former as being more inclined to indoctrinate than educate, how can they unblushingly present an ideal solution that is couched entirely in terms of storage of information and push-button control and make no references at all to developing or practising reasoning, discrimination or thinking? Of course, Reimer and Illich would not accept the relevance of reference to such resources as are available today, since they envisage something enormously more wide-spread, rid of élitist connotation and available to a deschooled generation. They may also care to believe that in changed circum-stances people will not only avail themselves of the networks of things, but will also seek to develop rational faculties rather than merely to get the right answer from the computer. None the less, in essence the networks of things are collections of static data.

It is impossible to miss the technological bias here, and indeed there are times when it seems to be this enthusiasm that sustains Reimer in particular. The received wisdom on this subject is that 'Reimer and Illich have looked to technotopia, with voluntary learning groups brought together by the computer' (*D* p. 91). But the relationship between deschooling and technology is in fact more ambivalent than that remark may suggest. Certainly Goodman was not enamoured of technology, and Illich himself apparently dislikes television and will not use it as a medium. It is also far from clear whether technology should be seen as a cause or a means of deschooling. Lister states that 'the revolution in media technology has made the school obsolete as a transmitter of information' (*D* p. 9), but that seems a double-edged remark. On the face of it it is simply untrue (the school is certainly not obsolete as a transmitter of all information); but more to the point is the implication yet again that schools should be judged as transmitters of information, which most of us, including deschoolers in another context, would roundly deny. Nor am I much impressed or reassured to learn that the 'new media are potentially more susceptible to learner control: you can turn off a TV'. How does that differ from shutting a book or just switching off oneself, which, it will be recalled, deschoolers have claimed most children do most of the time? Furthermore, it surely isn't this kind of control that we are particularly concerned about: we are anxious for the individual to be able to control what he does hear, see or read, in the sense of assess for himself rather than succumb to persuasion, indoctrination or brainwashing. There is no reason at all to suppose that the new media afford more opportunity for control in this sense. It may very well be true as a matter of fact that 'chalk boards and single textbooks are yielding to overheads, micro-film readers, tapes, dial-access systems, and a complex of mechanical devices aimed at helping the learner to paddle his own canoe' (Kajubi – *D* p. 83), but what is not clear is that they do that better than anything else. I can only see an argument either of the form that, if for other reasons we disband schools, technology offers an alternative, or of the form that schools might utilise some technological developments. I cannot see how technology in and by itself can render the school obsolete, even as a transmitter of information, for it cannot do the same thing; it cannot transmit information in the same kind of way.

Toys and games are singled out as 'a special class of objects with great potential for offsetting the educational disadvantages of a technological society' (*SD* p. 111). It is suggested that they provide a pleasant way of learning skills and have the particular merit of constituting a means of organising activities among peers without recourse to authority. The argument seems a little disingenuous (it may be true that the nature of the game determines the activities of the participants, but who determines which game to play?), but it is not as foolish as the unthinking conviction that games are 'paradigms of intellectual systems'. Once again we are forced to recognise the fact that, for all the talk of releasing people from the current indoctrination of the schooling system, the deschoolers do not have an adequate conception of autonomous and rational thinking. Games may require skill and intelligence in some sense; one may need to be clever in some sense to play some of them; they may be based on points of logic, embody rational procedures or give scope for thinking clearly. But by and large games make a minimal contribution to developing the capacity to discriminate sharply between concepts, to seek and to find appropriate evidence, reasons and arguments for things, and to avoid fallacious reasoning. There is only one way to improve people's standard of debate about, say, international politics, and that is to insist that they know as much as possible about the facts of the matter, that they question the factual status of alleged facts by inquiring into the evidence for them, and they reason soundly in relation to those facts. Playing 'Diplomacy' certainly will not help.

Sadly, Illich adds nothing of significance to Reimer's disturbingly empty account of networks of things, although it is interesting to note that he modifies his own position slightly. In *Celebration of Awareness* he seems to accept the idea of programmed maths and language teaching, and to advocate two months a year of formal schooling. In *Deschooling Society* however he places emphasis, with Reimer, on a lack of compulsion combined with free access to learning webs such that 'there should be no obstacle for anyone at any time of his life to be able to choose instruction among hundreds of definable skills' (*DS* p. 21). Like Reimer, he demands 'access to available resources at any time in their lives' (*DS* p. 78) for all. Like Reimer, he wants to do away with dominant institutions, but he terms them 'manipulative' and their opposite 'convivial', examples of the latter being 'telephone link-ups, subway lines, mail routes' (*DS* p. 59). Like Reimer, he wants to stress reality, which means in effect that he stresses knowledge of our immediate and observable surroundings and requires that study should take place *in situ*, so that learning about the car engine, for example, should take place in the local garage and not on a car brought to a special place of instruction. And like Reimer, he has a very hazy view of what he means by knowledge. He states that most of us would say that 'their knowledge of facts, their understanding of life and work came to them from friendship or love, while viewing TV or while reading, from examples of peers or the challenge of a street encounter' (*DS* p. 74) as opposed to from school or other institutionalised settings. I am not sure that I would say that, and it certainly must depend to some extent on what we count as 'knowledge of facts' and 'understanding of life and work': it is by no means obvious that all important knowledge was acquired in such ways. Besides, Illich and Reimer, seduced by technology perhaps, seem stuck with a grossly oversimplified picture of the acquisition of knowledge as something comparable to the camera recording what it witnesses; whereas in truth what we learn from television, reading or chance encounters depends to some extent on what we put in and how we interpret and understand what is set before us.[3] In a similar way Illich's view that a tape recorder for everyone (in Bolivia, as it happens) 'would provide opportunity for free expression: literate and illiterate alike could record, preserve, disseminate and repeat their opinions' (*DS* p. 80) seems to reduce thought and discussion to a mere concatenation of ideas. It seems quite beyond his grasp that reading might not be simply a means of recording and disseminating ideas, but that teaching people to read may be a way of teaching them to think. When the teacher explains the difference between 'the man who ...' and 'the man, who ...' he is not doing something equivalent to explaining which button to press on a recorder; he is introducing the learner to a potentially useful distinction, which in some contexts will allow of more precise thinking, and which the provision and use of tape recorders does nothing in itself to enhance or advance. Of course, in particular contexts (Bolivia perhaps being one), free expression and exchange of ideas may for good reason be a priority. But it certainly is not in Western industrial and technological culture. For us education should very obviously be concerned more with developing people's capacity to handle ideas than with the mere dissemination of ideas.

Besides webs or networks of things, Reimer and Illich also plan skill-exchanges, arrangements for peer-matching and access to education-at-large, all of which come under the heading of what Reimer calls 'networks of people'. Skill-exchanges are centres that provide access to skill-models, which is to say individuals proficient in a particular skill. The concession that such people may have something to offer is carefully qualified: the proficient typist, it is suggested, has more to offer the would-be learner than a fellow-learner or a teacher of typing could have, but the proficient typist is still less important than the thing itself, the typewriter. The feeling grows apace that Reimer and Illich are being suffocated by their own love of jargon and schemata, and are offering us a national bureaucracy for vocational training as a substitute for education. Does not the relative importance to the learner of thing, proficient expert, fellow-learners and teacher vary depending on what is being learned? In philosophy, for example, one can imagine one's fellow-learners being of crucial importance, whereas in physics a teacher might be worth more than a skill-model. And how can we take seriously the suggestion that teaching geography in relation to Africa without the physical presence of Africans and the Zambesi is analogous to teaching typewriting without a typewriter? (*SD* p. 115).[4]

It is ironic, but none the less welcome, that, having made such a song and dance about the supremacy of 'the thing', Illich and Reimer should then defend the provision of skill-models and other persons on the grounds that the learners' responses to things such as computers are not always predictable and the human beings can adapt to and cope with any unexpected responses. They argue that schools operate a closed shop in respect of skill-models by effectively preventing the individual from presenting himself as a skill-model unless he is a properly accredited and licensed teacher. The argument is a little clumsy since it suggests that schools would not recognise outsiders as *skill-models*, whereas all that can be said with certainty is that they will not recognise them as *competent teachers* of the skills they model. Of course, that too is arguably objectionable, since there may be many who would make excellent teachers and skill-models but who are not recognised as such because they are not duly accredited teachers. But equally, a system without any form of licensing runs the risk of subjecting would-be learners to incompetent models and teachers. The main point here should surely be that, although there are certain tasks that will be better learned through accompanying an expert on the job, it is not the most appropriate way to learn everything. We should resist the assumption that a skill-model is something essentially separate from a teacher. One might learn all that one needed or wanted to learn about, say, driving, cooking or carpentry through being put in touch with those who were competent and interested in these spheres. But, without denying the point that we probably tend to confuse bona fide competence with certified competence, it does not follow that we could not learn such skills from teachers in schools (even if it so happened that they were not particularly good practitioners or skill-models themselves); and despite Illich's observation that he can 'see no . . . reason why other complex skills such as the mechanical aspects of surgery and playing the fiddle [and] of reading' (*DS* p. 90) should not also be learned simply by watching others demonstrate them, since he offers no reasoning at all to support this implausible suggestion, we may perhaps be forgiven for merely registering our dissent.

It is further argued that, once individuals have dialled a model and seen the skill they wish to acquire practised, they themselves will need to practise it and for that purpose will require partners to practise with. To that end central agencies are set up through which people with similar interests and wishes can be contacted. 'Learners in search of peers need only identify themselves and their interests in order to find matches' (*SD* p. 121); alternatively, advertising through journals or newspapers might prove adequate. One might reasonably object that it is already open to people to make contact in this way (and many of course do), but that to make it the *only* way would be both cumbersome and in practice limiting, and that the school system, among other things, performs this function of bringing like-minded peers together. And yet again we note evidence of the view of human nature as something essentially innate and static that runs un-obtrusively and unconsciously through radical thought: at no stage is thought given to the idea of fostering, creating or developing interests. The entire discussion on networks of people is conducted on the implicit assumption that individuals have certain particular interests which they become aware of and then, by dialling a thing, a model or a peer or two, attempt to perfect.

Finally, educators are allowed back into the scheme of things. Reimer distinguishes between three types all of whom have their place: 'architects and administrators of the educational resource networks', 'pedagogues who can design effective individual educational pro-grammes, diagnose educational difficulties and prescribe remedies', and 'leaders in every branch of learning' (*SD* p. 122). In keeping with the computer-loving attitude consistently revealed, these functions are regarded as quite distinct.

So what we are being offered is everything and nothing. Every-thing, because in a crude way the taxonomy we have been given is supposed to embrace the whole field of human knowledge and experience. Nothing, because nobody necessarily learns anything, and we have not been told that there is anything that they should ideally learn. The deschoolers evidently think that all contingencies have been catered for, so that if the individual wants to learn this or that he will be able to do so. They have given little or no thought to the consequences, both for the individuals concerned and the community as a whole, of the fact that some may not want to learn anything much, because they do not think that a likely occurrence. For some reason not immediately obvious these networks and webs of things and persons will not choke the presumed innate enthusiasm to learn which the schools are alleged to choke. It is quite impossible to predict how this alternative to schooling will affect the degree and nature of freedom and equality or justice, despite Reimer's avowal that education should lead to a world based on those values.[5] But it seems reasonable to predict that it will lead to a greater degree of difference in terms of interest and competence between various people and to a diminution of any feeling of community and shared experience such as a system of schooling can provide.

VOUCHERS

The deschoolers are at pains to insist that it would be easy and cheaper to fund their alternatives. (I am not competent to judge that claim; I wonder whether anyone is, given the rather loose nature of the proposals.) They also evidently feel that their new proposal for financing education is more equitable or just than the present centralised system. That proposal is the adoption of the voucher system.

There have already been various experiments with voucher systems, so the idea is, in a crude sense at least, practicable. A recent scheme in California allowed parents to choose between schools and courses. Normally they were given vouchers worth the average cost to cover courses, but there were also some special compensatory ones (i.e. more valuable) for the very poor, so that schools might become eager to take in children of poor parents and hence compete to put on courses that will appeal to them in particular.

According to Rhodes Boyson (an advocate of the system), although he gives no evidence at all to support this, this scheme of compensatory vouchers has proved more successful than any scheme of reverse discrimination put into practice in Britain. He also deduces from the fact that '40 per cent of parents with two or more children chose different courses for their different children' that 'they did understand their children's individual differences of temperament and ability at least as well as did local bureaucrats' (Black Paper,

No. 3. p. 27). The deduction however clearly can be only tentative: the figure shows only what it shows: 40 per cent of such parents treat their children differently. They may have thought that they had good reason for what they did. They may have had. But then again they might not have had. Besides, 40 per cent is not really a particularly satisfactory figure in this context. So, despite Boyson's confidence here, we still cannot ignore one possible line of objection to a voucher system, namely that many parents will, for whatever reason, make unwise choices for their children. (There are of course many possible variations in detail to the sort of scheme outlined here, such as demanding some kind of parental contribution, possibly scaled. I shall ignore discussion of such possibilities.)

Boyson's main point is that with this system 'popular schools would continue and expand and unpopular schools would decline and close'. Now that presumably is true and is likely to make the idea seem attractive to anyone who at a particular time and place feels confident that the groundswell of popular opinion is running the way of his ideals, as Boyson may well feel. Again, it will make the idea seem attractive to those who believe strongly that we as individuals should be governed by majority views no matter what they are. What is difficult to see is how the system ever attracted the deschoolers. (Of course, they are not advocating vouchers for schools but for alternative webs, networks and resource centres; the principle however is the same.) For deschoolers are not democrats: they are first and last individualists. Yet there can be no doubt about it: the voucher system makes the popular vote the paymaster, and the tyranny of the majority does not answer to the requirements of the deschoolers.

There are other signs too that the deschoolers have not really done their homework on the precise details of a voucher system. Reimer certainly believes in compensatory financing such that the poor would, by whatever means, receive more from public funds for expenditure on education. In arguing for such compensation for underprivileged homes he explicitly states that it is the environment 'rather than deficient genes, which handicaps the learning of children' (*SD* p. 130). That is an important statement partly because, as I have argued, it is at a variance with most of the implications of deschooling theory with its emphasis on choice as something innate and static. But it is important also because it strongly suggests that **Reimer is committed to the ideal of an equal society in the sense** of a society in which people are as nearly as possible in the same material circumstances. Yet he is perfectly well aware that some parents will fail to make good use of their vouchers through ignorance and that others will cheerfully sell them for cash in hand (*SD* p. 131). How then can he be satisfied, as he suggests he is, that all our problems will become manageable once educational resources are put directly into the hands of the consumers? (The danger that some will make better use than others of exactly similar resources remains whether we assume that parents or children themselves control them.)

Illich is equally concerned that at present some, generally the already favoured, are getting more in the way of education than others, and he therefore goes so far as to propose a legal reform which would guarantee 'the right of each citizen to an equal share of educational resources, the right to verify his share of these resources, and the right to sue for them if they are denied ... an edu-credit card in the hands of every citizen would effectively implement this third guarantee' (*CA* p. 155). But the appalling-sounding edu-credit card surely misses the point. For most children today the problem is not that somebody is deliberately denying their rights: it is that nobody (including their parents) is taking advantage of their rights, and that situation would presumably become appreciably worse under a voucher system.

Though some would see the question of whether a voucher system should be adopted (whether in conjunction with schooling or de-schooling) as essentially an economic issue, it clearly is not; furthermore, ensuring that every individual or individual family has access to finance for education is neither necessary nor sufficient to solve any of our problems. In fact, seeing the issue of vouchers as significant at all is a ghastly blunder. To be sure, 'students could be furnished with educational vouchers which entitled them to ten hours yearly private consultation with the teacher of their choice – and for the rest of their learning depend upon the library, the peer-matching networks and apprenticeships' (*DS* p. 96), but what problems is that supposed to solve? What do we think we are talking about when we debate this issue? We are in a blind alley as a result of the deschoolers' obsession with waste, jargon and gimmickry. Certainly as things are money is wasted, but that means it achieves no good. To stop wasting it, it is necessary to use it to some good purpose. Certainly as things are resources are unevenly distributed. To remedy that in the sphere of education the same effort must be made in respect of education of each child. But why do the deschoolers imagine that the provision of vouchers will increase the amount of good achieved or result in a more equal distribution of real education?

We have come to the main and final point – and that is the whole question of the political consequences of a deschooling policy. Illich explicitly states that 'we cannot begin a reform of education unless we first understand that neither individual learning nor social equality can be enhanced by the ritual of schooling' (*DS* p. 43). There can be no doubt that his hope is to change society – 'a merely political revolution', by which is meant the mere improvement of existing institutions, is not wanted. A cultural revolution is called for, which implies a new outlook or 'the transformation of both public and personal reality' (*CA* p. 149). And Illich and Reimer have given us a vague but recognisable vision of the envisaged new society and educated man. It is a world in which we can choose action before consumption, can cope with change, difference and variety, are free to do as we want, are self-realised and, above all, are not schooled. And the vision is supplemented by more specific political statements such as: 'If any one phrase can sum up the nature of the new era, it is the end of privilege and licence' (*CA* p. 18). But can deschooling bring about the ideal?

If the ideal had already been realised, so that we lived in the Utopian educational *polis* desired and imagined, then the matter would be different. The problem of the chicken and the egg would have been solved: we would have a chicken (society) suitable to produce the egg (true education). But that is not the case. What happens if we deschool now, even supposing that we have made some major advances in setting up the proposed alternative networks and webs? One thing we will naturally *not* have done is changed everybody's attitudes, so what happens is that some of their own volition do this, others do that; some are pushed here by parents, others there; some take advantage of the increased freedom and opportunities in various ways, while others elect to do practically nothing. At the end of the day we have a lot of different people with a lot of different interests. There is nothing new in that. But what will be new will be the much greater variation in ability and interest between people, the much greater lack of ability to comprehend other people's interests, and the lack of common culture and a common stock of information, values and skills. It will be, as Goodman at least saw, a situation comparable more to the medieval situation than to what we are familiar with today. But why should it mean an end to privilege and licence or 'a world based on freedom and justice where freedom means a minimum of constraint by others and justice means a distribution of wealth, power and other values consistent with this kind of freedom'? (*SD* p. 99).

CHAPTER 7

NEIL POSTMAN and CHARLES WEINGARTNER

THE AIM

Neil Postman and Charles Weingartner, joint authors of *Teaching as a Subversive Activity*, share with the theorists already examined a dislike of what they perceive as going on in the school system at the present time. They feel that society faces certain enormous problems, failure in solving which would certainly be perilous and might put our survival as a society in jeopardy. The key problem is this: 'what, if anything, can we do about these problems?' (*TSA* p. 12). In essence, their answer is that the situation could be ameliorated through education. Not through the educational system as it is, however: in their view schools as they are teach lies and probably don't do any good at all. Unlike the deschoolers, however, Postman and Weingartner think that they could. In order to do so, the schools need to begin with the recognition that 'change – constant, accelerating, ubiquitous – is the most striking characteristic of the world we live in' (*TSA* p. 13). Therefore they need to develop 'the abilities and attitudes required to deal adequately with change' and to 'help young people to master concepts necessary to survival in a rapidly changing world'. As a result of being enabled to cope with change, these young people will be better placed to deal with the critical problems we face. The schooling system should provide 'an education that develops in youth a competence in applying the best available strategies for survival in a world filled with unprecedented troubles, uncertainties and opportunities'. Postman and Weingartner see their task as being to fill out this formal account by explaining to us precisely what the available strategies are.

The key concept in their argument is that of crap-detecting, which in essence is rationality, although Postman and Weingartner would not thank me for saying so. 'Crap-detecting' as a phrase is useful to them for a variety of reasons. First, it has impact. Second, it avoids the associative ideas that have grown up around such alternatives as 'rationality' – in particular, it is hard for us to think of the idea of rationality without thinking of examples of things that are usually and traditionally thought to be rational; but if we are really concerned to weed out the rubbish we must challenge all our preconceptions and presumptions including our stereotypical examples of rationality. Third, 'crap-detecting' is vague and to some extent flexible.[1]

The individual who has a developed and competent crap-detector as part of his intellectual equipment recognises change and is sensitive to the various problems that may be caused by the phenomenon of change itself (over and above any problems created by a specific change). He also has 'that most "subversive" intellectual instrument – the anthropological perspective' (*TSA* p. 17). By this Postman and Weingartner do not mean that he has studied anthropology but that he is aware of the myriad customs and prejudices to be found in the world, and is neither insular in outlook nor prone to assume that what he is familiar with is the only or best way of looking at things. He is free of prejudice. Since none of us is completely without prejudice, however, or completely unaffected by what he is familiar with, in practice, having a built-in crap-detector is a matter of degree rather than a simple quality. But it is the chief sign or indication of 'a competent "crap-detector" that he is not completely captivated by the arbitrary abstractions of the community in which he happened to grow up' (*TSA* p. 17). (The expression is used indiscriminately as the name of a characteristic that one may possess or as a description of the person who has it.) If we ignore the tendency to overplay the relativity of knowledge (so that it sounds at times as if it is being suggested that the concepts employed by any particular set of people are purely a matter of chance and bear no relation whatever to how the world actually is and how things actually are, which tendency is one of the idiocies of our age), this seems reasonable enough: to develop one's personal crap-detector is among other things to avoid uncritical and irrevocable commitment to the particular ideology, religion, world view or simply outlook of one's community. The subversion that Postman and Weingartner wish to promote is subversion of the uncritical acceptance of the *status quo*. The crap-detector detects it only if and when it is there; he does not automatically see everything as crap. Consequently, the fact that somebody is dismissive of some cultural norm and regards it as crap proves nothing in itself about whether that person is or is not a competent crap-detector. The crap-detector is not to be confused with the crapper.

On the grounds that the two central distinguishing features of our age are the domination of institutional bureaucracy and technology, in particular the newer mass media, it is argued that the school should develop the crap-detecting element in the individual with particular reference to them. We must bring children up so that they question such things, asking what they are good for, rather than submit to their domination, so that they subvert anything that fosters 'chaos and uselessness' and so that they do not suffer from what Alvin Tofler has called 'future shock'. (Future shock is what you experience when you realise that, or feel that, 'the world you were educated to believe in doesn't exist'.)

A particular contrast is then drawn between their ideal of education and what is alleged to be current educational practice, by reference to McLuhan's thesis that the medium is the message, which Postman and Weingartner swallow with considerable gusto and no reservations. That is perhaps a pity, since McLuhan's thesis is a typical example of the type of overstatement that currently excites attention and sometimes passes for insight; it is plainly false when taken literally, and plainly true when toned down. Thus it is simply false to assert that the way in which one presents a message is all that one ever conveys, and it is probably false to suggest that one ever conveys only what is implicit in one's manner of delivery. On the other hand, it is fairly obviously the case that, in addition to what one is trying to get across, sometimes to the virtual extinction of it, the manner of presentation or 'the environment itself conveys the critical and dominant messages by controlling the perceptions and attitudes of those who participate in it'. In fact, this is the hidden curriculum theory under its latest name with an added refinement: it is suggested not only that one teaches something else besides what one overtly teaches by one's style of teaching, but also that how one presents the content overtly modifies it. So method and content cannot be divorced, and in the view of Postman and Weingartner 'the critical content of any learning experience is the method or process through which the learning occurs' (*TSA* p. 30).

This brings them to one of their criticisms of current schooling practice. The emphasis, they maintain, is on recall by the student of what he has been told, rather than on his initiating, challenging or even reflecting (*TSA* p. 30). Children 'are almost never required to make observations, formulate definitions, ... to ask substantive questions ... to play any role in determining what problems are worth studying' (*TSA* p. 30). And because the manner of schooling is such, the chief thing they learn is that theirs is not to reason why, and that the world consists of various truths which teachers and a few other educated persons can hand to them (*TSA* p. 31). No wonder they are confused and at a loss when what were presented as certainties in their youth crumble and disintegrate as they emerge into adulthood (*TSA* p. 31).

So far so good. But at this point Postman and Weingartner seem to go to pieces.

THE MEANS

Postman and Weingartner attack what can only be described as a straw stereotype of current schooling, since it is both false and, in so far as it resembles reality, misunderstood by them. They suggest that 'what students mostly do in class is guess what the teacher wants them to say' (*TSA* p. 31), but that is a very emotive and misleading way of expressing the rather different point that (perhaps) typically children hope to please the teacher by giving what the teacher believes to be, and what they accept as, the correct answers to questions. Admittedly, Postman and Weingartner's whole point here is that there is no such thing as a correct answer. But the correct answer to that is that there very obviously is in many instances, and that even when there is not there may still be a distinction between plausible or reasonable answers and absurd or ridiculous ones. Consequently when the teacher asks 'What is the principal river of Uruguay?' the fact that he may be thinking of a particular answer does not mean that the child must be trying to guess what he wants him to say. The child may very sensibly seek to produce a reasonable answer.

The deschoolers regarded the tendency of the school to convey the message that there is usually one true and correct answer to any question as inevitable so long as there were institutions. But Postman and Weingartner differ in thinking that the school, by finding and using new techniques, a new process or a new medium, can thereby continue to exist while conveying a different message. They suggest, plausibly enough, that in the mind of the general public 'educated' and 'knowledge' are virtually indistinguishable from 'informed' and 'dogma'. Rather less plausibly, they maintain that the same confusion is exhibited by teachers, so that, although 'no teacher ever said "Don't value uncertainty"' (*TSA* p. 33), none the less, that message is quietly and insidiously communicated. What they want and propose is a new manner of teaching that does not by implication devalue uncertainty, tentativeness or an open admission of ignorance where appropriate. In contrast to their image of the traditional class-room, they envisage a situation in which students respond to questions with further questions such as 'What would I have to do in order to find an answer to that?', 'What is a fact?' or 'Why are we doing this work?'

We have now arrived at one of their central tenets: 'knowledge is produced in response to questions. And new knowledge results from the asking of new questions about old questions' (*TSA* p. 34). This is possibly true, but it is important to note that it is only a remark about how people come to know things. It must not be con-fused with remarks about the nature of knowledge; nor must it be forgotten that, even assuming it to be true, it might well be necessary to have already mastered some previous knowledge before further knowledge could be adequately and effectively gained in this way. Again, it is as yet an open question whether education necessarily has a great deal to do with *new* knowledge. While accepting the point made, one might go on to say that once knowledge has been produced it can be passed on to others in various different ways and that, at least for much of the time, schools are rightly concerned to pass on current knowledge, albeit as a basis from which the individual may move on to finding new knowledge for himself.

But Postman and Weingartner have already moved in a different direction towards a different conclusion. Their eyes are firmly set on enabling each individual to find new knowledge and, they maintain, 'once you have learned how to ask questions – relevant and appropriate and substantial questions – you have learned how to learn and no one can keep you from learning whatever you want or need to know' (*TSA* p. 35). They also regard this facility as the essential tool for survival in this era of rapid change. They are therefore satisfied that there are excellent reasons for developing such a questioning aptitude and are confident that the school can provide the environment in which to do it. The school must constitute the 'inquiry environment'. The use of the inquiry method may well contribute to other desirable objectives, including some espoused by traditionalists, we are told, but it is advocated because 'it generates a different, bolder and more potent kind of intelligence' (*TSA* p. 38). Other currently fashionable techniques such as programmed learning are specifically rejected on the grounds that they merely represent new ways of doing the same old thing – namely, preaching acceptance rather than criticism. Any notion of a predetermined syllabus is incompatible with the inquiry method, whereby 'students generate their own stories by becoming involved in the methods of learning' (*TSA* p. 39). In any case, any plan for a sequential curriculum deserves to be frowned upon since children themselves do not proceed sequentially. 'Learning is a happening in itself', and our object should be to 'increase their competence as learners ... by having students do what effective learners do' (*TSA* p. 41), which means, among other things, replacing a question such as 'Who discovered America?', which invites a right answer, with 'How do you discover who discovered America?' (which doesn't invite a right answer?).

The questions and problems that the above paragraph gives rise to are many. Why is it assumed that the best way to become good at doing something is necessarily to start by trying to do what a person who was already good at it would do? Sometimes it may be: throw the child in the water and sometimes he will start swimming. But sometimes he will drown. One would imagine at least that the advisability of the deep-end approach would vary between individuals and between different kinds of activity. It may very well be that the best way to learn to ride a bike is to be put in a position where you either do as the competent rider does or do nothing. On the other hand, it would seem absurd to suggest that the way to increase somebody's competence as a nuclear physicist is, from the beginning, to have him do what a nuclear physicist does. He cannot do that, unless he has something of the grounding of that physicist, for what the physicist does in his laboratory cannot be defined solely in terms of observable behaviour; what he is actually doing is crucially bound up with why he is doing it and how he perceives what he is doing. So, though practice may make perfect, it is monstrous to suggest that from the outset you can start to do anything and hence become good at it.

It is besides very unclear what being 'a good learner' without qualification is. No doubt there are common elements to good learning in any sphere, but there are also evident differences. There is no obvious reason to imagine that a good learner in matters scientific will be a good learner in matters athletic. The ability to learn in some areas of life does not necessarily entail ability in all spheres, and things that are perhaps common and necessary to all instances of learning – curiosity, possibly – are not sufficient for learning anything. For all the grandiose talk of 'potent intelligence', learning being 'a happening', and being 'an effective learner', all that is being said is that, if schools were to provide a setting that encouraged children to ask questions, to look for further problems lurking in received answers and to ask for the source of answers or the type of evidence appropriate to a particular question, that is the sort of thing they would learn. That is true, though they will not necessarily learn it. But one need not agree either that that is enough to cultivate the rational mind or that that is the only way to learn these specific habits. It is possible for a traditional manner of schooling to encourage people to take nothing on trust and to question away at received opinions in the manner apparently desired. Many individuals might be cited as proof of this, but perhaps it will be sufficient to mention Postman and Weingartner themselves, the crap-detecting products of the traditional school system.

Not only is the inquiry method not *necessary* as a means to the desired objective, but the more one pursues the matter the more one begins to suspect that it is not *sufficient*, either. The notion of the good learner, which for all practical purposes seems synonymous with the crap-detector, is now filled out by reference to a list of qualities that would make a Socrates blush. The good learner, ideally, is confident, aware of what is and what is not relevant to his survival, self-reliant, flexible, respectful of the facts, and a great deal more besides.

Postman and Weingartner are clearly guilty of the fallacy of assuming that the defining characteristics of a quality must also be present all the time, if one wishes to develop that quality. Autonomy means self-directing, but it follows neither that to develop someone's autonomy you must allow him to direct his own actions all the time, nor that that is all that you need to do. In the same way, if you want somebody to end up being a good learner, as defined, it does not follow that from the beginning you should treat him as if he were aware of what is relevant to his survival and so on. Postman and Weingartner's assumption that it does leads them into a lot of trouble because, under the misapprehension that the child must be given his head, they allow themselves to claim that the student should define what is germane and relevant (to his and society's needs) and what is not. That they are themselves uneasy over this is revealed by their subsequent assertion that 'no one has ever said that children themselves are the only, or necessarily the best, source for articulating relevant areas of inquiry' (*TSA* p. 59). But they themselves said just that when they wrote that 'the inquiry teacher is interested in students developing their own criteria or standards for judging the quality, precision and relevance of ideas' and that he should 'minimise' (the Manfred Syndrome) 'his role as arbiter of what is acceptable' and not 'exclude a student's idea because it is not germane' (*TSA* pp. 44, 45). At any rate the crucial point is that, even if we accept their ideal of the good learner and have a clear understanding of it in terms of the attributes and behavioural characteristics they list, it does not follow that the inquiry environment, defined as one 'in which these behaviours can flourish, in which they are the dominant messages of the medium' (*TSA* p. 43), is either necessary or sufficient to the realisation of that ideal. It is simply not the case that 'obviously' the objectives cannot be met 'if you teach self-reliance on Monday, enjoyment of problem-solving on Tuesday'. If it is the case that this is not a good way to produce good learners, it is a contingent matter to be established by empirical evidence; it is not an *a priori* truth. In short, although there may very well be good grounds for encouraging teachers to be more cautious than they are, more inclined to pluralise, more prone to asking open questions, less inclined to tell 'the students what he thinks they ought to know' (*TSA* p. 43) and more willing to encourage student interaction, no reason has yet been given for supposing that such an approach will necessarily produce better learners or more effective crap-detectors. (I make no further comment on the fact that we are drowning in the Manfred Syndrome.)

The emptiness and some of the weaknesses in their argument are thrown into relief by a little scenario which they now introduce.

Various educational views are parodied in the context of medicine. Thus one doctor removes gall-bladders simply because he regards it as inherently good to do so. Another performs pilioxidal-cyst excisions because he likes doing them and specialised in them in his degree course. When operations and cures fail the doctors blame it on bad patients. The reason that the play fails to make its point is that the analogy between medicine and education doesn't hold, because most of us (although not of course men such as Illich) would argue that there is not really room for dispute about the objective of medicine (health) or its definition; whereas the problems in education all stem from precisely the fact that we do not agree on what we want to achieve or, where we think we do, on how to define it. We can agree that to ignore the needs of patients is importantly wrong because it is generally clear what patients do need in terms of health; that issue becomes problematic in education where people disagree about what is needed. Although it may be true that particular teachers teach Shakespeare because they studied his work during their degree course, that is not their argument for teaching Shakespeare. Explanation and justification need to be distinguished, as do correlation and cause. Many people feel that there are good reasons for studying Shakespeare, and, while granting perhaps that their university courses (or school courses) explain why they want to teach Shakespeare and how they came to the judgement that they should, would legitimately deny that they justified it. Similarly, the fact that there is correlation between degree courses taken by teachers and school courses they teach does not mean that the latter are necessarily caused by the former. It is far more likely to mean that the same argument is being used to justify both. In the same way, although the notion of inherent value may have certain problems at a philosophical level, all that is illustrated here is the absurdity of a particular view of a particular thing as inherently worth while. It is the example and not the concept that is shown up as ridiculous.

We are not making much headway with the problem of how to teach for good learning, and in some respects we are back with familiar problems. We must agree that 'it is ... "insane" ... for a teacher to "teach" something unless his students require it for some identifiable and important purpose, which is to say for some purpose that is related to the life of the learner' (*TSA* p. 50). But that is the beginning not the end of the problem, for as we have seen before the real question is what purposes are important. We surely agree on the value of what we teach being related to the life of the learner, but related in what way? No doubt we agree too on the value of 'activities which produce knowledge' such as 'defining, questioning, observing, classifying, generalising, verifying, applying' (*TSA* p. 45), but how do you teach people to define, classify and verify well in some general way? Does the way in which you should proceed to verify not depend on what you are trying to verify, the way in which you should observe depend upon what you are trying to do?

Postman and Weingartner are superficially aware of the problems here and they attempt to clarify the situation negatively at least. They argue, as have all the radicals, that much of what goes on in schools today is irrelevant and useless to the lives of the learners and that the curriculum today is still 'largely designed to keep students from knowing themselves and their environment in any realistic sense' (*TSA* p. 54).

The claim is illustrated by reference to examples of examination papers set on the civilisations of Egypt and Greece which are referred to as 'pretentious trivia' (*TSA* p. 56). It will escape nobody that the illustration is rather special. Even in the traditional school few people nowadays are taught this subject matter and still fewer are tested on it in this way purely by examination. So even if we were to grant the irrelevance of the course cited, it would not establish much. But why should we unthinkingly grant the irrelevance? We are told that the children know that questions such as 'How were the Egyptians affected by the climate and geography of their country?' 'Why was Athens the leading city of Greece?' and 'What sort of religion did the Ancient Greeks have?' have nothing to do with them. Of course these questions are not relevant to the learners' lives in the sense that life cannot be lived without an answer to them or that a job in General Motors is dependent on them. Equally clearly, the course that lies behind them may have relation to one's life in a thousand ways, direct and indirect. The issue is whether developing some understanding of another time and place, having some knowledge of one of the bases of our civilisation, appreciating hundreds of different points such as the significance of climatic conditions on national characteristics or varying attitudes to religion, or developing critical faculties in response to some penetrating and beautiful literature might prove valuable for the individual or not. I should have thought that it might – more so than knowing how to mend a motor car, for instance.

But now is not the place to defend the study of ancient history and civilisations. The immediate points are (1) that Postman and Weingartner weaken the case that they are trying to make about the irrelevance of the typical curriculum by citing an atypical piece of curriculum content; (2) that by introducing it as something to be assessed by examination, which raises separate questions, they confuse the issue and seem forgetful of their own observation that it ain't what you do but the way that you do it; (3) that even on the level of information, let alone developing skills and promoting interests, this subject matter may obviously relate to the lives of the learners (especially while that idea remains thus unqualified and unexplicated); and (4) that some would argue, reasonably enough for anything said to the contrary so far, that it relates in such a way as to make the study valuable and important.

What is becoming clear is that the slogan 'the medium is the message' cannot take the strain of their argument and they know it. Refusal to make reference to any specific content, skills or knowledge leads to a plethora of general terms like 'thinker', 'crap-detector', 'questioner' and 'learner'. But one cannot be simply a thinker; one has to think about something, and good thinking may vary in kind from area to area and will often depend on familiarity and prior information. So even granted the value of some general technique or attitude in all areas of knowledge, we need to do more than just teach that technique, and indeed could not teach it except in some context. Besides which, there is the quite different point that even if there were such a thing as good thinking without further qualification, one might reasonably argue that to teach that is not enough: we require good thinking in respect of the good and the worth while. All this means in effect that Postman and Weingartner are partially right and partially wrong when they say that 'there is no way to help a learner to be disciplined, active and thoroughly engaged unless *he* perceives a problem to be a problem or whatever is to be learned as worth learning and unless he plays an active role in determining the process of the solution' (*TSA* p. 59). They are right that the student who doesn't see a problem or think something worth learning won't be active and thoroughly engaged; that is so by definition. They are wrong however to assert that it is impossible to be engaged unless playing a role in determining the solution and in the implication that the teacher cannot bring the child to see something as problematic or worth learning. They are wrong to say that one cannot proceed in a disciplined manner unless one sees something as worth learning. Above all, they are wrong to say that there is no other way to help a learner to be these things if by 'to be' they mean 'become'.

WHAT'S WORTH KNOWING?

Included in the crucial fifth chapter of *Teaching as a Subversive Activity* is some genuinely impressive evidence of the potentialities that may lie hidden in the inquiry approach being advocated in the form of some excellent and interesting discussions on a variety of topics transcribed from recordings of lessons. It is all the more distressing therefore that virtually nothing is said about the origins of this evidence; for we need to know the precise conditions under which the discussions took place. Have these students ever been taught by formal methods? Do all their lessons take this form? How old are they? What kind of people are they? It is undoubtedly very much to somebody or something's credit that there can be discussions such as those reported anywhere in the education system. If you like, here is evidence that the ideal is obtainable and not mere moonshine. But from what we are told it does not appear to constitute evidence that Postman and Weingartner's methods ought to be adopted throughout the school system 'from kindergarten to graduate school' (*TSA* p. 43), as they propose. For what the transcripts show is the inquiry method in action. They do not reveal anything about how people come to be able to use that method well and with profit. Once again we are back with the failure to distinguish between conditions necessary for performance and conditions necessary for generating the ability to perform.

There can be no doubt that there are teachers who can refrain from dominating or leading discussions and from anticipating the contributions of others, so that, while they take a back seat, one question generates others; nor that such open discussion may be fruitful, sensible and interesting. Certainly you *can* have a good discussion where the subject matter is the 'responses' of the participants 'to the questions they confront', and you can have it in school. But what does this show? That intelligent people, including children, can have intelligent discussions which may be illuminating to themselves and others. But what needs to be shown is that there is good reason to adopt this as the method of teaching from the beginning. It has not been shown that the sort of discussion illustrated must be the outcome of the widespread adoption of this style of teaching in schools from the kindergarten onwards, or even that it is likely to be.

One of the fundamental difficulties in estimating their thesis is that Postman and Weingartner evidently find it very difficult to delineate the limits of the responsibility of the teacher. They present a classic instance of the Manfred Syndrome. Sometimes it seems that they propose that he should not initiate any ideas himself, but then at times they seem not to want him even to contribute; certainly they do not want him to act as a source of information (*TSA* p. 83). We are told that 'question asking and answer finding go hand in hand' and that 'answer finding requires that students go to books, to laboratories', even 'to the streets', but not to the teacher. To insist on this as an absolute rule seems unnecessarily perverse, especially when society tends to select as teachers those who, for all their faults, are relatively well informed. Why is a book any more pure as a source of information than a teacher? This call for little interference and control is so vague as to be useless.

They offer more specific help in another direction. They give a long and varied list of questions which they think are 'worth seeking answers to'. But lest it seem that the teacher-figure is beginning to dominate too much, we are reminded that 'more importantly' questions must seem worth asking to the students. They 'play a central but not necessarily exclusive role in framing questions that they deem important' (*TSA* p. 65). Luckily a serious conflict between what we (society, teachers) regard as worth while and what the students do is not envisaged. Evidence in support of such confidence is provided by the fact that Postman and Weingartner's questions, we are informed, are deemed important by students even though they were selected by Postman and Weingartner as being in *their* judgement 'responsive to the actual and immediate as against the fancied and future needs of learners in the world as it is' (*TSA* p. 67).

The value of questions is partly measured in terms of their tendency to 'help the students to develop and internalise concepts that will help them to survive in the rapidly changing world'. Unfortunately it is far from clear how one discerns that a question has such properties. Further qualifications are placed on the sort of questions that should be asked when it is said that appropriate questions must meet certain standards. Ideally the sort of questions that should be selected are those that (1) increase the 'learner's will as well as his capacity to learn', (2) 'give him a sense of joy in learning', (3) 'provide confidence in his ability to learn', (4) involve him in making inquiries, (5) allow of 'alternative' answers, (6) 'tend to stress the uniqueness of the learner' in the process of answering, (7) involve 'different answers if asked at different stages of the learner's development', and (8) 'help the learner to sense and understand the universals in the human condition and so enhance his ability to draw closer to other people' (*TSA* p. 71).

Of these criteria only the fourth and seventh are unambiguous and absolutely clear. The second I take to mean that questions should be fascinating to the student; the third presumably implies that they should be answerable by the student. The fifth seems a peculiar criterion and I wonder whether what is meant might not be that questions should ideally allow of more than one answer. It is not at all clear to me how a question could meet the first criterion; the sixth seems to be gibberish and the eighth incomprehensible. It is not clear in any case why it is asserted that any valuable question must meet these criteria. Certainly there are some questions which *prima facie* have their uses and which do not meet them. But the more important point in the present context is that Postman and Weingartner can be seen to be placing severe restrictions on the kind of questions that should be asked. Consequently a true account of the situation is that they advocate that teachers should ensure that certain questions, which hopefully students will appreciate, are asked and examined. The idea is that by this means we shall be able 'to elicit from students the meanings that they have already stored up so that they may subject those meanings to a testing and verifying re-ordering process' (*TSA* p. 67).

But what children, of what age, and in what circumstances are we talking about? Just consider the nature of some of the proposed questions. They are momentous, provided that you can understand them and appreciate their significance, which no primary school child could. (It's true that it has been said that the individual should be able to give different answers at different stages of his development, but presumably he must understand the question.) A seminar based on the question, 'How can good be distinguished from evil?' with adults or teenagers is one thing; an education based on it is quite another. That we should at the end of the day ask and take seriously questions like 'What is progress?', 'What is change?', 'What are the most obvious causes of change?', 'Of the important changes going on in our society which should be encouraged and which resisted?', 'What are the conditions necessary for life to survive?' is one thing. But to conclude that education should consist of such questions would make sense only if you could establish that as a result of a school career based solely on such questions as trigger mechanisms people become eager and adept to cover important ground. There is no evidence at all for that. There is no evidence at all that relevant information and skills of reasoning cannot be more rapidly and more effectively instilled by other means.

Nor is the matter clarified when Postman and Weingartner conclude by putting forward their own list of basic necessities or fundamentals to replace the traditional three Rs. They begin by substituting the normative term 'thrive' for the neutral 'survive', which is not helpful, since most of us can agree on what counts as survival whereas we may legitimately argue about what counts as thriving. They themselves suggest that in order to thrive the organism needs other people, good communication, loving relationships, a workable concept of self, freedom and knowledge of how to learn. Some of this is not readily comprehensible and some of it is questionable. But the essential thing is that none of it is helpful. For the basic objection remains that nothing has been said to show that a curriculum based on asking these questions is a feasible way of attaining these objectives, still less that it is the only way.

KNOWLEDGE AND THE PERCEIVER

According to Postman and Weingartner, 'the meaning of what is out there is ascribed to it by the perceiver' (*TSA* p. 82). But this fashionable line of thought, like others we have met, can be shown to be either true but not very interesting or amazingly interesting and pretty obviously untrue. The purpose of their argument is to show that a system of education that to any marked extent relies on syllabus and teachers guiding towards the truth and a proper appraisal of what is, is unacceptable, because it ignores the fact that the meaning of what is out there is not a given, but is put there by each individual perceiver. They therefore need to show us that there is no qualitative difference between perceptions. No one would deny that the way we see things may vary, or that the significance we attach to what we perceive may vary. That is the trivially true interpretation of their claim. What many of us would deny is that that is all there is to it: that any perception is as good as any other. There are some perceptions, we would normally maintain, that, however sincere, are stupid, misguided, confused or incorrect.

Postman and Weingartner suggest that 'we "make" the reality we perceive rather than passively "receive" or "reflect" it' (*TSA* p. 89). Faced with something located in Parliament Square, some of us see the Houses of Parliament, which conjures up historical images, some of us see it as the hub of contemporary politics, some of us see it as a heap of stones, some as a large building difficult to clean and some as a magnificent piece of architecture. So far so true. Postman and Weingartner must (and do) admit that there is something out there; they are not saying that it is *all* in the mind (*TSA* p. 82). *We* must admit that different people will look at what is out there in different ways, with different associations and connotations, see it in different lights and attribute a different significance to it. Given both those admissions, it is very misleading to say as Postman and Weingartner do that '"reality" is a perception located somewhere behind the eyes' (*TSA* p. 93), since it suggests that there is no objective reality. But in the normal sense of those words there is, as has been admitted: the reality is the something out there, the building, which can have various aspects, but only a limited number. It would seem less tendentious and less confusing therefore to say that it is significance that is to some extent 'located behind the eyes' and not reality. Reality is by definition that which is not 'located behind the eyes'.

They now observe that 'it is only a slight exaggeration to say we see with our language' (*TSA* p. 93), meaning, which is true, that how you interpret what is before you is limited by your knowledge, which is embodied in concepts and, finally, in language. They conclude that the metaphor of 'meaning-making' is to be preferred to the usual static 'metaphors of the mind that are operative in the schools' (*TSA* p. 94). Their point has two aspects. First, they continue to stress that we do make meaning in the sense that what something signifies is to some extent the product of our way of looking at it, and it is therefore inappropriate to use metaphors that imply giving the one and only meaning of something to children. Second, they argue that to adopt the metaphor would make a difference because in itself it forces a shift of perspective and makes new meaning: 'if teachers *acted* as though their students were meaning makers, almost everything about the schooling process would change' (*TSA* p. 94).

Dewey's notion of 'transactional psychology', the view that 'what human beings are and what they make their environment into is a product of a mutually simultaneous, highly complex and continuing "bargaining" process between what is inside their skins and what is outside' (*TSA* p. 92), seems self-evidently plausible. We need have no hesitation in accepting the truth of the statement, 'you tend to perceive what you want and need to perceive, and what your past experience has led you to believe will "work" for you' (*TSA* p. 93). And certainly it is the case that 'the ability to learn can be seen as the ability to relinquish inappropriate perceptions'. But note that, now that they are drawing their conclusions, Postman and Weingartner tone down their claims considerably and couch them in tentative and relative terms ('you tend to ...', 'the ability to', 'can be seen'). Whatever all this amounts to, it clearly does not amount to an argument to the effect that how you see things cannot be faulted or corrected. If there are 'inappropriate' perceptions, as it has been admitted there are, then there must be 'appropriate' ones, which is to say perceptions that work and are correct and true.

The trouble here is that Postman and Weingartner are guilty of reductionism. They want to reduce the whole business of truth, knowledge and learning in such a way as to make it fit a theory dominated by one perception – their perception that the agent can alter the significance of what he sees. But for that gross oversimplification there is no warrant. We grant that when rain falls from the sky some head for shelter and others continue walking. We grant that 'their perceptions of what is happening are different as reflected in the fact that they do different things. The fact that both groups will agree to the sentence "it is raining" does not mean they perceive the event in the same way' (*TSA* p. 94). And we say: so what? It does not follow that the truth is how you see it or that the reality of what is going on here depends on the state of mind of each witness. It does not follow that it is not a matter of fact that it is raining.

It is certainly wrong to put *all* the emphasis on individual perception and judgement. But how important is it to stress it at all? Postman and Weingartner feel that, given the truth of what they say, the argument over whether we should have a subject- or student-centred curriculum is otiose. 'You end up with a student-centred curriculum ... because you don't in fact have any other choice' (*TSA* p. 95). Since students *are* meaning-makers they restructure what they are fed to suit themselves and their perceptions anyway. But this observation, far from carrying their argument through to a triumphant conclusion, would seem to expose it for the verbal by-play that it is. You end up with a student-centred curriculum by definition, if you make the tendency of people to see things from their own point of view the crucial determinant of the 'reality' they are learning. You certainly do not end up with an argument for any change. There is on this view strictly speaking no need for change, since it is provided already by each individual. Furthermore, accepting the meaning-making metaphor for what it is worth, it just does not follow that 'you would quite logically stop the practices of preparing and using syllabi and texts which state exactly what knowledge is to be learned' (*TSA* p. 95). Emphasising the occurrence of individual perspective might well make one inclined to be less dogmatic and to make more effort to understand the student's view of a situation; it might lead one to treat the material on a syllabus in a different manner. But whatever you do, nothing has been said to lead to the conclusion that the meaning-maker metaphor makes it absurd to expect children to study certain selected works of literature, areas of history or aspects of physics. Another consequence of adopting the new metaphor that they lay claim to – that you would not expect the 'same' knowledge to be learned by every student – is true but trivial. It means that you would expect different slants on what is learned from different students, as most of us do already without benefit of the new metaphor.

It is also claimed that 'using the metaphor "meaning-makers" would help us to abandon our notion of "fixed intelligence" which in turn would weaken almost all of our reasons for grouping children and labelling them' (*TSA* p. 97). This, if true, would indeed be significant, both as a justification for the preoccupation with this metaphor and as evidence of how crucial the metaphors in terms of which we think may be. But, despite the vagueness of the phrasing, it seems to be clearly untrue. Few people, if any, who believe in what may loosely be termed fixed intelligence believe in a predetermined level and range of intellectual competences. They mean at the most that innate factors will limit the possibilities open to the individual. Put crudely but graphically, the claim would be that some people could not have been Einsteins under any circumstances. It is quite clear that one could consistently believe that and at the same time use the meaning-maker metaphor, for the individual child as he develops may perfectly well be a meaning-maker even supposing that he is innately limited to an as yet unknown degree. Postman and Weingartner's point is that if we work with a notion of fixed intelligence we perceive what we expect to perceive, which means in practice that we interpret whatever a dumb boy does as dumb (buggery in Bootle again). There is obviously some truth in this, but it is crucial to note both that the whole argument presupposes that there is such a thing as dumb behaviour (the argument is about whether adopting a new way of looking at things would minimise the occurrence of dumb behaviour) and that the process of imposing our expectations on others does not have to take place. We are once again obstructed from sorting this out by Postman and Weingartner's uncertainty as to whether some things have to be perceived as objectively true or not. They are anxious to draw the conclusion that nothing that goes on in the inquiry seminar can be irrelevant, inappropriate or a waste of time, and that adopting the meaning-maker metaphor will encourage an appreciation of that fact. But although it may be true that the metaphor will encourage this assumption it will not guarantee this state of affairs; and very properly not, for some things are in some contexts, including discussions and inquiries, decidedly irrelevant, inappropriate and a waste of time. This is not to deny that 'as soon as students realise that their lessons are about their meanings, then the entire psychological context of school is different' (*TSA* p. 98), or indeed that school in one sense is (or should be) about their meanings. It is rather to insist that there are some things that are true, correct and appropriate, whatever anybody thinks, and that students should be encouraged to seek out those things rather than to treasure their idiosyncratic views because they are their own. The fact that education is in some sense ultimately about the meanings of the individual does not entail that the process of education should be dominated by his meanings from start to finish.

All that they have effectively said so far is that to some extent we interpret what we see rather than merely photograph it, from which nothing significant follows for their central theme that there can be no body of information or skills that ought to be taught. It is therefore disconcerting to find that in the next chapter they go so much further that they are now contradicting some of their own earlier pronouncements. Whereas previously we were told that of course 'we are not saying that there isn't anything out there' (*TSA* p. 82), it now transpires that 'whatever is out there isn't anything until we make it something and then it "is" whatever we make it' (*TSA* p. 101). To which it seems sufficient to reply: nonsense. There is a tree outside my window, and will be even if I forget about it or if it is observed by someone who has never heard the word or seen such a thing before. The fact that you may see it as evidence of God's existence, a thing of beauty, a bird perch or not see it at all will not stop it being a tree. While agreeing that we do not have to regard a tree as a tree, it none the less *is* what happens to be called a tree. Similarly, we don't have to divide the year up into days, nights, weeks and months, but whether we do or do not, those divisions are there to be made in our hemisphere in a way that a division into three nights in a row is not. For Postman and Weingartner to suggest that the belief 'that a thing is either A or not A and that it can never be both at the same time' is a consequence 'of our language system, of our methods of codifying reality, and may or may not bear much resemblance to the wiggles outside of our skin' (*TSA* p. 101) is either trite (if it means that we would not say precisely this, if we had not come to use words the way we do and to see that this is the case) or unintelligible. That a thing is either A or not A is not a consequence of us, our behaviour or our ways of looking at things. It is a consequence of the way things are and must be. Besides, what do they mean by the phrase 'wiggles outside of our skin' if not reality? They know as well as I do that we must distinguish between what is there, what is put there and what is not there – between what is read into a situation and what is undeniably part of it.

Where they have gone wrong is in confusing truth, knowledge and certainty. It may very well be the case that 'no man can be absolutely certain of anything' (*TSA* p. 100). Consequently any claim

to knowledge is, strictly speaking, provisional. But it does not follow
that there is no truth or that there is no knowledge. It follows only
that we can never be sure that we have either. The difference is
enormous, because the latter demands only caution, whereas the
former demands subjectivism. 'The best anyone can ever do is say
how something appears to him' (*TSA* p. 100) is a dangerous
truism that entirely misses the distinction: it is obviously true that
if you see it that way, that's the way you see it and you cannot be
expected to say how it appears to anyone other than yourself.
Equally obviously, how you see it may not be how it is, and our
concern in education is to map out what is rather than what appears
to be. All of this may be summarised by a brief look at their inadequate attempt to deny the reality of stupidity. They want to argue
that when I call someone stupid I am telling you something about
me, and that 'stupidity is a grammatical category. It does not exist
in nature' (*TSA* p. 36). The word certainly does have emotive meaning and may very often function purely emotively; furthermore, it
is true that stupidity does not exist in a physical form: you cannot
pick it up, smell it or point it out. The fact remains that people may
be stupid, regardless of other people's opinions, even though we concede that it may be a matter of argument as to whether they are.
When I see a man take a hammer to crack a walnut or cut off his
nose to spite his face, I say he is stupid, and in so doing I tell you
something about him, whatever I may also reveal about myself.

So what are they proposing that schools should actually try to
do? The answer, which must come as something of a shock to those
who have read the first three-quarters of their book with care, is
that behind talk of 'languaging', and despite emphasis on everything being as you see it, they want children's competence in various
familiar disciplines developed. Ideally they want to produce a genera-
ation of what the rest of us would call well-informed philosophers,
and they maintain that the ideal can most properly be approached
by what the rest of us call the Socratic method – and that remains
an accurate statement of their position, despite their avowed fear
that the reader might say precisely some such thing (*TSA* p. 36).[2]

Although they call them languages they recognise the various
disciplines or subjects classified by reference to a disciplined way
of proceeding and systems of interrelated symbols and rules for their
interaction. When they say that 'every teacher is a language teacher'
(*TSA* p. 103) they mean that every teacher has a job to initiate the

child into the language of history, politics, biology or whatever it may be. Because he is learning language in a context where there is a question of 'the relationship of language to reality' (that word unobtrusively back on to the field of play), 'the student can begin to develop standards by which he can judge the value of perceptions' (*TSA* p. 104) because, it is now conceded, although perceptions are unique, 'we still need to know if someone's statements about the world are "better" than someone else's'. Putting 'better' in quotation marks is presumably designed to minimise the transparent *volte-face* that we are here witnessing. For now all memory of everything being only how you see it is erased as we rapidly swing back to the conventional viewpoint that we must of course 'have ways of telling the difference between a lunatic and a scientist', between the good and the bad, between what works and what fails (*TSA* p. 105). In other words, the student is *not* the final arbiter of what is relevant, right and true, despite the contrary claim above; and so that there shall be no misunderstanding we are rapidly introduced to a number of crucial rules and truths that we will need to be aware of, most of which are old rules of logic such as the distinction between connotation and denotation, intensional and extensional, and warnings about the dangers of generalisation and oversimplification. (Those desperate for a trace of consistency, however small, will be pleased to see that the rule that nothing can be A and not A at the same time is not included here.)

One final thing that is worth commenting on is the tendency of Postman and Weingartner (a tendency shared by all the radicals) to use the word 'concept' in such a vague way that 'having a concept' comes to be identified with possessing a characteristic. Thus at the end of *Teaching as a Subversive Activity* we are told that

> the new education has as its purpose the development of a new kind of person, one who – as a result of internalising a different series of concepts – is an actively inquiring, flexible, creative, innovative, tolerant, liberal personality who can face uncertainty and ambiguity without disorientation, who can formulate viable new meanings to meet changes [*TSA* p. 204].

Many of us can probably embrace something like that as an ideal. The argument has been about how, assuming we can agree on the definition of these terms, we can best produce the qualities in question. The answer we have been given is, in essence, that the new education will produce them because 'it consists of having students use concepts most appropriate to the world'. That is to say, students are brought up to think in terms of dynamic metaphors like meaning-making and crap-detecting. But if that approach is presumed likely to deliver the goods, then we really have swallowed the medium and confused it with a coherent message. To insist that people think in terms of uncertainty (i.e. have the concept) certainly does not in itself suffice to make them tolerant of it or able to live with it. Nor is having the concept (i.e. being aware of the idea of uncertainty) necessary to being able to live with it. Postman and Weingartner are evidently not quite certain what they mean by 'having a concept', still less what it actually does mean. They are very confusedly caught by the idea that to enunciate something is to make it happen, or, at the very least, to provide a formidable impetus towards making it happen. It is as if their book, by outlining the changed circumstances we live in, thereby must necessarily enable the reader more easily to cope with these changed circumstances. But that is simply not true. By and large recognition of something is perhaps necessary or at least helpful in dealing with it; but even that is not always so, and recognition of something certainly isn't sufficient to enable one to cope with it. You do not produce competent, inquiring, flexible, creative, innovative, tolerant liberal-minded people who can face uncertainty without disorientation simply by thrusting those concepts at them and thinking in terms of dynamic metaphors and real and valid jargon. I have yet to be persuaded that such methods are even helpful, let alone necessary or sufficient.

The truth is that Postman and Weingartner have given us no more than the familiar message that our schooling may not be encouraging people to think critically, and that it may rather be initiating them into unquestioning acceptance of existing fashions and prejudices. The fact that others such as Rousseau have said it before is not to be held against it or them. But clearly what is needed is a solution, not a new discovery of the problem. Their solution is, to say the least, empty. But where they, as against the deschoolers, may be right is in thinking that, if the current education is producing too much conformism, we ought to take active steps through the schools to produce something else, and in thinking that the way to defeat the hidden curriculum is to give children the skills to enable them to recognise it and examine it for themselves.

CHAPTER 8

Last Words

I had originally planned to include considerably more material on the style and techniques of argument employed by the radicals and to document, by examples, such general charges laid against them as those of emotionalism, contradiction and incoherence. Space has prevented me, and I have had to leave the reader to do much of the work for himself, picking out the steady flow of reductionism, argument by analogy, retreat into metaphor, obscurity masquerading as profundity, jargon, assertion without the backing of evidence, and conceptual ambiguity. But I hope that the reader has taken such a synoptic overview of the nature of radical argument, because the question of style is itself pertinent to the radical theme and to mine. The medium is the message, they insist, and regrettably they are half correct: advertising does work; selling is a technique; a trite message well packaged can be mistaken for wisdom. And without question the writing, marketing and presentation of radical literature has gained it a wider and more respectful audience than the reasoning contained within it deserves.

Considerations of space have also prevented me from drawing out and underlining all the links, development of themes and interesting differences between the individual authors, and from overtly extracting many general conclusions. I have shown but not made an issue of the plain fact that certain specific ideas and errors run through most of their writing. They challenge a stereotype of schooling and education the inadequacy of which stereotype is shown by the fact that it has hardly changed between the writing of Rousseau and that of present-day radicals, while the actual practice of education has changed dramatically and beyond recognition in the intervening years. They vehemently attack theory, while indulging in it, failing to see that it is not any split between theory and practice that is problematic, but the distinction between the practical and the impractical; it is to some extent the impracticality of much of their theorising that makes it inadequate. They fail to appreciate that sometimes half-achieving an ideal is worse than not achieving it at all. (I am reminded of Plato's belief that in ideal circumstances democracy would be the worst form of government but that in practice it may be the best: cf. Plato's *Statesman* 293c.) While they theorise they take permanent refuge in the Manfred Syndrome and a host of 'likely stories'; they generalise from the particular at the drop of a hat, they confuse average with typical, and they commit the naturalistic fallacy with alarming regularity.

Their work also contains many recurring themes and insights that are extremely important in themselves, although scarcely sufficient to establish the overall theses. One such is the insistence that education should enable people to see through hypocrisy and humbug. But, though all the radicals, with the exception of Neill, lay great stress on developing critical thinking, not one of them has made any real contribution to the problem of how best to do it; not one of them has even thought out carefully and comprehensively what is involved in being a critical thinker; they confuse generative and defining characteristics and they hide the whole problem behind an absurdly simplistic view of the conditions under which learning can take place. Their whole argument is, of course, heavily dependent on a host of concepts that are actually formal and dynamic, but which they see as substantive and static (need, nature, reality, use, relevance). Just as they unnecessarily try to extend the reasonable point that how one presents information may itself alter the nature of the information into the absurd suggestion that all content is manner of imparting, so they substitute the ludicrous doctrine that there is no question or problem of value for the reasonable point that value judgements may differ. But there *is* a question of whether some things are more worth doing than others, and the radicals do not improve their case by pretending that it isn't there.

The most serious problem facing the radicals however is the internal contradiction between their ideals (what they are seeking to bring about) and their proposals. To varying degrees they are politically minded: they want and hope to produce a more just, equal and democratic society. But by temperament they are individualists. Even in most congenial circumstances individualism does not rest easy with those ideals. The tension is exacerbated by the uncertainty of the radicals as to whether they are opting out of the real world, proposing plans for changing it, or depicting an ideal pattern of education for an ideal world.

If the community itself were educative, as all the radicals would like it to be, well and good. Of course we should not need schools. And some of what the radicals have to say may contain useful hints on ways and means of making the community more educative. But nothing that is said can alter the fact that the community will in fact go on being predominantly anti-educational, at least until we have properly educated a complete generation. At the same time, one cannot properly educate a generation by the means proposed by radicals, since they are means that depend on an educative environment.

For many people, at least until fairly recently, the hope has been that schooling on a national scale and well carried out would be the means for providing the freedom, justice, equality and happiness desired by the radicals too. The radicals represent one kind of reaction to the growing feeling that that hope was misplaced. However, even if it is clear that the dream has not materialised, it is not clear that the whole idea was absurd. It is clear only that we have not been very successful. It could still be argued that it is at least a necessary condition of the happy and just society that individuals should have a sense of community and a common code of references, understanding of and access to a wide range of activities and life-styles, and the ability to reason well coupled with the desire to do so. And it could still be argued that some pattern of common schooling is the best way to achieve those goals.*

What is incontestable is that any form of upbringing that puts the stress on leaving children alone to develop, by chance, in reaction to the stimuli of their particular environment must be disastrous in terms of radical objectives so long as environments are different, sometimes disparate and always anti-educational. A world without the sort of effort currently being made by schools – Emile's world, a world of Summerhills or a world without schools – would in practice be a world in which the individual's background determines his future, and, since we start with varying backgrounds, a world in which difference, envy and inequality are perpetuated. On one score Postman and Weingartner are therefore more nearly right

---

* I have tried to argue just such a thesis in *Common Sense and the Curriculum* and, implicitly, in *Plato, Utilitarianism and Education*.

than the other radicals: to solve the sort of problems that we all perceive, we need to make better use of the schools. Through schooling we may develop a sense of community and harmony, awareness of possibilities and individual talents and resources.

But we will not succeed if we cannot produce something more coherent and specific than Postman and Weingartner did. Now it must be back to the drawing board. The radicals have told us sharply and wisely that something needs doing: they have set before us some goals and indicated many shortcomings in the school system. They have suggested that our aim should be to bring up a generation of concerned and critical thinkers. The individual who first tells us precisely what is involved in being a concerned and critical thinker and how best we may produce them in the world as it is at the moment is the theorist whom the world awaits. It is sad and ironic that the radicals should have done more by their style of argument to suspend critical thought in their readers than to help define the notion.

Bibliographical, Biographical and Stylistic Notes

JEAN-JACQUES ROUSSEAU

A biographical note

Jean-Jacques Rousseau was born in Geneva in 1712. His mother died shortly after his birth and he was brought up by an aunt. His father, a watchmaker, had to leave Geneva as a result of clashes with the authorities when Jean-Jacques was only ten years old. After this somewhat unsettled beginning Rousseau was apprenticed to a notary and then to an engraver, without obvious success in either case. (He was dismissed for stealing at one point, although he tried to put the blame on someone else.) In 1728 he was introduced, as a result of his interest in Catholicism, to Mme Warens who subsequently became his mistress. For the next ten years Rousseau may fairly be said to have dabbled, not without effect, in a variety of activities and with a number of people's affections. But always he seems to have returned to Mme Warens.

The aimlessness of his life took direction when in 1737, taking advantage of a serious illness which left him with time on his hands, he embarked upon a wide-ranging programme of self-education which culminated in his first published work, the *Discourse on the Arts and Sciences* (1750). In this he argues that so-called progress in the arts and sciences has in fact brought about moral stagnation and even corruption. The essay represents the beginning of a series of attacks on contemporaneous fashionable society, an attitude borne out by his newly formed attachment to the serving girl Thérèse Levasseur, who was to bear him five illegitimate children, all of whom were sent to a foundlings' home.

Although Rousseau now saw himself, with some bitterness, as an outsider, during the next ten to fifteen years he was in many respects very successful in worldly terms. He had an opera and a play performed; he became familiar with the leading intellectuals of the day such as d'Alembert and Diderot, to whose work on the great new Encyclopedia he contributed; and he continued to publish, until finally he produced *Emile* and *The Social Contract* (which were designed to be read together, although the latter was published first, in 1762).

He was a difficult man. Despite contributing his piece on music he did not get on with the Encyclopedists. The publication of *Emile* brought trouble, the remarks on religion causing particular offence, and Rousseau had to flee France in order to avoid arrest. At one point during his exile he stayed with the English philosopher David Hume, but his always suspicious nature now seems to have approached the stage of paranoia and he had to move on after he had begun to accuse his host of trying to defame him.

He finally settled in Paris and married Thérèse, wrote his extraordinary *Confessions*, which might more aptly have been entitled Justification, since it is an extended defence of all his actions, and in 1778 died much as he had lived – in relative poverty, dependent on the goodwill of a patron.

Rousseau detested society and was evidently not at home in the fashionable salons of the time. This complete alienation from what passed in conventional terms for civilised town life must have impelled him some way towards his idyllic conception of country life. Furthermore, it must account to some extent for certain obsessions that Rousseau had. Whatever the merits of *Emile*, no critical reader could miss the disproportionate emphasis that Rousseau places on certain things that he has it in for. For all his intellectual ability, he is a man dominated by passions, some at least of which were surely the outcome of his isolated position. The love, the peace, the security that he writes of represent what he wanted rather than anything that he gave or received. Would-be psychologists may care to pursue this line of thought further. I do not intend to. To explain is not to justify, and this information concerning details of his life will not make his arguments any the better or his conclusions the more true. But it may help us to see some of Rousseau's rather strange emphases in some sort of perspective.

A note of the radical themes in Rousseau

The number of themes and ideas of significance in contemporary radical thought that are to be found in Rousseau's writings is really quite extraordinary. Reference has been made to the idea of learning through experience and learning by doing, including specific mention of the desirability of apprenticeships; the idea that there is such a thing as learning *how to learn* which is more important than learning any particular skill or content; the insistence that we should teach useful or relevant knowledge; the hidden curriculum; suspicion of the value of art and abstract study and a complementary emphasis on the dignity and value of learning a trade; the distinction between education and instruction, and the realisation that the latter may take place without the former and the former may take place without schools; the concept of child-centred education, if that elusive phrase is understood to imply the sort of points mentioned above; the perception of the possibility and dangers of what Alvin Tofler called 'future shock', which is to say the state of being prepared for a type of existence and type of world that no longer exists; respect for persons, in some sense; awareness that teaching can be counter-productive if employed at unsuitable times; the appreciation that what is suitable and what is not, what a child is ready for and what he is not, is to some extent a matter of his state of conceptual awareness; the realisation that the truth or falsity of propositions is to some considerable extent dependent on meaning; the importance of example and, more generally, environmental influence; the difference between acting in accordance with authority and acting through, under or because of authority; the primacy of sense experience; the importance of finding the right motivation, coupled with the suggestion that individual interest is a most important motive power; the danger of a sense of alienation developing in people; the idea that readiness and need are important criteria for enabling us to determine educational provision; the idea of the tutor as something far more than a mere instructor; the radical notion that the solution to educational problems lies to some extent in getting children away from schools and all that they represent.

Rousseau wants to provide an education that will not be overtaken by the march of time ('How do you know that all this fine teaching ... will not do him more harm than good in the future'), and that will enable Emile to contribute to a stable and just society. There will be no competition, but only a striving against one's own previous record of achievement. Something very like what we now term 'compensatory education' is implied if not demanded when, addressing the sons of the rich, he says 'You owe more to others than if you had been born with nothing, since you were born under favourable conditions.' Always he is concerned with the reality rather than the appearance of things, as in his demand that we do not 'confuse the outward forms of religion with religion itself' (*E* pp. 146, 158, 259).

He has sometimes been regarded as a man against authority. But he was more precise than his disciples. He was anti-authoritarian and he could see the distinction between doing things in accordance with the dictates of authority and doing things because they were commanded by authority. The latter he rightly regards as in itself a poor reason for action. But there is nothing necessarily wrong with the former. His central theme, as we have seen, is not that people should do what they want, so much as that they should do what they ought to do. The radical change that he is after is that they should do what they ought to do because they understand that they ought to, because they see why it should be done, rather than because they are ordered to do it. That is the explanation of the remark, 'Let the child do nothing because he is told. Nothing is good for him but what he recognises as good' (*E* p. 141).

A. S. NEILL

A biographical note

Born in 1883 in Forfar, Scotland, A. S. Neill experienced an upbringing at the opposite end of the spectrum to Rousseau's ideals. His father, George Neill, was a schoolmaster and a disciplinarian, with something of a typically Calvinist puritanism in his soul. Neill attended his father's village school, but at the age of fourteen was sent as a clerk to Edinburgh. He was not happy and in 1899 he became a pupil teacher back at his father's school. At this stage he failed to become a fully qualified teacher and a judgement enshrined in a report of Her Majesty's Inspectors in 1901 describes his work as weak all round. After a couple of moves between schools he resolved on, and succeeded in, entering the University of Edinburgh, where he read English (changing over from agriculture). Despite ambitions to become a writer, he returned to teaching, and in 1921 was one of those who founded an international school in Dresden. That was the origin of the school that eventually became Summerhill in England, first at Lyme Regis and then at Leiston in Suffolk.

In one respect Neill is odd man out among the radicals discussed in this book. The others are not primarily, if at all, practitioners. Rousseau did a bit of teaching but was notably unsuccessful. Reimer has done many things, teaching not being one of them. Illich has been priest and pundit rather than pedagogue. Postman and Weingartner belong to the twilight world of teacher-training. But Neill was, first and last, a schoolmaster. What emerges very clearly from his writing, from reports by visitors to the school, and even from photographs of himself and children at Summerhill, is his love for children and his ability to rub along with them. All the authors with whom I am concerned *say* that they are concerned about children, but in Neill's case one *feels* or *senses* his warmth for children.

A note on Neill's style of argument

When one turns to Neill's own theorising one cannot fail to note his tendency to indulge in overstatement, sweeping generalisations, *non sequiturs* and unsupported assertions. To some extent this may be the consequence of a simple desire to shock the reader, which can be found in Rousseau too, and has now become the acme of respectability among bona fide radicals. It is dangerous to raise a voice against this tedious tendency, but shocking is not arguing. There is a particular danger with Neill in that his tendency to exaggerate may be counter-productive, for sometimes he apparently means what he says. For example, in the course of arguing that lack of freedom causes children to be unhappy he remarks: 'I saw a hundred thousand obedient, fawning dogs wag their tails in the Tempelhof, Berlin, when in 1935 the great trainer Hitler whistled his commands' (*S* p. 99). Despite the blatant emotivism of the example and despite the absurd simplicity of citing this as evidence (what about those brought up in the same conditions who resisted Hitler?), there is little doubt that here Neill is not trying to shock but is offering a serious argument to establish that we should give children the amount and type of freedom that he recommends. On the other hand, the not-dissimilar allusion in the claim that 'to beat a child at home . . . is basically the same thing as torturing a Jew in Belsen' (*S* p. 238) probably is designed to shock. One hopes so, for only a very blunt kind of intelligence could equate these two activities and thus reduce the latter to the level of being merely unattractive, unproductive and unnecessary.

The most marked feature of Neill's style is his willingness to extrapolate from isolated and individual cases some universal principle. Thus we are told the story of Jack (*S* p. 21): Jack tells his managing director that he thinks that Summerhill gave him self-confidence and his managing director thinks it more than likely. Neill interprets this little scene and regards it as sufficient to 'show' that 'learning in itself is not as important as personality and character. Jack failed in his university exams because he hated book learning. But his lack of knowledge about Lamb's essays or the French language did not handicap him in life. He is now a successful engineer.' Even if this case-study were documented and the interpretation of the events agreed, the single case would prove nothing. (There are of course a multiplicity of such isolated cases referred to by Neill in his writings, but they do not add up to anything because the story of each Tom, Dick and Harry is supposed to show something different.) Neill however is quite happy to generalise glibly and dogmatically from the particular, showing no awareness that a statement of generality, even if true, does not mean that it applies to each individual. The generalisation that traditional schools brutalise individuals, for example, if it were true as a generalisation, would precisely imply that some individuals are *not* brutalised by such schools, which carries the very important corollary that such schools do not *necessarily* brutalise and have not been shown by the argument to have an *inherent* capacity to do so. But, by and large, for Neill, to see something once is enough to establish some inevitable law: thus the alleged impossibility of children ever being interested in abstract matters is triumphantly established by a few glances at the behaviour pattern of Summerhill children: 'A boxer or a good tennis player is surrounded at once, but visitors who spout theory are left severely alone' (*S* p. 26.).

As with Rousseau, there is a touch of the 'likely story' running through all that Neill has to say. Admitting a certain lack of success with girls at Summerhill, Neill argues that the reason that latecomers to the school, as the girls usually are, fail is that they are usually the children of parents who do not appreciate freedom. The evidence for this conclusion is that 'if they had had [such appreciation] their girls would not have been problems' (*S* p. 29). The circularity of this argument makes it quite meaningless, let alone verifiable or falsifiable. Worth noting also is Neill's fondness for attempting to solve the problems of the limits to be drawn around something by distinguishing two concepts: using this approach, he attempts to delineate the limits of freedom by distinguishing between liberty, which corresponds to justifiable freedom, and licence, which corresponds to unjustifiable freedom (*S* p. 137). Manners and etiquette are similarly distinguished in order to locate the sort of politeness and consideration one should show for others and what one need not (*S* p. 172). Lying, which can be legitimate, is to be distinguished from dishonesty, which involves illegitimate lying and therefore cannot be justified. Such distinctions can be important for certain purposes, but Neill is not up to making good use of them. He fails to recognise that in itself this manoeuvre tells us nothing about what we should be free to do, what kinds of consideration are necessary, and when lying is legitimate. He has offered us a purely formal distinction and given us no clues at all as to how or by what criteria we should make the distinctions and hence decide whether a particular action is an example of liberty or licence, manners or etiquette, lying or dishonesty. The only contribution that Neill makes to that kind of question is to offer at scattered intervals some particular instances, without a hint of why they are taken to be instances of liberty rather than licence, or whatever it may be. And coupled with the vagueness inherent in that procedure is Neill's splendid panache in, if not actually contradicting himself, at any rate recouping his losses as fully as possible. No sooner have we been told that 'children should be allowed almost infinite responsibility' (*S* p. 171) than we are told that 'a child should not be asked to face responsibilities for which he is not ready, nor be saddled with decisions he is not yet old enough to make'. The Manfred Syndrome and Neill were made for each other.

Generally speaking, Neill is content with very little confirmation of his prejudices: he feels that because he has witnessed something, he has *ipso facto* become cognisant of an indisputable and un-

changeable fact about the world – the opposite of what he understands by the term 'theory'. But things are not as simple as that.
As Rousseau has conveniently reminded us, what we witness is partly
a product of our own idiosyncratic experience and interpretation.
There are therefore the questions of whether Neill sees what he sees
accurately, penetratingly and as others do, what his values are,
whether what may be agreed to have been shown to be a means
to a given end is necessarily the best means, and whether the world
is as static as Neill seems to assume. Neill can be very foolish as
when he announces that he has never seen acne on a happy face
(*S* p. 309); very muddled as when he writes that 'so-called bad habits
are natural tendencies' (*S* p. 311), which he does not actually mean
as a universal truth and would not say of homosexuality (cf. *S* pp.
206–7) (whereas he does say it of masturbation because he is obsessed
with the idea that masturbation is an entirely proper activity); and,
as he admits when revealing that he forbids strong drink at the school,
quite illogical (*S* p. 317). In 1973 Michael Duane concluded his
review of a book about Neill with this sentence: 'Never again can
Neill's achievement be brushed aside by ... philosophers as "lacking
intellectual or philosophical rigour".' The remark was the more silly
and inapposite since the book in question, Ray Hemmings' *Fifty
Years of Freedom*, is not even supposed by its author to be an
analysis and defence of Neill's ideas, as Duane's review implies, still
less a demonstration of his intellectual and philosophical rigour. It
purports to remain, and does remain, on the level of a descriptive
account of how Neill's ideas, whether coherent or otherwise,
developed. So the college lecturers need not fear Hemmings or Duane.
Nor, I think, need they actually reverse their judgement on Neill's
lack of rigour. (I am not convinced that the words 'intellectual' or
'philosophical' add much in this context. The point is not that Neill
was not an academic philosopher or a scholarly intellectual – he
never pretended to be either, nor is there any obvious reason why
he should have been. The point is that he does not give a clear and
consistent set of reasons, amounting to a convincing argument, that
he is on to anything.)

The fact is that some of what Neill says is unclear, some is plainly
contradictory, some is mere verbiage and some is false. We therefore do not as yet have any clear and demanding reason to found
a Summerhill or for supposing it to be desirable to do so.

What we do have amounts to a statement of faith that this kind of upbringing will produce happy individuals and a value judgement to the effect that that is all that matters. Let us concede that for all we know to the contrary education of the type proposed may provide present happiness and could contribute to and maintain happiness generally in a certain kind of society – one in broad respects comparable to Summerhill. But in the meantime, society being what it is, could widespread education of this type meet its own objectives? Conversely, could such education bring about the desired changes in society? There seems no obvious reason to answer either question in the affirmative. It seems at least as likely that such an education, if adopted generally, could lead rapidly to a backward, resourceless and unequal society and hence a most unhappy one: backward in respect of technological control and advance; resourceless in the sense of a community of persons lacking individual resources of knowledge and skills, to a significant degree; and unequal inasmuch as this is unashamedly an education to bring out the differences in people and one that carries it so far as to have no concern at all for any kind of common reference points.

PAUL GOODMAN

A bibliographical and stylistic note

Paul Goodman is in some ways the most approachable of the deschoolers. His style of writing is straightforward and simple compared with the opaqueness of Illich's. The development of his thought from the general social criticism of *Growing Up Absurd* to the specific educational solution proposed in the article 'Freedom and Learning' is continuous and comprehensible. He knows what he objects to and he can evoke our anger in the same cause; he knows what he wants, and his (on the whole) good-hearted determination is liable to be persuasive.

But 'persuasive' is the key word. Attractive and simple though the gospel according to Goodman is, it is far from clear that he has offered us a coherent case for adopting a specific course of action. He is inclined to rely on rhetorical techniques to make the worse cause appear the better. He makes important statements purely on the strength of anecdotes he has heard or acquaintances he has met.

He relies on analogies and metaphors that beg the question. He uses tendentious and emotive phraseology. There does not appear to be any malice aforethought in any of this – on the contrary, he embraces such stratagems with gusto and frankness. But it is precisely what makes him popular and readable, this frank unashamed commitment, that makes him slightly suspect: can the whole matter be quite as simple as this prophet would have it?

'Fundamentally,' says Goodman, 'there is no right education except growing up into a worthwhile world.... A decent education aims at, prepares for, a more worthwhile future, with a different community spirit, different occupations, and more real utility than attaining status and salary' (*CM* p. 55). There is the basic message: we need to re-orientate society completely, and a proper education system could and should devote itself to that end. Unfortunately, a great deal of the argument leading to the indictment of society as it is, and the holding out of hope for a brighter tomorrow, consists of evidence from unnamed and hence unverifiable sources. For example, Goodman asserts that 'informed labour people tell' him this and 'it has been shown that....' (*CM* p. 51; FL p. 109). The latter bland statement is of particular interest since what has apparently 'been shown' is that 'whatever is useful in the present eight year ... curriculum can be learned in four months by a normal child of twelve'. Since that is the lynchpin of Goodman's whole thesis, it is astonishing to find that no evidence to support the contention is given at all. The claim crops up repeatedly in his writings, but it is difficult to trace its origins and therefore impossible to check its adequacy.

It is characteristic of Goodman to continue using a particular claim or piece of evidence over the years, notwithstanding the fact that his own views changed or developed and the possibility that new research might have discredited previous research. The best example of this tenacity is probably his allegiance to the research of James Conant, which he first cites in *Growing Up Absurd* and which, virtually twenty years later, serves as one of the main plants for the argument in 'Freedom and Learning'. There is nothing wrong with that, you may say. Nor perhaps is there, until one realises that in *Growing Up Absurd* Goodman took a very dim view of Conant's research. It transpires therefore that what is presented in 'Freedom and Learning' as important and unimpeachable evidence is the product of twenty-year-old research summarised in a report which, according to Goodman's earlier views, was 'superficial' and 'a minor national disaster' (*GA* pp. 14, 84). This discrepancy seems so blatant that I am tempted to wonder whether different bits of research are referred to in either case. But there is no way of knowing, since (again fairly typically in radical literature) scorn for the ritual of scholarship leads to an absurd debunking of everything to do with scholarship: there are no references at all, and it is literally impossible to follow anything up, relying on the texts alone.

Sometimes a source of evidence is revealed, as when Goodman himself visits a school and, apparently solely on the strength of his interpretation of his observation of limited aspects of that one school, writes a chapter on the 'kind of alternative environment to the home' that the school (generically) does 'in fact give' (*CM* Ch. 2). Sometimes he presents crude and gross claims backed by no evidence at all, as for instance the statement that 'increasingly the best young people resist authority' (FL p. 108). Assuming that Goodman does not wish to make this emptily true by definition (i.e. to explain the remark by saying that, increasingly, what he means by 'the best' are 'those who resist authority'), it is a quite preposterous remark in the absence of both a definition of 'best' and any research carried out into the way such people are behaving. Even the very different proposition, 'increasingly ... young people resist authority', is not obviously true. We need some evidence, just as we need evidence that allowing children to conduct their lives according to their voluntary choices affords them 'the likeliest ways of growing up reasonably' (FL p. 111).

There are times when Goodman, like Neill, is no less cavalier about verbal precision than he is about empirical evidence. He sneers at what he calls verbal philosophy and contrasts it with something called real philosophy, the exact meaning of which is not made clear. It is, of course, only as a result of not clarifying his terms that he can make some of his claims seem plausible. And just as he trades (unconsciously, no doubt) on the ambiguity of words, so he trades on their emotive connotations and power: in 'Freedom and Learning' the word 'schooling', itself acquiring unattractive connotations thanks to the deschoolers themselves, is replaced by the unambiguously unpleasant phrase 'prior processing' (FL p. 107) at one point. But perhaps one should not complain: in *Compulsory Miseducation* schools had been dismissed as 'concentration camps' (*CM* p. 51).

One final point should be made. Despite his tendency to indulge in unscholarly and inept argument, Goodman is certainly not anti-intellectual even in the sense of anti-academic. His own preferred interests show this: more than any of the other individuals considered in this book he shows the conventional marks and signs of the cultivated mind – a genuine acquaintanceship with the classics, with the milestones of literature, with music and with art. He has no desire to force these traditional values down the throats of others, but he does have such values himself. In particular, he values intellectual achievement in a conventional sense. At one point in *Growing Up Absurd* his hostility to popular culture is hardly different in kind to that of a moderate Black Paper contributor such as G. H. Bantock (*GA* p. 25, cf. *GA* pp. 83, 137, 223). His general attitude is well exemplified by his deploring the fact that nowadays there is so much attention paid to extramural goals and 'no devotion to intellectual goals'. In similar vein he laments that colleges and universities 'in the foreseeable future' will cease to 'pass on the tradition of disinterested learning'. Such preoccupations mark him out as distinct among radicals. He has in this respect strong affinities with an altogether different kind of radical such as William Morris, who is in no way to be associated with those who despise the cultural heritage, but who, rather, emphasises in addition the cultural possibilities and dimensions of what are commonly considered non-cultural everyday activities. Goodman values the cultural tastes of the so-called educated minority, but he does not think that education should be defined in such terms, nor does he believe that such tastes will appeal or be of interest to the majority.

A note on Goodman's ideals

Goodman's personal values are never concealed in his writings: he has a personal affection for what he calls the liberal arts. But he believes that it is counter-productive for the schools to treat them as *the* unquestionably worthwhile body of knowledge and that most other trades have no less a value. Neither those opinions nor his ultimate aim of a world in which individuals do their own thing but do it in harmony are at all ridiculous, odd or to be scorned. But it seems undeniable that if we were to adopt Goodman's educational proposals in the world as it is, we would get something like this: in a community made up of a number of disparate groups (plumbers, Latinists, farmers, engineers, dustmen), some individuals would have knowledge of a variety of trades, most would know their own trade well and very little else, and few individuals would have anything in common with those of different trade and background. The scholar would pursue his trade like anybody else in isolation. In that respect, as Goodman acknowledges, he is advocating a return to the medieval world and it is no accident that he cites Plato, who likewise wanted scholarship to be a profession, with approval.

Perhaps this would be acceptable if academics were only a trade and scholarship a profession. But academics as a whole is not quite comparable to plumbing or journalism, even if specific items like studying Sanskrit might be seen in such a light. However difficult it may be to describe and assess, the study of things like history and English offer more than a mere initiation into the trade of historian or literary critic. As Goodman himself has said, there is also the hidden curriculum to be considered: schools covertly give children a sense of community and countless values. Can we afford to leave all such things to chance? Although it must remain speculative, it seems reasonable enough to predict that mini-schools and apprenticeships in the world as it is would intensify a class society in the sense of a community in which there are distinct alien groups, and one might add that the group most likely to take control and dominate is that which is most 'educated' in something approaching the current sense of that word. 'I have been accused', Goodman writes, 'of being a racist–élitist who thinks that some people are not good enough to go to school. But I am not an élitist and I do not think that some people are not good enough. The scholastic disposition is a beautiful and useful one; we are lucky that a minority of people are so inclined. But I do not think it is the moon and stars' (*CM* p. 119). Of course, he is neither a racist nor an élitist, but it is perhaps not surprising that he should be accused of being one. For he does apparently believe in differences that are innate and he naively wishes upon us a system which, given that possibly true assumption, will magnify the differences between people and minimise communal feeling, while very likely making the most of the capacities of those from favoured backgrounds and the least of those from unfavoured backgrounds. The favoured few are likely to retain their favoured position partly because, although the radicals cannot see it, much of the traditional school fare, the academic trade in Goodman's terms, has considerable use, not least for one who wants to understand and control his world, and partly because academic prowess has a mystique that can only increase, if we regress to a situation where it is shared by only a few. After all, in the Middle Ages, too, it was the academic minority, the schooled few, who did all right for themselves; and, incidentally, their mystique owed little to the paraphernalia of schools, examinations and certification.

IVAN ILLICH

Aspects of Illich's style

We should look briefly at the language of ritual and service which Illich uses prominently in respect of schools and note the nature of the kind of argument they typify. I do not question whether schooling is, as Illich insistently maintains, a new religion so much as whether it is wise or helpful to think in these terms. Illich has a genuine interest in religion and it would not be fair therefore to dismiss his use of religious language in the context of schooling as mere figure of speech or just rhetorical technique. None the less, the religious terminology has come to assume that status in the popular mind: all sorts of people, who couldn't tell a priest from a piano-tuner, parrot and cry that schooling is the new religion.

Much of *Celebration of Awareness* in fact consists of essays on disestablishing the church, that being one of Illich's earlier concerns. Very crudely, what worries him is that the trappings of religion have come to mean more than what they stand for, and he sees the church as being much of a muchness with General Motors. There are therefore two points here: one is the observation that even a religious foundation or organisation can become predominantly an institution (which is to say, worried about 1·8 million full-time employees rather than about the faith itself) and, as such, will fail to a great extent to do what it ought to be doing and do what it wots not of (preaches a hidden curriculum, in other words). Second is the observation that the supposed beneficiaries (the flock) may come to adulate the bureaucracy, the institution and its demands, rather than what lies behind it. At that stage we have a godless religion on our hands.

Consequently, when Illich says that 'the school has become the established Church of secular times' and that to equate equal educational opportunity with compulsory schooling 'is to confuse salvation with the Church', he means that we are worshipping the trappings of education (the system, its offices, its bureaucratic demands) and have lost sight of the thing itself: that which the system is supposed to provide.

But suddenly it doesn't seem to be a very good analogy. The whole point is that schools are *not* as churches (just as education is not comparable to medicine). It is obviously possible to worship God without the help of churches, and it is obvious that one ought not to worship the priest in and for himself. But schools are not means for worshipping education: they are means for acquiring it, and it is not at all clear, at any rate as things are, that one could acquire everything easily without them. And one might quite reasonably respect the 'trappings' of schooling, such as the teacher, the school and the degree, for these are not trappings in the sense of irrelevant ritualistic extras: the calibre and quality of the school and teacher may materially determine whether one is well or badly educated, and although the degree in itself is merely a sign or symbol, it may none the less be a sign of something valuable. (Money is not the less valuable because it is a mere symbol of exchange.) Nor is Illich's further observation that schools divide the educational school from the rest of the non-educational world, just as the church divides its religious self from the profane everyday world, confirmation of the soundness of the analogy. The analogy breaks down because it is essential to the church that it should be seen as something sacred and distinguishable from the outside world, whereas it is not essential that the school should peddle the myth that it and it alone is the source of all true education, even if as a matter of fact it has tended to do so. The truth is simple but important: this kind of rich and persuasive metaphor, which has perhaps a grain of truth in it and may capture the popular imagination, prevents us from thinking. It suggests that it is inherent in schooling that people should mistakenly see schools as necessary and sufficient for all education, and it thereby pre-empts the possibility of our considering ways in which we might counter the contingent likelihood of this view arising. That is why this manner of argument is unfortunate.

Similar objections arise in relation to the image of the service industry. What is generally meant by a service industry is one that does not produce consumer durables or, more generally, something material and usable. Thus medicine and sewage disposal are service industries, while ball-bearing manufacture, coal and steel industries are not. Illich's argument is that increased automation and technological development reduces the rate of employment in producing industries and thus, in the industrial West, leads to a rapid growth in service industries. The need to maintain full (or as nearly full as is practicably possible) employment creates an increase in leisure time, as people work shorter hours, while the need to maintain or increase sales leads to the growth of advertising, which is regarded as the epitome of the service industry: producing nothing, but crucial to the smooth running of everything else as a result of the wide employment it provides and its ability to create demand for whatever there is available. So far there is nothing particularly remarkable in this picture. But Illich now suggests that education should be regarded as an aspect of, or something comparable to, advertising, since 'it creates the need for its own products and it validates its own activities' (*D* p. 7). Nor does the bandwagon stop when things are going badly: when education runs into a period of trouble, we do not call a halt or curtail our activities. We step them up, producing research, studies and inquiries. Our response to the emergence of a sense that the school curriculum is absurd is to set up panels of schooled experts to engage in curriculum research. 'The greater the failure, the greater the expansion.' The substance of this view is of course by now familiar: the immediate point is the use of the epithet 'service industry' to stamp home the message that the education system creates the demand for its own services.

But once again the analogy creaks a bit. In this case the basic distinction between service and producer industries is itself rather rough and ready. Nominally coal-mining is a producer industry and television a service industry, for example. But every so often the Coal Board, worried about competing sources of energy supply, has to start selling itself and its product, and thus becomes effectively a service industry. Conversely, television companies can also be involved in production in crude industrial terms: making and selling programmes abroad can be big business. Quite apart from the difficulty of locating industries that are clearly either purely service or production industries, it is fairly obvious that certain activities, such as education itself, are in fact by their nature both. If Illich wishes to call education exclusively a service industry we need not object, provided that it is not assumed that it is a service industry in the way that, say, a firm that produces five hundred prints in a limited edition, just to create and cash in on a limited demand, is a service industry. This brings us to the nub of the matter: advertising may be a thoroughly pernicious activity and it may be a service industry, but it is at best *one example* of a service industry. It is not the definition of the term. The question is whether schooling is comparable in all important essentials to advertising. The answer is that it is not, even if there are one or two interesting and important similarities. But the point here is that once again the analogy obscures thought. If it really held, then indeed the only solution would be to sweep away schooling; but it does not hold. Unlike advertising, which by its nature creates demand regardless of value or people's actual wants, schools do not have to go on legitimising everything they touch. There is nothing inherently absurd about the idea that schools should be reformed in such a way that they provide only what is otherwise thought to be desirable.

Notes to Chapters

CHAPTER 1

1 There is some evidence that Neill did not entirely reciprocate the feeling. See Hemmings (1972, p. xi).

2 It is Goodman's perspective (amazingly, since it is less true and less productive than Rousseau's) that predominates in subsequent radical literature. The source for this view in every instance appears to be Ariès's *Centuries of Childhood*. A little more research would have revealed that the basic claim is not even true: as far back as Plato people have been aware that, as Rousseau was to insist, the child is not a miniature adult. The view reaches its most extreme and absurd form in the writings of John Holt who, on the strength of it, suggests that we should give everyone, including new-born babies, the right to vote, to work, to own property and to use drugs.

3 An 'institution which requires full-time attendance of specific age-groups in teacher supervised classrooms for the study of graded curricula' (cf. *DS* p. 32).

CHAPTER 2

1 The contemporary tone of much of this speaks for itself, but it is worth noting that he also anticipates one of the central deschooling theses to the effect that we are in danger of being overrun by service industries which create need for their own ministrations. In Rousseau's words, we are 'governed by artificial needs which can be satisfied only with the help of other people'.

2 Rousseau states that he is not interested in weak or sickly children: they are more trouble than they are worth.

3 As Josh Billings put it, 'The trouble ain't that people are ignorant; it's that they know so much that ain't so.'

4 Rousseau has the practical wit to add that, when adopting this mode of moral teaching, if you have anything of value that might be damaged you should keep it out of the 'reach of the ill-tempered' (*E* p. 64).

5 But Rousseau is not anti-books. It is 'the misuse of books that is the death of sound learning. People think they know what they have read, and so take no pains to learn' (*E* p. 414).

6 Cf. Plato, *Republic* 378. D for the observation that the child cannot comprehend allegory. This is by no means the only case in which the radicals are anticipated by Plato.

7 If Rousseau is to be believed, Emile's contact with such people as Robert the Gardener and the conjuror has been exceptional – the result of odd forays into the wider world.

8 See p. 183 for a further note on Rousseau's themes and ideas.

CHAPTER 3

1 A second point arising from the examples is that whether something is or is not natural in the specific sense of precivilised is itself a contentious matter. One need only consider that Locke assumed that life in a precivilised state of nature would be easy-going, co-operative and friendly, while Hobbes stated tersely that it would be 'nasty, brutish and short' to appreciate that.

2 If reading books counts as a verbal lesson, this total embargo on verbal lessons is later lifted, though even then it is said that children should 'learn nothing from books which they can learn from experience'. The embargo on overt instruction is never lifted. (May the teacher respond to requests for information?)

3 'Your job is to give him a taste for [the sciences] and methods of learning them when the taste is more mature' (*E* p. 135).

4 It is true that Rousseau asserts that 'there is no original sin in the human heart; the how and why of the entrance of every vice can be traced', but this need not be interpreted as implying original virtue. It is quite consistent with the idea of original vacuity provided that we accept the corollary that in principle the how and why of the entrance of every virtue can be traced, which Rousseau would (*E* p. 56).

5 The radicals by definition want to change both society and education. Each of them envisages an ideal such that proposed changes in one make proposed changes in the other more plausible. What is less clear is how far in any particular case it is presumed that one could make changes in one without the other. The overall vagueness and uncertainty on this matter I refer to as the chicken-and-egg problem: granted that *if* we had a different society we could do with a different kind of education (and vice versa), what are we supposed to do in practice? What comes first: a new society or a new system of upbringing?

CHAPTER 4

1 Whom Neill never read. The similarities and differences are fortuitous and of interest to us, not them.

2 Neill himself recognises that there is actually no such thing as a self-regulating child, but he seems to regard that as an unfortunate contingent fact.

3 It is true that Neill is reacting against the doctrine of original sin. That may constitute an explanation of why he is so concerned about this matter. It is also true that all he needs to do to reject that doctrine is to replace it with a *tabula rasa* theory. But what he needs to do and explanations of how he came to be obsessed by this and oblivious of that are not to the immediate point. His interest in repudiating the theory that we are born in a state of sin does to some extent influence the emphasis of his remarks and sometimes causes him to stress the negative aspect at the expense of the positive. But he clearly does believe in innate goodness, as I argue in the text.

4 Neill is fond of contrasting pairs of words. See p. 187.

CHAPTER 5

1 Consider, for example, the almost too casual 'somewhere we missed out on equality' followed by what seems to Goodman to be the real objection: 'and this is now threatening our flexibility and stability' (*GA* p. 59).

2 Teaching too is a vain profession in Goodman's view. He insists, though his grounds for this assertion are not at all clear, that although teaching may be thought to be a 'manly job', it is not really necessary and dignified because it does not really have the exalted aims that it lays claim to and is sometimes thought to have. This, incidentally, is a characteristic line of attack among the radicals: they cannot or will not believe that there may be a large part of the educational establishment that sincerely aims to do something other than what the radicals claim it does do.

3 Goodman claims here to be subscribing to what he says is Dewey's view that 'with guidance whatever a child experiences is educational. It makes no difference what is learned at this stage, so long as the child goes on wanting to learn something' (FL p. 108). 'For a small child everything in the environment is educative, if he attends to it with guidance' (MS p. 36). It remains unclear quite what 'educative' means for Goodman and what exactly we are to understand by 'with guidance'. But it would seem in any case that Goodman has misunderstood Dewey. Dewey was not a radical in my sense of the word. There are odd passages in his writings that harmonise well with some of the views of the radicals I have mentioned. Like Rousseau, Dewey believes that there will be no friction in society if individuals see social constraint as the demand of impersonal laws rather than the arbitrary imposition of other persons (Dewey, 1973, p. 52; cf. p. 55). Like Neill, he envisages self-generated interest as sufficient to promote learning. In keeping with the thinking of most of them he asserts that 'there is no such thing as educational value in the abstract' (p. 46). None the less, he is not a radical because he is not critical, root and branch, of either society or the educational objectives generally canvassed in his time. Unlike Rousseau and Neill, he is a democrat for whom the reality has not turned sour. He believes in the American democracy of his time and is concerned only to improve it by making education more suited to it.

Dewey's educational theory is built round an empirical thesis to the effect that a certain means will prove more efficacious in arriving at the accepted goal of producing sound, democratic and inventive citizens. He argues, as does Rousseau, that education should be based on experience, but he is very careful to qualify that vague phrase precisely and heavily. Some experiences, he assures us, are mis-educative. Worried by the empirical observation that many people in the past have 'lost the impetus to learn because of the way in which learning was experienced by them' (p. 26), Dewey proposes to motivate and achieve his object as a result of ensuring that children are presented with experiences that exhibit what he calls continuity and interaction. An experience has interaction if it is one that is suited to the individual or seems meaningful and important to him (i.e. if there is interaction between agent and activity). It has continuity in so far as it leads on to the chance to enjoy further experiences. 'Continuity and interaction in their active union with each other provide the measure of the educative significance and value of an experience' (p. 44). But Dewey is emphatic that the mature adult can judge the value of an experience, at least as regards continuity, better than the young themselves. Thus the educator, who must be able to judge 'what attitudes are actually conducive to continued growth' (p. 39), is properly bound 'to select those things within the range of existing experience that have the promise and potentiality of presenting new problems which by stimulating new ways of observation and judgement will expand the area of further experience' (p. 75).

Whereas Rousseau wants to do away with both the system of schooling and the type of society with which he was familiar, Dewey wants neither. Some kind of organised institutional setup is necessary to his purpose, for he wants an artificially controlled democratic society to mirror his perception of the outside world. And he approves the kind of society of which, theoretically, he is part. For Dewey freedom was something to be seen in positive terms: a man is free not in so far as restraint is absent, but in so far as he has 'the power to frame purposes' (p. 67), which encompasses the ability to achieve his chosen ends. To promote people's freedom it is therefore necessary, among other things, to give them knowledge, skills and certain attitudes. The main point of Dewey's programme was to ensure rather than to subvert the American Dream. It was 'more in accord with the democratic ideal to which [the American] people is committed' (p. 33) than the traditional methodology, and that, for Dewey, was its chief recommendation.

4 Goodman tends to cling like a fox terrier to isolated fragments of research, through thick and thin. Throughout his life he quotes Conant's verdict on this point (e.g. *FL* p. 110 for a late statement), notwithstanding the fact when he first referred to it he very reasonably questioned it: 'Dr. Conant does not seem to wonder why there are so few ... who are academically talented' (*GA* p. 84). (In fact, Goodman there refers to Conant's report as 'a minor national disaster'.) Notwithstanding that remark, Goodman's belief in innate aptitudes is demonstrated by such claims as that in *CM* p. 119 where, referring back to the year 1900 when only 6 per cent graduated from high school, he remarks 'maybe another 10 per cent would have graduated if they could have afforded it' to bring it into line with Conant's 15 per cent.

5 By this definition parrot-learning and rote-learning are properly so-called. But although they are species of learning they are usually not very valuable because the things that one learns in this way are usually not very valuable or interesting in their own right. One learns about the exploits of kings but one learns to parrot their dates. It is not learning to recite that is bad (or not true learning) but, usually, that what one learns to recite is futile. To learn to recite a poem is without question to learn something. But if that is all one learns, as opposed to learning about the meaning of the poem, one learns very little.

CHAPTER 6

1 The two are not contradictory. 'Beating the game is one form of conformity' (*SD* p. 18).

2 Perhaps worth mentioning is that Reimer seems to assume that, because the various rituals he refers to function to perpetuate certain (false) messages, they must be hollow and meaningless rituals. But clearly the so-called ritual of research or democratic procedures are not *just* hollow rituals. Things do happen as a result of such procedures.

3 As the radicals themselves *overstress* in other contexts. See Chapter 7.

4 The alert reader will note that argument by analogy keeps cropping up in the

radical theses and that on every occasion noted it begs the question at issue.
5 'Education should lead to a world based on freedom and justice; where freedom means a minimum of constraint by others, and justice means a distribution of wealth, power and other values consistent with this kind of freedom' (*SD* p. 99).

CHAPTER 7

1 It is perhaps more significant than its progenitors realise that the term was first produced by Hemingway in a context where he was at a loss as to what the key characteristics of a great writer might be: it was born of a situation where one phrase was sought to express something that couldn't easily be expressed in a simple phrase.
2 'In instances where someone wishes to dismiss the inquiry method, it is common to hear, "Oh, all you mean is the Socratic method".'

Bibliography

Barrow, Robin (1975) *Plato, Utilitarianism and Education* London and Boston, Routledge and Kegan Paul.

Barrow, Robin (1976) *Common Sense and the Curriculum* London, Allen and Unwin.

Dewey, John (1973) *Experience and Education* London, Collier-Macmillan.

Flew, Antony (1976) *Sociology, Equality and Education* London, Macmillan.

Goodman, Paul (1960) *Growing up Absurd* London, Gollancz; and New York, Random House (1960).

Goodman, Paul (1971a) *Compulsory Miseducation* Harmondsworth, Middx, Penguin; and New York, Horizon Press (1964).

Goodman, Paul (1971b) 'Freedom and Learning: the Need for Choice' in R. Hooper (ed.) *The Curriculum* Edinburgh, Oliver & Boyd.

Goodman, Paul (1975) 'Mini-Schools: a Prescription for the Reading Problem' in I. Lister (ed.) *Deschooling* Cambridge, Cambridge University Press.

Grimsley, Ronald (1973) *The Philosophy of Rousseau* Oxford, Oxford University Press.

Hemmings, R. (1972) *Fifty Years of Freedom* London, Allen & Unwin.

Holt, John (1975) *Escape from Childhood* Harmondsworth, Middx, Penguin.

Illich, Ivan (1973a) *Celebration of Awareness* Harmondsworth, Middx, Penguin; and Garden City, New York, Doubleday (1970).

Illich, Ivan (1973b) *Deschooling Society* Harmondsworth, Middx, Penguin; and New York, Harper and Row (1971).

Illich, Ivan (1975) *Medical Nemesis* London, Calder & Boyars.

Lister, I. (ed.) (1975) *Deschooling* Cambridge, Cambridge University Press.

Neill, A. S. (1961) *Summerhill* Harmondsworth, Middx, Penguin; and New York, Hart Publishing Co. (1960).

Plato *The Republic*

Plato *The Statesman*

Postman, N. and Weingartner, C. (1971) *Teaching as a Subversive Activity* Harmondsworth, Middx, Penguin; and New York, Delacorte Press (1969).

Reimer, Everett (1971) *School is Dead* Harmondsworth, Middx, Penguin; and Garden City, New York, Doubleday, (1971).

Rousseau, Jean-Jacques (1935) *The Social Contract* London, J. M. Dent and Everyman.

Rousseau, Jean-Jacques (1971) *The Confessions* Harmondsworth, Middx, Penguin.

Rousseau, Jean-Jacques (1972) *Emile* London, J. M. Dent and Everyman; and New York, E. P. Dutton and Co. (1911).

Index